Moses Roper
and
Harriet Jacobs

A drawing of Moses Roper of which appeared in some versions of the British and American editions of his autobiography.

Photograph of Harriet Jacobs in the 1890s shortly before her death in 1897. This is the only known image of her.

Moses Roper and Harriet Jacobs

Two Unforgettable Autobiographies about the Ugly Reality of American Slavery

SPECIAL EDITION
Edited by Gary Brin

LIST OF TITLES USED FOR THIS COLLECTION

Narrative of My Escape from American Slavery was originally published in a British Edition in 1837 and an American Edition in 1838—both under the title *A Narrative of the Adventures and Escape of Moses Roper from American Slavery*. It has been republished in various editions and varying titles by multiple publishing companies.

Incidents in the Life of a Slave Girl was originally published in 1861 and has republished in various editions by multiple publishing companies.

BOTH TITLES CAN BE FOUND AT THE SITE LISTED BELOW
www.nancyhankslincolnpubliclibrary.org

Spelling errors and publishing mistakes found in the original versions were corrected or adjusted when necessary for this edition. Incorrect spelling of biographical and geographical names mentioned was adjusted whenever possible as well. Original text was left intact to preserve the historical accuracy of the writings.

BOTH BOOKS USED FOR THIS EDITION HAS BEEN REFORMATTED FROM THE ORIGINAL 1838 AND 1861 PUBLISHED VERSIONS.

Images of Moses Roper and Harriet Jacobs displayed in this book are courtesy of the Library of Congress. Both photographs were digitally restored for this edition.
Cover design and book layout © 2021 by Standish Press
Compilation © 2021 by Standish Press

FIRST EDITION

ALL NEW MATERIAL AND CORRECTIONS
Copyright © 2021 by Standish Press

All rights reserved. No part of this book may be reproduced by any means whatsoever without written permission from the publisher.

For more information about reprint rights please visit
www.standishpress.com

ISBN—978-1-945510-06-9

Library of Congress Control Number
2021946474

MANUFACTURED IN THE UNITED STATES OF AMERICA

In Remembrance of

Moses Roper and Harriet Jacobs

They lived in a time when the future appeared impossible and
dreams seemed out of reach for enslaved people.
Today their stories make it possible for future generations to
remember the past and improve the future.

This book is also dedicated in memory of

Mary Stace Willis and Cornelia Grinnell Willis

Two excellent examples of decent human beings who showed
that it doesn't take much effort to be honorable.

Contents

Page 11
Foreword

Page 13
Moses Roper

Page 54
Harriet Jacobs

Page 249
Afterword

Page 255
Additional Notes

Page 258
About the Series Editor

Foreword

When someone takes a look at these riveting memoirs written by two brave individuals who lived through extraordinary times, they will experience a time machine where not even the best science fiction writers could hope to recreate. The harrowing accounts described by Moses Roper and Harriet Jacobs seem impossible to have happened in America—but they did as well as many others also. Originally published in 1838 and 1861—both accounts have remained in print since their initial publication.

Moses Roper was born in the early part of the nineteenth century, although the exact date is unknown. Horribly treated by most of the white so-called Christians who owned him, he persevered and managed to outsmart his captors escaping to freedom after several failed attempts. Nevertheless, throughout his ordeal he never seemed to give up hope that one day he would be free and strived to fulfill his goal despite how hopeless it seemed at the time. Today it's hard to imagine someone could have lived through such cruelty inflicted by strangers and relatives alike, but all anyone needs to do is look at present events in the news and it's easy to see that despite almost two hundred later after these events played out, there are still people who harbor deep hatred toward their fellow citizens—and of whom would easily do the wrong thing both ethically and morally if given a choice. Reading Roper's book is painful—it's not a fun tell-all by any means in case anyone was wondering beforehand, but that said, it is one of the most unforgettable accounts written by someone who experienced the worst of human behavior.

Harriet Jacobs lived a life worthy of a feature film or a television miniseries. Mistreated by those who claimed ownership of her, she refused to surrender her will and forged ahead dreaming about freedom from American slavery during the middle of the nineteenth century. Seeing firsthand how dark the souls of many so-called Christian slave owners were—based on their treatment of fellow human beings whom they gleefully subjected to extreme cruelty—she nevertheless learned that not every God-fearing person she met was an example of what religion sometimes brings out in people who claim to be disciples. Once she secured her freedom upon her escape, she published her unforgettable autobiography in the years following with the help of abolitionist and civil rights leader Lydia Maria Child.

Today her memoir is considered one of the most important documents ever published detailing the cruelties about slavery in the United States prior to the Civil War. Over a century later Harriet Jacobs continues to inspire new generations of readers through her bravery and heroism—despite how hopeless it must have seemed to her at the time when she thought about the future and what seemed like an impossible dream.

Gary Brin
Series Editor

Moses Roper

A Narrative of the Adventures and Escape of Moses Roper from American Slavery

I was born in North Carolina, in Caswell County. I am not able to tell in what year or month. What I shall now relate, is what was told me by my mother and grandmother. A few months before I was born, my father married my mother's young mistress. As soon as my father's wife heard of my birth, she sent one of my mother's sisters to see whether I was white or black, and when my aunt had seen me, she returned back as soon as she could, and told her mistress that I was white, and resembled Mr. Roper very much. Mr. R.'s wife being not pleased with this report, she got a large club stick and knife, and hastened to the place in which my mother was confined. She went into my mother's room with full intention to murder me with her knife and club, but as she was going to stick the knife into me, my grandmother happening to come in, caught the knife and saved my life.

But as well as I can recollect from what my mother told me, my father sold her and myself soon after her confinement. I cannot recollect anything that is worth notice till I was six or seven years old. My mother being half-white and my father a white man, I was at that time very white. Soon after I was six or seven years of age, my mother's old master died, that is my father's wife's father. All his slaves had to be divided among the children. I have mentioned before of my father disposing of me, I am not sure whether he exchanged me and my mother for another slave or not, but think it very likely he did exchange me with one of his wife's brothers or sisters, because I remember when my mother's old master died, I was living with my father's wife's brother-in-law, whose name was Mr. Durham. My mother was drawn with the other slaves. The way they divide their slaves is this, they write the names of different slaves on a small piece of paper, and put it into a box and let them all draw. I think that Mr. Durham drew my mother, and Mr. Fowler drew me, so we were separated a considerable distance, I cannot say how far. My resembling my father so very much, and being whiter than the other slaves, caused me to be soon sold to what they call a Negro trader, who took me to the Southern States of America, several hundred miles from my mother. As well as I can recollect, I was then about six years old. The trader, Mr. Michael, after traveling several hundred miles, and selling a good many of his slaves, found he could not sell me very well, (as I was so much whiter than the other slaves were), for he had been trying several months—left me with a Mr. Sneed, who kept a large boardinghouse, who took me to wait at table, and sell me if he could. I think I stayed with Mr. Sneed about a year, but he could not sell me. When Mr. Michael had sold his slaves, he went to the North and brought up another drove, and returned to the South with them, and sent his son-in-law into Washington, in Georgia, after me, so he came and took me from Mr. Sneed, and met his father-in-law with me, in a town called Lancaster, with his drove of slaves. We stayed in Lancaster a week, because it was court week, and there were a great many people there, and it was a good opportunity for selling the slaves, and there he was enabled to sell me to a gentleman, Doctor Jones, who was both a doctor and a cotton planter. He took me into his shop to beat up and to mix medicines, which was not a very hard employment, but I did not keep it long, as the doctor soon sent me to his cotton plantation that I might be burnt darker by the sun. He sent for me to be with a tailor to learn the trade, but all the journeymen being white men, Mr. Bryant, the tailor, did not let me work in the shop, I cannot say whether it was the prejudice of his journeymen in not wanting me to sit in the shop with them, or whether Mr. Bryant wanted to keep me about the house to do the domestic work instead of teaching me the trade. After several months my master came to know how I got on with the trade, I am not able to tell Mr. Bryant's answer, but it was either that I could not learn, or that his journeymen were not willing that I should sit in the shop with them. I was only once in the shop all the time I was there, and then only for an hour or two, before his wife called me out to do some other work. So my master took me home, and as he was going to send a load of cotton to Camden, about forty miles distance, he sent me with the bales of cotton to be sold with it, where I was soon sold to a gentleman named Allen, but Mr. Allen soon exchanged me for a female slave to please his wife. The traders who bought me were named Cooper and Linsey, who took me for sale, but could not sell me, people objecting to my being rather white. They then took me to the city of Fayetteville, North Carolina, where he swapped me for a boy that was blacker than me, to Mr. Smith, who lived several miles off. I was with Mr. Smith nearly a year. I arrived at the first knowledge of my age when I lived with him. I was then between twelve and thirteen years old, it was when President Jackson was elected the first time, and he has been president eight years, so I must be nearly twenty-one years of age. At this time I was quite a small boy, and was sold to Mr. Hodge, a Negro trader.

Here I began to enter into hardships. After traveling several hundred miles, Mr. Hodge sold me to Mr. Gooch the cotton planter, Kershaw County, South Carolina, he purchased me at a town called Liberty Hill, about three miles from his home. As soon as he had got home, he immediately put me on his cotton plantation to work and put me under overseers, gave me allowance of meat and bread with the other slaves, which was not half enough for me to live upon, and very laborious work, here my heart was almost broke with grief at leaving my fellow slaves. Mr. Gooch did not mind my grief, for he flogged me nearly every day, and very severely. Mr. Gooch bought me for his son-in-law, Mr. Hammond, about five miles from his residence. This man had but two slaves besides myself, he treated me very kindly for a week or two, but in summer when cotton was ready to hoe, he gave me task work connected with this department, which I could not get done, not having worked on cotton farms before. When I failed in my task, he commenced flogging me, and set me to work without any shirt, in the field in a very hot sun, in the month of July.

In August, Mr. Condell, his overseer, gave me a task of pulling fodder, having finished my task before night, I left the field, the rain came on which soaked the fodder, on discovering this he threatened to flog me for not getting in the fodder before the rain came. This was the first time I attempted to run away, knowing that I should get a flogging. I was then between thirteen and fourteen years of age, I ran away to the woods half-naked, I was caught by a slaveholder, who put me in Lancaster gaol. When they put slaves in gaol they advertise for their masters to own them, but if the master does not claim his slave in six months from the time of imprisonment, the slave is sold for gaol fees. When the slave runs away, the master always adopts a more vigorous system of flogging, this was the case in the present instance. After this, having determined from my youth to gain my freedom, I made several attempts, was caught, and got a severe flogging of 100 lashes each time. Mr. Hammond was a very severe and cruel master, and his wife still worse, she used to tie me up and flog me while naked. After Mr. Hammond saw that I was determined to die in the woods, and not live with him, he tried to obtain a piece of land from his father-in-law, Mr. Gooch, not having the means of purchasing it, he exchanged me for the land. As soon as Mr. Gooch had possession of me again, knowing that I was averse to going back to him, he chained me by the neck to his chaise. In this manner he took me to his home at McDaniel's Ferry, in the county of Chester, a distance of fifteen miles. After which, he put me into a swamp, to cut trees, the heaviest work which men of twenty-five or thirty years of age have to do, I being but sixteen. Here, I was on very short allowance of food, and having heavy work, was too weak to fulfill my tasks. For this I got many severe floggings, and, after I had got my irons off, I made another attempt at running away. He took my irons off in the full anticipation that I could never get across the Catawba River, even when at liberty. On this I procured a small Indian canoe, which was tied to a tree, and ultimately got across the river in it. I then wandered through the wilderness for several days without any food, and but a drop of water to allay my thirst, till I became so starved, that I was obliged to go to a house to beg for something to eat, when I was captured, and again imprisoned. Mr. Gooch having heard of me through an advertisement, sent his son after me, he tied me up, and took me back to his father. Mr. Gooch then obtained the assistance of another slaveholder, and tied me up in his blacksmith's shop, and gave me fifty lashes with a cowhide. He then put a long chain, weighing twenty-five pounds, round my neck, and sent me into a field, into which he followed me with the cowhide, intending to set his slaves to flog me again. Knowing this, and dreading to suffer again in this way, I gave him the slip, and got out of his sight, he having stopped to speak with the other slaveholder.

  I got to a canal on the Catawba River, on the banks of which, and near to a lock, I procured a stone and a piece of iron, with which I forced the ring off my chain, and got it off, and then crossed the river, and walked about twenty miles, when I fell in with a slaveholder named Ballad, who had married the sister of Mr. Hammond. I knew that he was not so cruel as Mr. Gooch, and, therefore, begged of him to buy me. Mr. Ballad, who was one of the best planters in the neighborhood, said, that he was not able to buy me, and stated that he was obliged to take me back to my master, on account of the heavy fine attaching to a man harboring a slave. Mr. Ballad proceeded to take me back, as we came in sight of Mr. Gooch's, all the treatment that I had met with there, came forcibly upon my mind, the powerful influence of which is beyond description. On my knees, with tears in my eyes, with terror in my countenance, and fervency in all my features, I implored Mr. Ballad to buy me, but he again refused, and I was taken back to my dreaded and cruel master. Having reached Mr. Gooch's, he proceeded to punish me. This he did by first tying my wrists together and placing them over the knees, he then put a stick through, under my knees and over my arms, and having thus secured my arms, he proceeded to flog me, and gave me 500 lashes on the bare back. This may appear incredible, but the marks which they left at present remain on my body a standing testimony to the truth of this statement of his severity. He then chained me down in a log pen with a forty pound chain, and made me lie on the damp earth all night. In the morning, after his breakfast, he came to me, and without giving me any breakfast, tied me to a large heavy barrow, which is usually drawn by a horse, and made me drag it to the cotton field for the horse to use in the field. Thus, the reader will see, that it was of no possible use to my master to make me drag it to the field and not through it, his cruelty went so far as actually to make me the slave of his horse, and thus to degrade me. He then flogged me again, and set me to work in the cornfield the whole of that day, and at night chained me down in the log pen as before. The next morning, he took me to the cotton field, and gave me a third flogging, and set me to hoe cotton. At this time, I was dreadfully sore and weak with the repeated floggings and harsh treatment I had endured. He put me under a black man, with orders, that if I did not keep my row up in hoeing with this man, he was to flog me. The reader must recollect here, that not being used to this kind of work, having been a domestic slave, it was quite impossible for me to keep up with him, and, therefore, I was repeatedly flogged during the day. Mr. Gooch had a female slave about eighteen years old, who had also been a domestic slave, and through not being able to fulfill her task, had run away, which slave he was at this time punishing for that offense. On the third day, he chained me to this female slave with a large chain of forty pounds weight, round the neck. It was most harrowing to my feelings, thus to be chained to a young female slave, for whom I would rather have suffered 100 lashes than she should have been thus treated, he kept me chained to her during the week, and repeatedly flogged us both while thus chained together, and forced us to keep up with the other slaves, although retarded by the heavy weight of the log chain. Here again words are insufficient to describe the misery which possessed both body and mind whilst under this treatment, and which was most dreadfully increased by the sympathy which I felt for my poor degraded fellow sufferer. On the Friday morning, I entreated my master to set me free from my chains, and promised him to do the task which was given me, and more, if possible, if he would desist from flogging me. This he refused to do until Saturday night, when he did set me free. This must rather be ascribed to his own interest in preserving me from death, as it was very evident I could no longer have survived under such treatment. After this, though still determined in my own mind to escape, I stayed with him several months, during which he frequently flogged me, but not so severely as before related.

During this time I had opportunity for recovering my health, and using means to heal my wounds. My master's cruelty was not confined to me, it was his general conduct to all his slaves. I might relate many instances to substantiate this, but will confine myself to one or two. Mr. Gooch, it is proper to observe, was a member of a Baptist church, called Black Jack Meeting House, in Kershaw County, which church I attended for several years, but was never inside. This is accounted for by the fact, that the colored population are not permitted to mix with the white population. Mr. Gooch had a slave named Phil, who was a member of a Methodist church, this man was between seventy and eighty years of age, he was so feeble that he could not accomplish his tasks, for which his master used to chain him round the neck, and run him down a steep hill, this treatment he never relinquished to the time of his death. Another case, was that of a slave named Peter, who, for not doing his task, he flogged nearly to death, and afterwards pulled out his pistol to shoot him, but his (Mr. Gooch's) daughter snatched the pistol from his hand. Another mode of punishment which this man adopted was, that of using iron horns, with bells, attached to the back of the slave's neck. This instrument he used to prevent the Negroes running away, being a very ponderous machine seven feet in height, and the cross pieces being two feet four, and six feet in length. This custom is generally adopted among the slaveholders in South Carolina, and some other slave states. One morning, about an hour before daybreak, I was going on an errand for my master, having proceeded about a quarter of a mile, I came up to a man named King, (Mr. Sumlin's overseer) who had caught a young girl that had run away with the above described machine on her. She had proceeded four miles from her station with the intention of getting into the hands of a more humane master. She came up with this overseer, nearly dead, and could get no farther, he immediately secured her, and took her back to her master, a Mr. Johnston. Having been in the habit of going over many slaves states with my master, I had good opportunities of witnessing the harsh treatment which was adopted by masters towards their slaves. As I have never read nor heard of anything connected with slavery so cruel as what I have myself witnessed, it will be well to mention a case or two. A large farmer, Colonel McQuiller, in Kershaw County, South Carolina, was in the habit of driving nails into a hogshead so as to leave the point of the nail just protruding in the inside of the cask, into this he used to put his slaves for punishment, and roll them down a very long and steep hill. I have heard from several slaves (though I had no means of ascertaining the truth of the statement) that in this way he killed six or seven of his slaves. This plan was first adopted by a Mr. Perry, who lived on the Catawba River, and has since been adopted by several planters. Another was that of a young lad, who had been hired by Mr. Bell, a member of a Methodist church, to hoe three-quarters of an acre of cotton per day. Having been brought up as a domestic slave, he was not able to accomplish the task assigned to him. On the Saturday night, he left three or four rows to do on the Sunday, on the same night it rained very hard, by which the master could tell that he had done some of the rows on Sunday. On Monday his master took and tied him up to a tree in the field, and kept him there the whole of that day, and flogged him at intervals. At night, when he was taken down he was so weak that he could not get home, having a mile to go. Two white men, who were employed by Mr. Bell, put him on a horse, took him home, and threw him down on the kitchen floor, while they proceeded to their supper. In a little time they heard some deep groans proceeding from the kitchen, they went to see him die, he had groaned his last. Thus, Mr. Bell flogged this poor boy even to death, for what? For breaking the Sabbath, when he (his master) had set him a task on Saturday which it was not possible for him to do, and which, if he did not do, no mercy would be extended towards him. So much for the regard of this Methodist for the observance of the Sabbath.

The general custom in this respect is, that if a man kills his own slave, no notice is taken of it by the civil functionaries, but if a man kills a slave belonging to another master, he is compelled to pay the worth of the slave. In this case, a jury met, returned a verdict of "willful murder" against this man, and ordered him to pay the value. Mr. Bell was unable to do this, but a Mr. Cunningham paid the debt, and took this Mr. Bell, with this recommendation for cruelty, to be his overseer. It will be observed, that most of the cases here cited are those in respect to males. Many instances, however, in respect to females might be mentioned, but are too disgusting to appear in this narrative. The cases here brought forward are not rare, but the continued feature of slavery. But I must now follow up the narrative as regards myself in particular. I stayed with this master for several months, during which time we went on very well in general. In August, 1831, (this was my first acquaintance with any date) I happened to hear a man mention this date, and as it excited my curiosity, I asked what it meant? They told me it was the number of the year from the birth of Christ. On this date, August, 1831, some cows broke into a crib where the corn is kept, and ate a great deal. For this his slaves were tied up and received several floggings, but myself and another man hearing the groans of those who were being flogged, stayed back in the field, and would not come up. Upon this I thought to escape punishment. On the Monday morning, however, I heard my master flogging the other man who was in the field, he could not see me, it being a field of Indian corn, which grows to a great height. Being afraid that he would catch me, and dreading a flogging more than many others, I determined to run for it, and after traveling forty miles I arrived at the estate of Mr. Crawford, in North Carolina, Mecklenburg County. Having formerly heard people talk about the Free States, I determined upon going thither, and if possible, in my way, to find out my poor mother who was in slavery several hundred miles from Chester, but the hope of doing the latter was very faint, and even if I did, it was not likely that she would know me, having been separated from her when between five and six years old. The first night I slept in a barn upon Mr. Crawford's estate, and, having overslept myself, was awoke by Mr. Crawford's overseer, upon which I was dreadfully frightened. He asked me what I was doing there? I made no reply to him then, and he, making sure that he had secured a runaway slave, did not press me for an answer. On my way to his house, however, I made up the following story, which I told him in the presence of his wife—I said, that I had been bound to a very cruel master when I was a little boy, and that having been treated very badly, I wanted to get home to see my mother. This statement may appear to some to be a direct lie, but as I understood the word *bound*, I considered it to apply to my case, having been sold to him, and thereby bound to serve him, though still, I did rather hope that he would understand it, that I was bound, when a boy, till twenty-one years of age. Though I was white at that time, he would not believe my story, on account of my hair being curly and woolly, which led him to conclude I was possessed of enslaved blood. The overseer's wife, however, who seemed much interested in me, said she did not think I was of African origin, and that she had seen white men still darker than me, her persuasion prevailed, and after the overseer had given me as much buttermilk as I could drink, and something to eat, which was very acceptable, having had nothing for two days, I set off for Charlotte in North Carolina, the largest town in the county. I went on very quickly the whole of that day, fearful of being pursued. The trees were very thick on each side of the road, and only a few houses at the distance of two or three miles apart, as I proceeded I turned round in all directions to see if I was pursued, and if I caught a glimpse of anyone coming along the road, I immediately rushed into the thickest part of the wood to elude the grasp, of what I was afraid might be my master. I went on this way the whole day, at night I came up with two wagons, they had been to market, the regular road wagons do not generally put up at inns, but encamp in the roads and fields. When I came to them, I told them the same story I had told Mr. Crawford's overseer, with the assurance that the statement would meet the same success. After they had heard me, they gave me something to eat and also lodging in the camp with them. I then went on with them about five miles, and they agreed to take me with them as far as they went, if I would assist them. This I promised to do. In the morning, however, I was much frightened by one of the men putting several questions to me—we were then about three miles from Charlotte. When within a mile of that town, we stopped at a brook to water the horses, while stopping here, I saw the men whispering, and fancying I overheard them say they would put me in Charlotte gaol, when they got there, I made my escape into the woods, pretending to be looking after something till I got out of their sight. I then ran on as fast as I could, but did not go through the town of Charlotte as had been my intention, being a large town, I was fearful it might prove fatal to my escape.

  Here I was at a loss how to get on, as houses were not very distant from each other for near 200 miles. While thinking what I should do, I observed some wagons before, which I determined to keep behind, and never go nearer to them than a quarter of a mile—in this way I traveled till I got to Salisbury. If I happened to meet any person on the road, I was afraid they would take me up, I asked them how far the wagons had got on before me, to make them suppose I belonged to the wagons. At night, I slept on the ground in the woods, some little distance from the wagons, but not near enough to be seen by the men belonging to them.

All this time I had but little food, principally fruit, which I found on the road. On Thursday night, I got into Salisbury, having left Chester on the Monday morning preceding. After this, being afraid my master was in pursuit of me, I left the usual line of road and took another direction, through Huntsville and Salem, principally through fields and woods, on my way to Caswell Courthouse, a distance of nearly 200 miles from Salisbury, I was stopped by a white man, to whom I told my old story, and again succeeded in my escape. I also came up with a small cart, driven by a poor man who had been moving into some of the western territories, and was going back to Virginia to move some more of his luggage. On this, I told him I was going the same way to Hilton, thirteen miles from Caswell Courthouse, he took me up in his cart and we went to the Red House, two miles from Hilton, the place where Mr. Mitchell took me from when six years old, to go to the Southern States. This was a very providential circumstance, for it happened that at the time I had to pass through Caswell Courthouse, a fair or election was going on, which caused the place to be much crowded with people, and rendered it more dangerous for me to pass through. At the Red House I left the cart and wandered about a long time, not knowing which way to go to find my mother. After some time, I took the road leading over Ikeo Creek. I shortly came up with a little girl about six years old, and asked her where she was going, she said to her mother's, pointing to a house on a hill about half a mile off. She had been to the overseer's house, and was returning to her mother. I then felt some emotions arising in my breast, which I cannot describe, but will be fully explained in the sequel. I told her that I was very thirsty, and would go with her to get something to drink. On our way, I asked her several questions, such as her name, that of her mother, she said hers was Maria, and her mother's Nancy. I inquired if her mother had any more children? She said five besides herself, and that they had been told that one had been sold when a little boy. I then asked the name of this child, she said it was Moses. These answers, as we approached the house, led me nearer and nearer to the finding out the object of my pursuit, and of recognizing in the little girl the person of my own sister. At last I got to my mother's house, my mother was at home, I asked her if she knew me? She said no. Her master was having a house built just by, and the men were digging a well, she supposed that I was one of the diggers.

I told her I knew her very well, and thought that if she looked at me a little she would know me, but this had no effect.

I then asked her if she had any sons? She said yes, but none so large as me. I then waited a few minutes, and narrated some circumstances to her, attending my being sold into slavery, and how she grieved at my loss. Here the mother's feelings on that dire occasion, and which a mother only can know, rushed to her mind, she saw her own son before her, for whom she had so often wept, and in an instant we were clasped in each other's arms, amidst the ardent interchange of caresses and tears of joy. Ten years had elapsed since I had seen my dear mother.

My own feelings, and the circumstances attending my coming home, have often been brought to mind since, on a perusal of the 42nd, 43rd, 44th, and 45th chapters of *Genesis*. What could picture my feelings so well, as I once more beheld the mother who had brought me into the world and had nourished me, not with the anticipation of my being torn from her maternal care when only six years old, to become the prey of a mercenary and bloodstained slaveholder. I say, what picture so vivid in description of this part of my tale, as the 7th and 8th verses of the 42nd chapter of *Genesis*, "and Joseph saw his brethren and he knew them, but made himself strange unto them. And Joseph knew his brethren, but they knew not him." After the first emotion of the mother, on recognizing her firstborn, had somewhat subsided, could the reader not fancy the little one, my sister, as she told her simple tale of meeting with me to her mother, how she would say, while the parent listened with intense interest. "The man asked me straightly of our state and of our kindred, saying, is your father yet alive, and have ye another brother?" Or, when at last, I could no longer refrain from making myself known, I say I was ready to burst into a frenzy of joy.

How applicable the 1st, 2nd, and 3rd verses of the 45th chapter, "then Joseph could not refrain himself before all them that stood by him, and he wept aloud, and said unto his brethren, I am Joseph, doth my father still live?" Then when the mother knew her son, when the brothers and sisters owned their brother, "he kissed all his brethren and wept over them, and after that his brethren talked with him," 15th verse. At night, my mother's husband, a blacksmith, belonging to Mr. Jefferson, at the Red House, came home, he was surprised to see me with the family, not knowing who I was. He had been married to my mother when I was a babe, and had always been very fond of me. After the same tale had been told him, and the same emotions filled his soul, he again kissed the object of his early affection. The next morning I wanted to go on my journey, in order to make sure of my escape to the Free States. But, as might be expected, my mother, father, brothers, and sisters, could ill part with their long lost one, and persuaded me to go into the woods in the daytime, and at night come home and sleep there. This I did for about a week, on the next Sunday night, I had laid me down to sleep between my two brothers, on a pallet which my mother had prepared for me, about twelve o'clock, I was suddenly awoke, and found my bed surrounded by twelve slaveholders with pistols in hand, who took me away (not allowing me to bid farewell to those I loved so dearly) to the Red House, where they confined me in a room the rest of the night, and in the morning lodged me in the gaol of Caswell Courthouse. What was the scene at home, what sorrow possessed their hearts, I am unable to describe, as I never after saw any of them more. I heard, however, that my mother, who was in the family way when I went home, was soon after confined, and was very long before she recovered the effects of this disaster. I was told afterwards, that some of those men who took me, were professing Christians, but to me they did not seem to live up to what they professed, they did not seem, by their practices, at least, to recognize that God as their God, who hath said, "thou shalt not deliver unto his master, the servant which is escaped from his master unto thee, he shall dwell with thee, even among you, in that place which he shall choose, in one of thy gates, where it liketh him best, thou shalt not oppress him." (*Deuteronomy* XXIII 15 and 16) I was confined here in a dungeon underground, the grating of which looked to the door of the gaoler's house. His wife had a great antipathy to me. She was Mr. Roper's wife's cousin. My grandmother used to come to me nearly every day, and bring me something to eat, besides the regular gaol allowance, by which my sufferings were somewhat decreased. Whenever the gaoler went out, which he often did, his wife used to come to my dungeon and shut the wooden door over the grating, by which I was nearly suffocated, the place being very damp and noisome. My master did not hear of my being in gaol for thirty-one days after I had been placed there. He immediately sent his son, and son-in-law, Mr. Anderson, after me. They came in a horse and chaise, took me from the gaol to a blacksmith's shop, and got an iron collar fitted round my neck, with a heavy chain attached, then tied up my hands, and fastened the other end of the chain on another horse, and put me on its back. Just before we started, my grandmother came to bid me farewell, I gave her my hand as well as I could, and she having given me two or three presents, we parted. I had felt enough, far too much, for the weak state I was in, but how shall I describe my feelings upon parting with the *last* relative that I ever *saw*. The reader must judge by what would be his own feelings under similar circumstances. We then went on for fifty miles, I was very weak, and could hardly sit on the horse. Having been in prison so long, I had lost the Southern tan, and, as the people could not see my hair, having my hat on, they thought I was a white man—a criminal—and asked what crime I had committed. We arrived late at night at the house of Mr. Britton. I shall never forget the journey that night. The thunder was one continued roar, and the lightning blazing all around. I expected every minute that my iron collar would attract it, and I should be knocked off the horse and dragged along the ground. This gentleman, a year or two before, had liberated his slaves, and sent them into Ohio, having joined the Society of Friends, which society does not allow the holding of slaves. I was, therefore, treated very well there, and they gave me a hearty supper, which did me much good in my weak state. They secured me in the night by locking me to the post of the bed on which they slept. The next morning we went on to Salisbury.

At that place we stopped to water the horses, they chained me to a tree in the yard, by the side of their chaise. On my horse they had put the saddlebags which contained the provisions. As I was in the yard, a black man came and asked me what I had been doing, I told him I had run away from my master, after which he told me several tales about the slaves, and among them, he mentioned the case of a Quaker, who was then in prison, waiting to be hung, for giving a free pass to a slave.

I had been considering all the way how I could escape from my horse, and once had an idea of cutting his head off, but thought it too cruel, and at last thought of trying to get a rasp and cut the chain by which I was fastened to the horse. As they often let me get on nearly a quarter of a mile before them, I thought I should have a good opportunity of doing this without being seen. The black man procured me a rasp, and I put it into the saddlebags which contained the provisions. We then went on our journey, and one of the sons asked me if I wanted anything to eat, I answered no, though very hungry at the time, as I was afraid of their going to the bags and discovering the rasp. However, they had not had their own meal at the inn, as I supposed, and went to the bags to supply themselves, where they discovered the rasp.

Upon this, they fastened my horse beside the horse in their chaise, and kept a stricter watch over me. Nothing remarkable occurred till we got within eight miles of Mr. Gooch's, where we for giving a free pass stopped a short time, and taking advantage of their absence, I broke a switch from some boughs above my head, lashed my horse, and set off at full speed. I had got about a quarter of a mile before they could get their horse loose from the chaise, one then rode the horse, and the other ran as fast as he could after me. When I caught sight of them, I turned off the main road into the woods, hoping to escape their sight, their horse, however, being much swifter than mine, they soon got within a short distance of me. I then came to a rail fence, which I found it very difficult to get over, but breaking several rails away, I effected my object. They then called upon me to stop, more than three times, and I not doing so, they fired after me, but the pistol only snapped. This is according to law, after three calls they may shoot a runaway slave. Soon after, the one on the horse came up with me, and catching hold of the bridle of my horse, pushed the pistol to my side, the other soon came up, and breaking off several stout branches from the trees, they gave me about 100 blows. They did this very near to a planter's house, the gentleman was not at home, but his wife came out, and begged them not to *kill* me *so near the house*, they took no notice of this, but kept on beating me. They then fastened me to the axle tree of their chaise, one of them got into the chaise, the other took my horse, and they run me all the eight miles as fast as they could, the one on my horse going behind to guard me.

    In this way we came to my old master, Mr. Gooch. The first person I saw was himself, he unchained me from the chaise, and, at first, seemed to treat me very gently, asking me where I had been, and etc. The first thing the sons did, was to show the rasp which I had got to cut my chain. My master gave me a hearty dinner, the best he ever did give me, but it was to keep me from dying before he had given me all the flogging he intended. After dinner he took me to a log house, stripped me quite naked, fastened a rail up very high, tied my hands to the rail, fastened my feet together, put a rail between my feet and stood on one end of it to hold it down, the two sons then gave me fifty lashes each, the eldest another fifty, and Mr. Gooch himself, fifty more. While doing this, his wife came out and begged him not to kill me, the first act of sympathy I ever noticed in her. When I called for water, they brought a pail full, and threw it over my back, plowed up by the lashes. After this, they took me to the blacksmith's shop, got two large bars of iron, which they bent round my feet, each bar weighing twenty pounds, and put a heavy log chain on my neck. This was on Saturday. On the Monday he chained me to the same female slave as before.

As he had to go out that day, he did not give me the punishment which he intended to give me every day, but at night when he came home, he made us walk round his estate, and by all the houses of his slaves, for them to taunt us, when we came home he told us we must be up very early in the morning, and go to the fields before the other slaves. We were up at daybreak, but we could not get on fast, on account of the heavy irons on my feet. We walked about a mile in two hours, but knowing the punishment he was going to inflict on us, we made up our minds to escape into the woods, and secret ourselves. This we did, and he not being able to find us, sent all his slaves, about forty, and his sons, to find us, which they could not do, and about twelve o'clock, when we thought they would give up looking for us at that time, we went on and came to the banks of the Catawba.

Here I got a stone, and prized the ring off the chain on her neck, and got it off, and as the chain round my neck was only passed through a ring, as soon as I had got hers off I slipped the chain through my ring and got it off my own neck. We then went on by the banks of the river for some distance, and found a little canoe about two feet wide. I managed to get in, although the irons on my feet made it very dangerous, for if I had upset the canoe I could not swim. The female got in after me, and gave me the paddles, by which we got some distance down the river. The current being very strong, it drove us against a small island, we paddled round the island to the other side, and then made towards the opposite bank. Here again we were stopped by the current, and made up to a large rock in the river, between the island and the opposite shore. As the weather was very rough, we landed on the rock and secured the canoe, as it was not possible to get back to the island. It was a very dark night, and rained tremendously, and as the water was rising rapidly towards the top of the rock, we gave all up for lost, and sometimes hoped, and sometimes feared to hope, that we should never see the morning. But Providence was moving in our favor, the rain ceased, the water reached the edge of the rock, then receded, and we were out of danger from this cause. We remained all night upon the rock, and in the morning reached the opposite shore, and then made our way through the woods till we came to a field of Indian corn, where we plucked some of the green ears and ate them, having had nothing for two days and nights. We came to an estate, where we met with a colored man who knew me, and, having run away himself from a bad master, he gave us some food, and told us we might sleep in the barn that night. Being very fatigued we overslept ourselves, the proprietor came to the barn, but as I was in one corner under some Indian corn tops, and she in another, he did not perceive us, and we did not leave the barn before night. (Wednesday) We then went out, got something to eat, and stayed about the estate till Sunday.

On that day I met with some men, one of whom had, had irons on his feet the same as me, he told me that his master was going out to see his friends, and that he would try and get my feet loose, for this purpose I parted with this female, fearing that if she were caught with me, she would be forced to tell who took my irons off. The man tried some time without effect, he then gave me a file, and I tried myself, but was disappointed, on account of their thickness. On the Monday I went on towards Lancaster, and got within three miles of it that night, and went towards the plantation of Mr. Crockett, as I knew some of his slaves, and hoped to get some food given me. When I got there, however, the dogs smelt me out and barked, upon which Mr. Crockett came out, followed me with his rifle and came up with me. He put me on a horse's back, which put me to extreme pain, from the great weight hanging from my feet. We reached Lancaster gaol that night, and he lodged me there. I was placed in the next dungeon to a man who was going to be hung.

I shall never forget his cries and groans, as he prayed all night for the mercy of God. Mr. Gooch did not hear of me for several weeks, when he did, he sent his son-in-law, Mr. Anderson, after me. Mr. Gooch, himself, came within a mile of Lancaster and waited until Mr. Anderson brought me. At this time I had but one of the irons on my feet, having got so thin round my ankles that I had slipped one off while in gaol. His son-in-law tied my hands, and made me walk along till we came to Mr. Gooch.

As soon as we arrived at McDaniel's Ford, two miles above the ferry, on the Catawba River, they made me wade across, themselves going on horseback. The water was very deep, and having irons on one foot, and round my neck, I could not keep a footing. They dragged me along by my chain, floating on the top of the water. It was as much as they could do to hold me by the chain, the current being very strong. They then took me home, flogged me, put extra irons on my neck and feet, and put me under the driver, with more work than ever I had before. He did not flog me so severely as before, but continued it every day. Among the instruments of torture employed, I here describe one—this machine was used for packing and pressing cotton.

By it he hung me up by the hands—a horse moving round the screw—and carrying it up and down—and pressing the block into the box—into which the cotton is put. At this time he hung me up for a quarter of an hour. I was carried up ten feet from the ground, when Mr. Gooch asked me if I was tired. He then let me rest for five minutes, then carried me round again, after which he let me down and put me into the box—and shut me down in it for about ten minutes. After this torture, I stayed with him several months, and did my work very well. It was about the beginning of 1832, when he took off my irons, and being in dread of him, he having threatened me with more punishment, I attempted again to escape from him. At this time, I got into North Carolina, but a reward having been offered for me, a Mr. Robinson caught me, and chained me to a chair, upon which he sat up with me all night, and next day proceeded home with me. This was Saturday. Mr. Gooch had gone to church, several miles from his house. When he came back, the first thing he did, was to pour some tar on my head, then rubbed it all over my face, took a torch, with pitch on, and set it on fire, he put it out before it did me very great injury, but the pain which I endured was most excruciating, nearly all my hair having been burnt off. On Monday, he put irons on me again, weighing nearly fifty pounds. He threatened me again on the Sunday with another flogging, and on the Monday morning, before daybreak, I got away again, with my irons on, and was about three hours going a distance of two miles. I had gone a good distance, when I met with a colored man, who got some wedges and took my irons off. However, I was caught again, and put into prison in Charlotte, where Mr. Gooch came, and took me back to Chester. He asked me how I got my irons off? They having been got off by a slave, I would not answer his question, for fear of getting the man punished. Upon this he put the fingers of my left hand into a vice, and squeezed all my nails off.

    He then had my feet put on an anvil, and ordered a man to beat my toes, till he smashed some of my nails off. The marks of this treatment still remain upon me, my nails never having grown perfect since. He inflicted this punishment in order to get out of me how I got my irons off, but never succeeded. After this, he hardly knew what to do with me, the whole stock of his cruelties seemed to be exhausted. He chained me down in the log house. Soon after this, he sent a female slave to see if I was safe.

    Mr. Gooch had not secured me as he thought, but had only run my chain through the ring without locking it. This I observed, and while the slave was coming, I was employed in loosening the chain with the hand that was not wounded. As soon as I observed her coming, I drew the chain up tight, and she observing that I seemed fast, went away and told her master, who was in the field ordering the slaves. When she was gone, I drew the chain through the ring, escaped under the flooring of the log house, and went on under his house, till I came out at the other side, and ran on, but, being sore and weak, I had not got a mile before I was caught, and again carried back. He tied me up to a tree in the woods at night, and made his slaves flog me. I cannot say how many lashes I received, but it was the worst flogging I ever had, and the last which Mr. Gooch ever gave me. There are several circumstances which occurred on this estate while I was there, relative to other slaves, which it may be interesting to mention. Hardly a day ever passed without someone being flogged. To one of his female slaves he had given a dose of castor oil and salts, together, as much as she could take, he then got a box, about six feet by two and a half, and one and a half feet deep, he put this slave under the box, and made the men fetch as many stones as they could get, and put them on the top of it, under this, she was made to stay all night. I believe that if he had given this slave one, he had given her three thousand lashes. Mr. Gooch was a member of a Baptist church. His slaves thinking him a very bad sample of what a professing Christian ought to be, would not join the connection he belonged to, thinking they must be a very bad set of people, there were many of them members of the Methodist church. On Sunday, the slaves can only go to church at the will of their master, when he gives them a pass for the time they are to be out. If they are found by the patrol after the time to which their pass extends, they are severely flogged. On Sunday nights, a slave, named Allen, used to come to Mr. Gooch's estate for the purpose of exhorting and praying with his brother slaves, by whose instrumentality many of them had been converted. One evening, Mr. Gooch caught them all in a room, turned Allen out, and threatened his slaves with one hundred lashes each if they ever brought him there again. At one time, Mr. Gooch was ill and confined to his room, if any of the slaves had done anything, which he thought deserving a flogging, he would have them brought into his bedroom and flogged before his eyes. With respect to food, he used to allow us one peck of Indian meal each, per week, which, after being sifted and the bran taken from it, would not be much more than half a peck. Meat we did not get for sometimes several weeks together, however, he was proverbial for giving his slaves more food than any other slaveholder. I stayed with Mr. Gooch a year and a half. During that time, the scenes of cruelty I witnessed and experienced, are not at all fitted for these pages. There is much to excite disgust in what has been narrated, but hundreds of other cases might be mentioned. After this, Mr. Gooch, seeing that I was determined to get away from him, chained me, and sent me with another female slave, whom he had treated very cruelly, to Mr. Britton, son of the before-mentioned, a slave dealer. We were to have gone to Georgia to be sold, but a bargain was struck before we arrived there. Mr. Britton had put chains on me to please Mr. Gooch, but having gone some little distance, we came up with a white man, who begged Mr. Britton to unchain me, he then took off my handcuffs. We then went on to Union Courthouse, where we met a drove of slaves, the driver came to me, and ultimately bought me, and sent me to his drove, the girl was sold to a planter in the neighborhood, as bad as Mr. Gooch.

In court week, the Negro traders and slaves encamp a little way out of the town. The traders here will often sleep with the best looking female slaves among them, and they will often have many children in the year, which are said to be slaveholder's children, by which means, through his villainy, he will make an immense profit of this intercourse, by selling the babe with its mother. They often keep an immense stock of slaves on hand.

Many of them, will be with the trader a year or more, before they are sold. Mr. Marcus Rowland, the drover who bought me, then returned with his slaves to his brother's house (Mr. John Rowland) where he kept his drove, on his way to Virginia. He kept me as a kind of servant. I had to grease the faces of the blacks every morning with sweet oil, to make them shine before they are put up to sell. After he had been round several weeks and sold many slaves, he left me and some more at his brother's house, while he went on to Washington, about 600 miles, to buy some more slaves, the drove having got very small. We were treated very well while there, having plenty to eat, and little work to do, in order to make us fat. I was brought up more as a domestic slave, as they generally prefer slaves of my color for that purpose. When Mr. Rowland came back, having been absent about five months, he found all the slaves well, except one female, who had been grieving very much at being parted from her parents, and at last died of grief. He dressed us very nicely, and went on again. I traveled with him for a year, and had to look over the slaves, and see that they were dressed well, had plenty of food, and to oil their faces. During this time, we stopped once at White House Church, a Baptist association, a protracted camp meeting was holding there, on the plan of the revival meetings in this country. We got there at the time of the meeting, and sold two female slaves on the Sunday morning, at the time the meeting broke up, to a gentleman who had been attending the meeting the whole of the week. While I was with Mr. Rowland, we were at many such meetings, and the members of the churches are by this means so well-influenced towards their fellow creatures, at these meetings for the worship of God, that it becomes a fruitful season for the drover, who carries on immense traffic with the attendants at these places. This is common to Baptists and Methodists. At the end of the year, he exchanged me to a farmer, Mr. David Goodley, for a female slave, in Greenville, about fourteen miles from Greenville Courthouse. The gentleman was going to Missouri to settle, and on his way had to pass through Ohio, a free state. But, having learnt, after he bought me, that I had before tried to get away to the Free States, he was afraid to take me with him, and I was again exchanged to a Mr. Marvel Louis. He was in the habit of traveling a great deal, and took me as a domestic slave to wait on him. Mr. Louis boarded at the house of Mr. Clevelin, a very rich planter at Greenville, South Carolina. Mr. L. was paying his addresses to the daughter of this gentleman, but was surprised and routed in his approaches, by a Colonel Dorkin, of Union Courthouse, who ultimately carried her off in triumph. After this, Mr. Louis took to drinking, to drown his recollection of disappointed love.

One day he went to Pendleton Races, and I waited on the road for him, returning intoxicated, he was thrown from his horse into a brook, and was picked up by a gentleman, and taken to an inn, and I went there to take care of him. Next day he went on to Pumpkintown with Mr. Warren R. Davis, a member of Congress, I went with him. This was at the time of the agitation of the Union and Nullifier Party, which was expected to end in a general war.

The Nullifier Party had a grand dinner on the occasion, after which, they gave their slaves all the refuse, for the purpose of bribing them to fight on the side of their party. The scene on this occasion was most humorous, all the slaves scrambling after bare bones and crumbs, as if they had, had nothing for months. When Mr. Louis had got over this fit of drunkenness, we returned to Greenville, where I had little to do, except in the warehouse.

    There was preaching in the courthouse on the Sunday, but scarcely had the sweet savor of the worship of God passed away, when, on Monday, a public auction was held for the sale of slaves, cattle, sugar, iron, and etc., by Z. Davis, the high constable, and others. On these days, I was generally very busy in handing out the different articles for inspection, and was employed in this way for several months, after which, Mr. Louis left this place for Pendleton, but his health getting worse, and fast approaching consumption, he determined to travel. I went with him over Georgia to the Indian Springs, and from there to Columbus, here he left me with Lawyer Kemp, a member of the State Assembly, to take care of his horses and carriage till he came back from Cuba, where he went for the benefit of his health. I traveled round with Mr. Kemp, waiting until my master came back. I soon after heard that Mr. Louis had died at Apalachicola, and had been buried at Tennessee Bluff. I was very much attached to the neighborhood of Pendleton and Greenville, and feared, from Mr. Louis's death, I should not get back there. As soon as this information arrived, Mr. Kemp put me, the carriage and horses, a gold watch, and cigars, up to auction, on which I was much frightened, knowing there would be some very cruel masters at the sale, and fearing I should again be disappointed in my attempt to escape from bondage. Mr. Beveridge, a Scotchman, from Apalachicola, bought me, the horses, and cigars. He was not a cruel master, he had been in America eighteen years, and I believe I was the first slave he ever bought. Mr. Kemp had no right to sell me, which he did before he had written to Mr. Louis's brother. Shortly after this, Mr. Kemp having some altercation with General Woodfork, it ended in a duel, in which Mr. W. was killed. A few weeks after, as Mr. Kemp was passing down a street, he was suddenly shot dead by Mr. Milton, a rival lawyer. When I heard this, I considered it a visitation of God on Mr. Kemp for having sold me unjustly, as I did not belong to him. This was soon discovered by me, Mr. Louis's brother having called at Mackintosh Hotel, Columbus, to claim me, but which he could not effect. After this, I traveled with Mr. Beveridge through Georgia, to the Warm Springs, and then came back to Columbus, going on to Marianna, his summer house in Florida. Here I met with better treatment than I had ever experienced before, we traveled on the whole summer, at the fall, Mr. Beveridge went to Apalachicola on business. Mr. Beveridge was contractor for the mail from Columbus to Apalachicola, and owner of three steamboats, the *Versailles*, *Andrew Jackson* and *Van Buren*.

He made me steward on board the *Versailles* the whole winter. The river then got so low that the boats could not run. At this time, Mr. Beveridge went to Mount Vernon. On our way we had to pass through the Indian nation. We arrived at Columbus, where I was taken dangerously ill of a fever. After I got well, Mr. Beveridge returned to Marianna, through the Indian nation. Having gone about twelve miles he was taken very ill. I took him out of the carriage to a brook, and washed his hands and feet until he got better, when I got him into the carriage again, and drove off till we came to General Irving's, where he stopped several days, on account of his health. While there, I observed on the floor of the kitchen several children, one about three months old, without anybody to take care of her, I asked where her mother was, and was told that Mrs. Irving had given her a very hard task to do at washing, in a brook about a quarter of a mile distant. We heard after, that not being able to get it done she had got some cords, tied them round her neck, climbed up a tree, swung off, and hung herself. Being missed, persons were sent after her, who observed several buzzards flying about a particular spot, to which they directed their steps, and found the poor woman nearly eaten up. After this, we traveled several months without anything remarkable taking place. In the year 1834, Mr. Beveridge, who was now residing in Apalachicola, a town in West Florida, became a bankrupt, when all his property was sold, and I fell into the hands of a very cruel master, Mr. Register, a planter in the same state, of whom, knowing his savage character, I always had a dread. Previously to his purchasing me, he had frequently taunted me, by saying, "You have been a gentleman long enough, and, whatever may be the consequences, I intend to buy you." To which I remarked, that I would, on no account, live with him if I could help it. Nevertheless, intent upon his purpose, in the month of July, 1834, he bought me, after which, I was so exasperated that I cared not whether I lived or died, in fact, whilst I was on my passage from Apalachicola, I procured a quart bottle of whiskey, for the purpose of so intoxicating myself, that I might be able, either to plunge myself into the river, or so to enrage my master, that he should dispatch me forthwith. I was however, by a kind Providence, prevented from committing this horrid deed by an old slave on board, who knowing my intention, secretly took the bottle from me, after which, my hands were tied, and I was led into the town of Ochesa, to a warehouse, where my master was asked by the proprietor of the place, the reason for his confining my hands, in answer to which, Mr. Register said, that he had purchased me. The proprietor, however, persuaded him to untie me, after which, my master being excessively drunk, asked for a cowhide, intending to flog me, from which the proprietor dissuaded him, saying that he had known me for some time, and he was sure that I did not require to be flogged. From this place, we proceeded about mid-day on our way, he placing me on the bare back of a half-starved old horse, which he had purchased, and upon which sharp *surface* he kindly intended, I should ride about eighty miles, the distance we were then from his home. In this unpleasant situation, I could not help reflecting upon the prospects before me, not forgetting that I had heard that my new master had been in the habit of stealing cattle and other property, and among other things, a slave woman, and that I had said, as it afterwards turned out, in the hearing of someone who communicated the saying to my master, that I had been accustomed to live with a gentleman and not with a rogue, and, finding that he had been informed of this, I had the additional dread of a few hundred lashes for it, on my arrival at my destination. About two hours after we started, it began to rain very heavily, and continued to do so until we arrived at Marianna about twelve at night, where we were to rest till morning.

My master here questioned me, as to whether I intended to run away or not, and I, not then knowing the sin of lying, at once told him that I would not. He then gave me his clothes to dry, I took them to the kitchen for that purpose, and he retired to bed, taking a bag of clothes belonging to me with him, as a kind of security, I presume, for my safety. In an hour or two afterwards, I took his clothes to him dried, and found him fast asleep. I placed them by his side, and said that I would then take my own to dry too, taking care to speak loud enough to ascertain whether he was asleep or not, knowing that he had a dirk and pistol by his side, which he would not have hesitated using against me, if I had attempted secretly to have procured them.

I was glad to find, that the effects of his drinking the day before had caused his sleeping very soundly, and I immediately resolved on making my escape, and without loss of time, started with my few clothes into the woods, which were in the immediate neighborhood, and, after running many miles, I came to the river Chipola, which is very deep, and so beset with alligators, that I dared not attempt to swim across. I paced up and down this river, with the hope of finding a conveyance across, for a whole day, the succeeding night, and till noon the following day, which was Saturday. About twelve o'clock on that day I discovered an Indian canoe, which had not, from all appearance, been used for some time, this, of course, I used to convey myself across, and after being obliged to go a little way down the river, by means of a piece of wood I providentially found in the boat, I landed on the opposite side. Here I found myself surrounded by planters looking for me, in consequence of which I hid myself in the bushes until night, when I again traveled several miles, to the farm of a Mr. Robinson, a large sugar planter, where I rested till morning in a field. Afterwards I set out, working my way through the woods about twenty miles towards the east, this I knew by my knowledge of the position of the sun at its rising. Having reached the Chattahoochee River, which divides Florida from Georgia, I was again puzzled to know how to cross, it was three o'clock in the day, when a number of persons were fishing, having walked for some hours along the banks, I at last, after dark, procured a ferry boat, which not being able, from the swiftness of the river, to steer direct across, I was carried many miles down the river, landing on the Georgian side, from whence I proceeded on through the woods two or three miles, and came to a little farmhouse about twelve at night, at a short distance from the house, I found an old slave hut, into which I went, and informed the old man, who appeared seventy or eighty years old, that I had, had a very bad master, from whom I had run away, and asked him if he could give me something to eat, having had no suitable food for three or four days, he told me he had nothing but a piece of dry Indian bread, which he cheerfully gave me, having eaten it, I went on a short distance from the hut, and laid down in the wood to rest for an hour or two. All the following day (Monday) I continued traveling through the woods, I was greatly distressed for want of water to quench my thirst, it being a very dry country, till I came to Spring Creek, which is a wide, deep stream, and with some of which I gladly quenched my thirst. I then proceeded to cross the same by a bridge close by, and continued my way till dusk. I came to a gentleman's house in the woods, where I inquired how far it was to the next house, taking care to watch an opportunity to ask some individual whom I could master, and get away from, if any interruption to my progress was attempted. I went on for some time, it being a very fine moonlight night, and was presently alarmed by the howling of a wolf very near me, which I concluded was calling other wolves to join him in attacking me, having understood that they always assemble in numbers for such a purpose, the howling increased, and I was still pursued, and the numbers were evidently increasing fast, but I was happily rescued from my dreadful fright, by coming to some cattle, which attracted the wolves, and saved my life, for I could not get up the trees for safety, they being very tall pines, the lowest branches of which were at least forty or fifty feet from the ground, and the trunks very large and smooth.

 About two o'clock, I came to the house of a Mr. Cherry, on the borders of the Flint River, I went up to the house, and called them up to beg something to eat, but having nothing cooked, they kindly allowed me to lie down in the porch, where they made me a bed. In conversation with this Mr. Cherry, I discovered that I had known him before, having been in a steamboat, the *Versailles*, some month previous, which sunk very near his house, but which I did not at first discern to be the same. I then thought that it would not be prudent for me to stop there, and therefore told them I was in a hurry to get on, and must start very early again, he having no idea who I was, and I gave his son six cents to take me across the river, which he did when the sun was about half an hour high, and unfortunately landed me where there was a man building a boat, who knew me very well, and my former master too—he calling me by name, asked me where I was going. I was very much frightened at being discovered, but summoned up courage, and said, that my master had gone on to Tallahassee by the coach, and that there was not room for me, and I had to walk round to meet him. I then asked the man to put me into the best road to get there, which, however, I knew as well as he did, having traveled there before, he directed me the best way, but I of course took the contrary direction, wanting to get on to Savannah. By this hasty and wicked deception, I saved myself from going to Bainbridge prison, which was close by, and to which I should surely have been taken, had it been known that I was making my escape. Leaving Bainbridge, I proceeded about forty miles, traveling all day under a scorching sun through the woods, in which I saw many deer and serpents, until I reached Thomas Town in the evening. I there inquired the way to Augusta of a man whom I met, and also asked where I could obtain lodgings and was told that there was a poor minister about a mile from the place, who would give me lodgings. I accordingly went and found them in a little log house, where, having awakened the family, I found them all lying on the bare boards, where I joined them for the remainder of the night. In the morning, the old gentleman prayed for me that I might be preserved on my journey, he had previously asked me where I was going, and I knowing, that if I told him the right place, any that inquired of him for me would be able to find me, asked the way to Augusta instead of Savannah, my real destination. I also told him, that I was partly Indian and partly white, but I am also partly African, but this I omitted to tell him, knowing if I did, I should be apprehended. After I had left this hut, I again inquired for Augusta, for the purpose of misleading my pursuers, but I afterwards took my course through the woods, and came into a road, called the Coffee Road, which General Jackson cut down for his troops at the time of the war, between the Americans and Spaniards, in Florida, in which road there are but few houses, and which I preferred for the purpose of avoiding detection.

After several days I left this road and took a more direct way to Savannah, where I had to wade through two rivers before I came to the Altamaha, which I crossed in a ferry boat, about a mile below the place where the rivers Oconee and Ocmulgee run together into one river, called the Altamaha. I here met with some cattle drovers, who were collecting cattle to drive to Savannah. On walking on before them, I began to consider in what way I could obtain a passport for Savannah, and determined on the following plan—I called at a cottage, and after I had talked some time with the wife, who began to feel greatly for me, in consequence of my telling her a little of my history, (her husband being out hunting) I pretended to show her my passport, feeling for it everywhere about my coat and hat, and not finding it, I went back a little way pretending to look for it, but came back saying, I was very sorry, but I did not know where it was. At last the man came home, carrying a deer upon his shoulders, which he brought into the yard and began to dress it. The wife then went out to tell him my situation, and after long persuasion he said he could not write, but that if I could tell his son what was in my passport he should write me one, and knowing that I should not be able to pass Savannah without one, and having heard several free colored men read theirs, I thought I could tell the lad what to write. The lad sat down and wrote what I told him, nearly filling a large sheet of paper for the passport, and another sheet with recommendations. These being completed, I was invited to partake of some of the fresh venison, which the woman of the house had prepared for dinner, and having done so, and feeling grateful for their kindness, I proceeded on my way. Going along, I took my papers out of my pocket, and looking at them, although I could not read a word, I perceived that the boy's writing was very unlike other writing that I had seen, and was greatly blotted besides, consequently, I was afraid that these documents would not answer my purpose, and began to consider what other plan I could pursue to obtain another pass. I had now to wade through another river to which I came, and which I had great difficulty in crossing in consequence of the water overflowing the banks of several rivers to the extent of upwards of twenty miles.

In the midst of the water, I passed one night upon a small island, and the next day I went through the remainder of the water. On many occasions I was obliged to walk upon my toes, and consequently found the advantage of being six feet two inches high, and at other times was obliged to swim. In the middle of this extremity, I felt it would be imprudent for me to return, for if my master was in pursuit of me, my safest place from him was in the water, if I could keep my head above the surface. I was, however, most dreadfully frightened, and most earnestly prayed that I might be kept from a watery grave, and resolved that, if again I landed, I would spend my life in the service of God. Having through mercy again started on my journey, I met with the drovers, and having, whilst in the waters, taken the pass out of my hat, and so dipped it in the water as to spoil it, I showed it to the men, and asked them where I could get another. They told me that in the neighborhood there lived a rich cotton merchant, who would write me one. They took me to him, and gave their word that they saw the passport before it was wet, (for I had previously showed it to them) upon which the cotton planter wrote a free pass and a recommendation, to which the cow drovers affixed their marks. The recommendation was as follows, "John Roper, a very interesting young lad, whom I have seen and traveled with for eighty or ninety miles on his road from Florida, is a free man, descended from Indian and White. I trust he will be allowed to pass on without interruption, being convinced from what I have seen that he is free, and though dark, is not an African. I had seen his papers before they were wetted."

These cow drovers, who procured me the passport and recommendation from the cotton planter, could not read, and they were intoxicated when they went with me to him. I am part African, as well as Indian and White, my father being a white man, Henry Roper, Esquire, Caswell County, North Carolina, United States, a very wealthy slaveholder, who sold me when quite a child, for the strong resemblance I bore to him. My mother is part Indian, part African, but I dared not disclose that, or I should have been taken up. I then had eleven miles to go to Savannah, one of the greatest slaveholding cities in America, and where they are always looking out for runaway slaves.

When at this city, I had traveled about five hundred miles. It required great courage to pass through this place. I went through the main street with apparent confidence, though much alarmed, did not stop at any house in the city, but went down immediately to the dock, and inquired for a berth, as a steward to a vessel to New York. I had been in this capacity before on the Apalachicola River. The person whom I asked to procure me a berth was steward of one of the New York packets, he knew Captain Deckay, of the schooner *Fox*, and got me a situation on board that vessel, in five minutes after I had been at the docks. The schooner *Fox* was a very old vessel, twenty-seven years old, laden with lumber and cattle for New York, she was rotten and could not be insured. The sailors were afraid of her, but I ventured on board, and five minutes after we dropped from the docks into the river. My spirits then began to revive, and I thought I should get to a free country directly. We cast anchor in the stream, to keep the sailors on, as they were so dissatisfied with the vessel, and lay there four days, during which time I had to go into the city several times, which exposed me to great danger, as my master was after me, and I dreaded meeting with him in the city.

Fearing the *Fox* would not sail before I should be seized, I deserted her, and went on board a brig sailing to Providence, that was towed out by a steamboat, and got thirty miles from Savannah. During this time I endeavored to persuade the steward to take me as an assistant, and hoped to have accomplished my purpose, but the captain had observed me attentively, and thought I was a slave, he therefore ordered me, when the steamboat was sent back, to go on board her to Savannah, as the fine for taking a slave from that city to any of the Free States is five hundred dollars. I reluctantly went back to Savannah, among slaveholders and slaves. My mind was in a sad state, and I was under strong temptation to throw myself into the river. I had deserted the schooner *Fox*, and knew that the captain might put me into prison till the vessel was ready to sail, if this had happened, and my master had come to the jail in search of me, I must have gone back to slavery. But when I reached the docks at Savannah, the first person I met was the captain of the *Fox*, looking for another steward in my place. He was a very kind man, belonging to the Free States, and inquired if I would go back to his vessel. This usage was very different to what I expected, and I gladly accepted his offer. This captain did not know that I was a slave. In about two days we sailed from Savannah for New York. I am (August 1834) unable to express the joy I now felt. I never was at sea before, and, after I had been out about an hour, was taken with seasickness, which continued five days. I was scarcely able to stand up, and one of the sailors was obliged to take my place.

The captain was very kind to me all this time, but even after I recovered, I was not sufficiently well to do my duty properly, and could not give satisfaction to the sailors, who swore at me, and asked me why I shipped, as I was not used to the sea. We had a very quick passage, and in six days, after leaving Savannah, we were in the harbor at Staten Island, where the vessel was quarantined for two days, six miles from New York. The captain went to the city, but left me aboard with the sailors who had most of them been brought up in the slaveholding states, and were very cruel men. One of the sailors was particularly angry with me because he had to perform the duties of my place, and while the captain was in the city, the sailors called me to the fore-hatch, where they said they would treat me. I went, and while I was talking, they threw a rope round my neck and nearly choked me. The blood streamed from my nose profusely. They also took up ropes with large knots, and knocked me over the head. They said I was a Negro, they despised me, and I expected they would have thrown me into the water. When we arrived at the city these men, who had so ill-treated me, ran away that they might escape the punishment which would otherwise have been inflicted on them. When I arrived in the city of New York, I thought I was free, but learned I was not, and could be taken there. I went out into the country several miles, and tried to get employment, but failed, as I had no recommendation. I then returned to New York, but finding the same difficulty there to get work, as in the country, I went back to the vessel, which was to sail eighty miles up the Hudson River, to Poughkeepsie.

When I arrived, I obtained employment at an inn, and after I had been there about two days, was seized with the cholera, which was at that place. The complaint was, without doubt, brought on by my having subsisted on fruit only, for several days, while I was in the slave states. The landlord of the inn came to me when I was in bed, suffering violently from cholera, and told me he knew I had that complaint, and as it had never been in his house, I could not stop there any longer. No one would enter my room, except a young lady, who appeared very pious and amiable, and had visited persons with the cholera.

She immediately procured me some medicine at her own expense and administered it herself, and, whilst I was groaning with agony, the landlord came up and ordered me out of the house directly. Most of the persons in Poughkeepsie had retired for the night, and I lay under a shed on some cotton bales. The medicine relieved me, having been given so promptly, and next morning I went from the shed and laid on the banks of the river below the city. Towards evening, I felt much better, and went on in a steamboat to the city of Albany, about eighty miles.

When I reached there, I went into the country, and tried for three or four days to procure employment, but failed.

At that time, I had scarcely any money, and lived upon fruit, so I returned to Albany, where I could get no work, as I could not show the recommendations I possessed, which were only from slave states, and I did not wish anyone to know I came from them. After a time, I went up the western canal as steward in one of the boats. When I had gone about 350 miles up the canal, I found I was going too much towards the slave states, in consequence of which, I returned to Albany, and went up the northern canal, into one of the New England states—Vermont. The distance I had traveled, including the 350 miles I had to return from the west, and the 100 to Vermont, was 2,300 miles.

When I reached Vermont, I found the people very hospitable and kind, they seemed opposed to slavery, so I told them, I was a runaway slave. I hired myself to a firm in Sudbury.[1] After I had been in Sudbury some time, the neighboring farmers told me that I had hired myself for much less money than I ought. I mentioned it to my employers, who were very angry about it, I was advised to leave by some of the people round, who thought the gentlemen I was with would write to my former master, informing him where I was, and obtain the reward fixed upon me. Fearing I should be taken, I immediately left and went into the town of Ludlow, where I met with a kind friend, who sent me to school for several weeks. At this time, I was advertised in the papers and was obliged to leave, I went a little way out of Ludlow to a retired place, and lived two weeks with a deacon of a church at Ludlow, at this place, I could have obtained education, had it been safe to have remained.[2] From there I went to New Hampshire, where I was not safe, so went to Boston, Massachusetts, with the hope of returning to Ludlow, to which place I was much attached. At Boston, I met with a friend who kept a shop, and took me to assist him for several weeks.

[1] During my stay in this town, I thought of the vow I made in the water (during escape from slavery), and I became more thoughtful about the salvation of my soul. I attended the Methodist chapel, where a Mr. Benton preached, and there I began to feel that I was a great sinner. During the latter part of my stay here, I became more anxious about salvation, and I entertained the absurd notion that religion would come to me in some extraordinary way. With this impression I used to go into the woods two hours before daylight to pray, and expected something would take place, and I should become religious.

[2] Whilst in this neighborhood, I attended the Baptist meeting, and trust the preaching of the gospel was much blessed to my soul. As this was the first time I was ever favored with any education, I was very intent upon learning to read the Bible, and in a few weeks I was able, from my own reading, to repeat by heart the whole of the last chapter of *Matthew*. I also attended the prayer and inquiry meetings, where the attendants used to relate their experience, and I was requested to do the same. I found these (prayer) meetings a great blessing, and they were the means, under God, of communicating to my mind a more clear and distinct knowledge of the way of salvation by Jesus Christ.

Here I did not consider myself safe, as persons from all parts of the country were continually coming to the shop, and I feared some might come who knew me. I now had my head shaved and bought a wig, and engaged myself to a Mr. Perkins of Brookline, three miles from Boston, where I remained about a month. Some of the family discovered that I wore a wig, and said that I was a runaway slave, but the neighbors all round thought I was a white, to prove which, I have a document in my possession to call me to military duty. The law is, that no slave or colored person performs this, but every other person in America of the age of twenty-one is called upon to perform military duty, once or twice in the year, or pay a fine. I then returned to the city of Boston, to the shop where I was before.[3] Several weeks after I had returned to my situation two colored men informed me that a gentleman had been inquiring for a person whom, from the description, I knew to be myself, and offered them a considerable sum if they would disclose my place of abode, but they being much opposed to slavery, came and told me, upon which information I secreted myself till I could get off. I went into the Green Mountains for several weeks, from thence to the city of

New York, and remained in secret several days, till I heard of a ship, the *Napoleon*, sailing to England, and on the 11th of November, 1835, I sailed, taking with me (several) letters of recommendation to the Reverends Morison and Raffles, and the Reverend Alex Fletcher. The time I first started from slavery was in July, 1834, so that I was nearly sixteen months in making my escape. On the 29th of November, 1835, I reached Liverpool, and my feelings when I first touched the shores of Britain were indescribable, and can only be properly understood by those who have escaped from the cruel bondage of (American) slavery.

[3]During the first part of my abode in this city, I attended at the colored church in Belknap Street, and I hope I found both profit and pleasure in attending the means of divine grace. I now saw the wicked part I had taken in using so much deception in making my escape. After a time, I found slave owners were in the habit of going to this colored chapel to look for runaway slaves. I became alarmed, and afterwards attended the preaching of the Reverend Sharp. I waited upon the Reverend to request he would baptize me and admit me a member of his church, and after hearing my experience, he wished me to call again. This I did, but he was gone into the country, and I saw him no more.

(Copy of the Document) Mr. Moses Roper, You being duly enrolled as a soldier in the company, under the command of Captain Benjamin Bradley, are hereby notified and ordered to appear at the Town House in Brookline, on Friday, 28th instant, at 3 o'clock PM, for the purpose of filling the vacancy in said Company, occasioned by the promotion of Lieutenant Nathaniel M. Weeks, and of filling any other vacancy which may then and there occur in said Company, and there wait further orders.

By order of the Captain, E. P. Wentworth, Clerk
Brookline, August 14th, 1835

Tis liberty alone that gives the flower of fleeting life its luster and perfume, and we are weeds without it. Slaves cannot breathe in England, if their lungs receive our air, that moment they are free. They touch our country and their shackles fall. (William Cowper)

When I reached Liverpool, I proceeded to Dr. Raffles, and handed my letters of recommendation to him. He received me very kindly, and introduced me to a member of his church, with whom I stayed the night. Here I met with the greatest attention and kindness. The next day, I went on to Manchester, where I met with many kind friends, among others Mr. Adshead, a hosier of that town, to whom I desire, through this medium, to return my most sincere thanks for the many great services which he rendered me, adding both to my spiritual and temporal comfort. I would not, however, forget to remember here, Mr. Leese, Mr. Childs, Mr. Crewdson, and Mr. Clare, the latter of whom gave me a letter to Mr. Scoble, the Secretary of the Anti-Slavery Society. I remained here several days, and then proceeded to London, December 12th, 1835, and immediately called on Mr. Scoble, to whom I delivered my letter, this gentleman procured me lodging. I then lost no time in delivering my letters to Reverend Morison and the Reverend Alexander Fletcher, who received me with the greatest kindness, and shortly after this Reverend Morison sent my letter from New York, with another from himself, to the *Patriot* newspaper, in which he kindly implored the sympathy of the public in my behalf. The appeal was read by Mr. Christopherson, a member of Reverend Morison's church, of which gentleman I express but little of my feelings and gratitude, when I say that throughout he has been towards me a parent, and for whose tenderness and sympathy I desire ever to feel that attachment which I do not know how to express. I stayed at his house several weeks, being treated as one of the family.

The appeal in the *Patriot*, referred to getting a suitable academy for me, which the Reverend Cox recommended at Hackney, where I remained half a year, going through the rudiments of an English education. At this time, I attended the ministry of Reverend Cox, which I enjoyed very much, and to which I ascribe the attainment of clearer views of divine grace than I had before. I had attended here several months, when I expressed my wish to Reverend Cox to become a member of his church, I was proposed, and after stating my experience was admitted, March 31st, 1836. Here I feel it a duty to present my tribute of thankfulness, however feebly expressed, to the affectionate and devoted attention of the Reverend Doctor, from whom, under God, I received very much indeed of spiritual advice and consolation, as well as a plentiful administration to my temporal necessities. I would not forget also to mention the kindness of his church generally, by whom I was received with Christian love and charity. Never, I trust, will be effaced from my memory, the parental care of the Reverend Morison, from whom I can strictly say I received the greatest kindness I ever met with, and to whom, as long as God gives me lips to utter, or mind to reflect, I desire to attribute the comfort which I have experienced since I set my foot upon the happy shores of England.

Here it is necessary that I should draw this narrative to a close, not that my materials are exhausted, but that I am unwilling to extend it to a size which might preclude many well wishers from the possession of it. But I must remark, that my feelings of happiness, at having escaped from cruel bondage, are not unmixed with sorrow of a very touching kind. "*The land of the free*" still contains the mother, the brothers and the sisters of Moses Roper, not enjoying liberty, not the possessors of like feelings with me, not having even a distant glimpse of advancing towards freedom, but still slaves. This is a weight which hangs heavy on me. As circumstances at present stand, there is not much prospect of ever again seeing those dear ones—that dear mother, from whom, on the Sunday night, I was torn away by armed slaveholders, and carried into cruel bondage. And nothing would contribute so much to my entire happiness, if the kindness of a gracious Providence should ever place me in such favorable circumstances, as to be able to purchase the freedom of so beloved a parent. But I desire to express my entire resignation to the will of God. Should that Divine Being, who made of one flesh all the kindreds of the earth, see fit that I should again clasp them to my breast, and see in them the reality of free men and free women, how shall I, a poor mortal, be enabled to sing a strain of praise sufficiently appropriate to such a boon from heaven. But if the all-wise Disposer of all things should see fit to keep them still in suffering and bondage, it is a mercy to know that he orders all things well, that he is still the Judge of all the earth, and that under such dispensations of his Providence, he is working out that which shall be most for the advantage of his creatures.

Whatever I may have experienced in America, at the hands of cruel taskmasters, yet I am unwilling to speak in any but respectful terms of the land of my birth. It is far from my wish to attempt to degrade America in the eyes of Britons. I love her institutions in the Free States, her zeal for Christ, I bear no enmity even to the slaveholders, but regret their delusions, many, I am aware, are deeply sensible of the fault, but some, I regret to say, are not, and I could wish to open their eyes to their sin, may the period come when God shall wipe off this deep stain from her constitution, and may America soon be *indeed* the land of the free. In conclusion, I thank my dear friends in England for their affectionate attentions, and may God help me to show, by my future walk in life, that I'm not wanting in my acknowledgements of their kindness. But above all, to the God of all grace, I desire here, before his people, to acknowledge that all the way in which he has led me has been the right way, and as in his mercy and wisdom he has led me to this country, where I am allowed to go free, may all my actions tend to lead me on, through the mercy of God in Christ, in the right way, to a city of habitation.

Harriet Jacobs

A Note about the Present Edition

In writing her memoir Harriet Jacobs used fictional names for the people mentioned in her book as well as herself. Below are the real identities of some of the people mentioned by Harriet Jacobs in *Incidents in the Life of a Slave Girl*. All names listed below have been verified and can be found in various sites on the Internet.

Linda Brent—Harriet Jacobs
Dr. Flint—Dr. James Norcom Sr.
Mrs. Flint—Mary Matilda Horniblow Norcom
Benny Sands—Joseph Jacobs (Sawyer)
Aunt Martha—Molly Horniblow
Father—Elijah (Daniel) Knox (Jacobs)
Mother—Delilah Horniblow
Ellen Sands—Louisa Jacobs (Sawyer)
William Brent—John S. Jacobs
Uncle Phillip—Mark Ramsey
Aunt Nancy—Betty Horniblow
Mr. Sands—Samuel Tredwell Sawyer
Martha's friend—Martha Hoskins Rombough Blount

Uncle Benjamin—Joseph Horniblow
Miss Fanny—Hannah Pritchard
Ruth Nash—Margaret Horniblow
Reverend Jeremiah Durham—Himself
Mr. Bruce—Nathaniel Parker Willis
Mrs. Bruce—Mary Stace Willis
Baby Mary—Imogen Willis
Gertrude Bruce—Cornelia Grinnell Willis
Emily Flint Dodge—Mary Norcom Messmore
Mr. Thorne—Joseph Blount
Mr. Hobbs—James Iredell Tredwell
Mrs. Hobbs—Mary Bonner Blount Tredwell
Mrs. Sands—Lavinia Peyton Sawyer
Young Mr. Flint—James Norcom Jr.
Young Mrs. Flint—Penelope Hoskins Norcom
Mr. Dodge—Daniel Messmore
Aggie (slave)—Sue Bent
Amy Post—Herself
Isaac Post—Himself
Harriet Beecher Stowe—Herself
Lydia Marie Child—Herself
Hamlin—James Hamlet (fugitive slave)
Miss Murray—Amelia Murray*

*The "honorable" Amelia Murray wrote a supposedly "truthful" account of her experiences visiting America in an 1856 book titled *Letters from the United States, Cuba and Canada* which detailed the issues of slavery "firsthand." Unfortunately Murray was not as honorable as she deemed herself to be as she easily (or carelessly) let herself be led astray by the people she spoke to concerning the question of slavery. Obviously the slaveholders she met had no problem with the issues of owning slaves—it was also clear *they* let her speak only to the slaves *they* chose in order to further bolster their fictionalization of their actions. But yet this fact apparently never occurred to Murray despite thinking she was an intelligent woman. If she really wanted to know if slavery was the great evil it was as described by former slaves, maybe she should have tried being a slave for one month herself. It is doubtful she would have made such loose comments after such an experience. Ignorance truly is bliss.

Incidents in the Life of a Slave Girl
Seven Years Concealed

I was born a slave, but I never knew it till six years of happy childhood had passed away. My father was a carpenter, and considered so intelligent and skillful in his trade, that, when buildings out of the common line were to be erected, he was sent for from long distances, to be head workman. On condition of paying his mistress two hundred dollars a year, and supporting himself, he was allowed to work at his trade, and manage his own affairs. His strongest wish was to purchase his children, but, though he several times offered his hard earnings for that purpose, he never succeeded. In complexion my parents were a light shade of brownish yellow, and were termed mulattoes.

They lived together in a comfortable home, and, though we were all slaves, I was so fondly shielded that I never dreamed I was a piece of merchandise, trusted to them for safekeeping, and liable to be demanded of them at any moment. I had one brother, William, who was two years younger than myself—a bright, affectionate child. I had also a great treasure in my maternal grandmother, who was a remarkable woman in many respects.

She was the daughter of a planter in South Carolina, who, at his death, left her mother and his three children free, with money to go to St. Augustine, where they had relatives.

It was during the Revolutionary War, and they were captured on their passage, carried back, and sold to different purchasers. Such was the story my grandmother used to tell me, but I do not remember all the particulars. She was a little girl when she was captured and sold to the keeper of a large hotel. I have often heard her tell how hard she fared during childhood. But as she grew older she evinced so much intelligence, and was so faithful, that her master and mistress could not help seeing it was for their interest to take care of such a valuable piece of property. She became an indispensable personage in the household, officiating in all capacities, from cook and wet nurse to seamstress. She was much praised for her cooking, and her nice crackers became so famous in the neighborhood that many people were desirous of obtaining them. In consequence of numerous requests of this kind, she asked permission of her mistress to bake crackers at night, after all the household work was done, and she obtained leave to do it, provided she would clothe herself and her children from the profits. Upon these terms, after working hard all day for her mistress, she began her midnight bakings, assisted by her two oldest children.

The business proved profitable, and each year she laid by little, which was saved for a fund to purchase her children. Her master died, and the property was divided among his heirs. The widow had her dower in the hotel, which she continued to keep open. My grandmother remained in her service as a slave, but her children were divided among her master's children. As she had five, Benjamin, the youngest one, was sold, in order that each heir might have an equal portion of dollars and cents.

There was so little difference in our ages that he seemed more like my brother than my uncle. He was a bright, handsome lad, nearly white, for he inherited the complexion my grandmother had derived from Anglo-Saxon ancestors. Though only ten years old, seven hundred and twenty dollars were paid for him. His sale was a terrible blow to my grandmother, but she was naturally hopeful, and she went to work with renewed energy, trusting in time to be able to purchase some of her children. She had laid up three hundred dollars, which her mistress one day begged as a loan, promising to pay her soon. The reader probably knows that no promise or writing given to a slave is legally binding, for, according to Southern laws, a slave, *being* property, can *hold* no property. When my grandmother lent her hard earnings to her mistress, she trusted solely to her honor. The honor of a slaveholder to a slave! To this good grandmother I was indebted for many comforts. My brother Willie and I often received portions of the crackers, cakes, and preserves, she made to sell, and after we ceased to be children we were indebted to her for many more important services. Such were the unusually fortunate circumstances of my early childhood. When I was six years old, my mother died, and then, for the first time, I learned, by the talk around me, that I was a slave. My mother's mistress was the daughter of my grandmother's mistress. She was the foster sister of my mother, they were both nourished at my grandmother's breast. In fact, my mother had been weaned at three months old, that the babe of the mistress might obtain sufficient food. They played together as children, and, when they became women, my mother was a most faithful servant to her whiter foster sister. On her deathbed her mistress promised that her children should never suffer for anything, and during her lifetime she kept her word. They all spoke kindly of my dead mother, who had been a slave merely in name, but in nature was noble and womanly. I grieved for her, and my young mind was troubled with the thought who would now take care of me and my little brother. I was told that my home was now to be with her mistress, and I found it a happy one. No toilsome or disagreeable duties were imposed upon me. My mistress was so kind to me that I was always glad to do her bidding, and proud to labor for her as much as my young years would permit. I would sit by her side for hours, sewing diligently, with a heart as free from care as that of any free-born white child. When she thought I was tired, she would send me out to run and jump, and away I bounded, to gather berries or flowers to decorate her room. Those were happy days—too happy to last. The slave child had no thought for the morrow, but there came that blight, which too surely waits on every human being born to be a chattel. When I was nearly twelve years old, my kind mistress sickened and died. As I saw the cheek grow paler, and the eye more glassy, how earnestly I prayed in my heart that she might live! I loved her, for she had been almost like a mother to me. My prayers were not answered.

She died, and they buried her in the little churchyard, where, day after day, my tears fell upon her grave. I was sent to spend a week with my grandmother. I was now old enough to begin to think of the future, and again and again I asked myself what they would do with me. I felt sure I should never find another mistress so kind as the one who was gone. She had promised my dying mother that her children should never suffer for anything, and when I remembered that, and recalled her many proofs of attachment to me, I could not help having some hopes that she had left me free. My friends were almost certain it would be so. They thought she would be sure to do it, on account of my mother's love and faithful service. But, alas! We all know that the memory of a faithful slave does not avail much to save her children from the auction block. After a brief period of suspense, the Will of my mistress was read, and we learned that she had bequeathed me to her sister's daughter, a child of five years old. So vanished our hopes. My mistress had taught me the precepts of God's word "Thou shalt love thy neighbor as thyself." "Whatsoever ye would that men should do unto you, do ye even so unto them." But I was her slave, and I suppose she did not recognize me as her neighbor. I would give much to blot out from my memory that one great wrong. As a child, I loved my mistress, and, looking back on the happy days I spent with her, I try to think with less bitterness of this act of injustice. While I was with her, she taught me to read and spell, and for this privilege, which so rarely falls to the lot of a slave, I bless her memory. She possessed but few slaves, and at her death those were all distributed among her relatives. Five of them were my grandmother's children, and had shared the same milk that nourished her mother's children. Notwithstanding my grandmother's long and faithful service to her owners, not one of her children escaped the auction block. These God-breathing machines are no more, in the sight of their masters, than the cotton they plant, or the horses they tend.

☐☐☐☐☐☐☐☐☐☐

Dr. Flint, a physician in the neighborhood, had married the sister of my mistress, and I was now the property of their little daughter. It was not without murmuring that I prepared for my new home, and what added to my unhappiness, was the fact that my brother William was purchased by the same family. My father, by his nature, as well as by the habit of transacting business as a skillful mechanic, had more of the feelings of a free man than is common among slaves. My brother was a spirited boy, and being brought up under such influences, he early detested the name of master and mistress. One day, when his father and his mistress both happened to call him at the same time, he hesitated between the two, being perplexed to know which had the strongest claim upon his obedience. He finally concluded to go to his mistress. When my father reproved him for it, he said, "You both called me, and I didn't know which I ought to go to first." "You are *my* child," replied our father, "and when I call you, you should come immediately, if you have to pass through fire and water." Poor Willie! He was now to learn his first lesson of obedience to a master. Grandmother tried to cheer us with hopeful words, and they found an echo in the credulous hearts of youth. When we entered our new home we encountered cold looks, cold words, and cold treatment. We were glad when the night came. On my narrow bed I moaned and wept, I felt so desolate and alone. I had been there nearly a year, when a dear little friend of mine was buried. I heard her mother sob, as the clods fell on the coffin of her only child, and I turned away from the grave, feeling thankful that I still had something left to love. I met my grandmother, who said, "Come with me, Linda," and from her tone I knew that something sad had happened. She led me apart from the people, and then said, "My child, your father is dead." Dead! How could I believe it? He had died so suddenly I had not even heard that he was sick. I went home with my grandmother. My heart rebelled against God, who had taken from me mother, father, mistress, and friend. The good grandmother tried to comfort me. "Who knows the ways of God?" said she. "Perhaps they have been kindly taken from the evil days to come." Years afterwards I often thought of this. She promised to be a mother to her grandchildren, so far as she might be permitted to do so, and strengthened by her love, I returned to my master's. I thought I should be allowed to go to my father's house the next morning, but I was ordered to go for flowers, that my mistress's house might be decorated for an evening party.

I spent the day gathering flowers and weaving them into festoons, while the dead body of my father was lying within a mile of me. What cared my owners for that? He was merely a piece of property. Moreover, they thought he had spoiled his children, by teaching them to feel that they were human beings. This was blasphemous doctrine for a slave to teach, presumptuous in him, and dangerous to the masters. The next day I followed his remains to a humble grave beside that of my dear mother. There were those who knew my father's worth, and respected his memory. My home now seemed more dreary than ever. The laugh of the little slave children sounded harsh and cruel. It was selfish to feel so about the joy of others. My brother moved about with a very grave face. I tried to comfort him, by saying, "Take courage, Willie, brighter days will come by and by." "You don't know anything about it, Linda," he replied. "We shall have to stay here all our days, we shall never be free." I argued that we were growing older and stronger, and that perhaps we might, before long, be allowed to hire our own time, and then we could earn money to buy our freedom. William declared this was much easier to say than to do, moreover, he did not intend to *buy* his freedom. We held daily controversies upon this subject. Little attention was paid to the slaves meals in Dr. Flint's house. If they could catch a bit of food while it was going, well and good. I gave myself no trouble on that score, for on my various errands I passed my grandmother's house, where there was always something to spare for me. I was frequently threatened with punishment if I stopped there, and my grandmother, to avoid detaining me, often stood at the gate with something for my breakfast or dinner. I was indebted to *her* for all my comforts, spiritual or temporal. It was *her* labor that supplied my scanty wardrobe. I have a vivid recollection of the linsey-woolsey dress given me every winter by Mrs. Flint. How I hated it! It was one of the badges of slavery. While my grandmother was thus helping to support me from her hard earnings, the three hundred dollars she had lent her mistress were never repaid. When her mistress died her son-in-law, Dr. Flint, was appointed executor.

When grandmother applied to him for payment, he said the estate was insolvent, and the law prohibited payment. It did not, however, prohibit him from retaining the silver candelabra, which had been purchased with that money. I presume they will be handed down in the family, from generation to generation. My grandmother's mistress had always promised her that, at her death, she should be free, and it was said that in her Will she made good the promise. But when the estate was settled, Dr. Flint told the faithful old servant that, under existing circumstances, it was necessary she should be sold. On the appointed day, the customary advertisement was posted up, proclaiming that there would be a "public sale of Negroes, horses, and etc." Dr. Flint called to tell my grandmother that he was unwilling to wound her feelings by putting her up at auction, and that he would prefer to dispose of her at a private sale.

My grandmother saw through his hypocrisy, she understood very well that he was ashamed of the job. She was a very spirited woman, and if he was base enough to sell her, when her mistress intended she should be free, she was determined the public should know it. She had for a long time supplied many families with crackers and preserves, consequently, "Aunt Marthy," as she was called, was generally known, and everybody who knew her respected her intelligence and good character. Her long and faithful service in the family was also well-known, and the intention of her mistress to leave her free. When the day of sale came, she took her place among the chattels, and at the first call she sprang upon the auction block. Many voices called out, "Shame! Shame! Who is going to sell *you*, Aunt Marthy? Don't stand there! That is no place for *you*." Without saying a word, she quietly awaited her fate. No one bid for her. At last, a feeble voice said, "Fifty dollars." It came from a maiden lady, seventy years old, the sister of my grandmother's deceased mistress.

She had lived forty years under the same roof with my grandmother, she knew how faithfully she had served her owners, and how cruelly she had been defrauded of her rights, and she resolved to protect her. The auctioneer waited for a higher bid, but her wishes were respected, no one bid above her. She could neither read nor write, and when the bill of sale was made out, she signed it with a cross. But what consequence was that, when she had a big heart overflowing with human kindness? She gave the old servant her freedom. At that time, my grandmother was just fifty years old. Laborious years had passed since then, and now my brother and I were slaves to the man who had defrauded her of her money, and tried to defraud her of her freedom. One of my mother's sisters, called Aunt Nancy, was also a slave in his family. She was a kind, good aunt to me, and supplied the place of both housekeeper and waiting maid to her mistress. She was, in fact, at the beginning and end of everything. Mrs. Flint, like many Southern women, was totally deficient in energy. She had not strength to superintend her household affairs, but her nerves were so strong, that she could sit in her easy chair and see a woman whipped, till the blood trickled from every stroke of the lash. She was a member of the church, but partaking of the Lord's Supper did not seem to put her in a Christian frame of mind. If dinner was not served at the exact time on that particular Sunday, she would station herself in the kitchen, and wait till it was dished, and then spit in all the kettles and pans that had been used for cooking. She did this to prevent the cook and her children from eking out their meager fare with the remains of the gravy and other scrapings. The slaves could get nothing to eat except what she chose to give them. Provisions were weighed out by the pound and ounce, three times a day. I can assure you she gave them no chance to eat wheat bread from her flour barrel. She knew how many biscuits a quart of flour would make, and exactly what size they ought to be. Dr. Flint was an epicure. The cook never sent a dinner to his table without fear and trembling, for if there happened to be a dish not to his liking, he would either order her to be whipped, or compel her to eat every mouthful of it in his presence.

  The poor, hungry creature might not have objected to eating it, but she did object to having her master cram it down her throat till she choked. They had a pet dog, that was a nuisance in the house. The cook was ordered to make some Indian mush for him. He refused to eat, and when his head was held over it, the froth flowed from his mouth into the basin. He died a few minutes after. When Dr. Flint came in, he said the mush had not been well-cooked, and that was the reason the animal would not eat it. He sent for the cook, and compelled her to eat it. He thought that the woman's stomach was stronger than the dog's, but her sufferings afterwards proved that he was mistaken. This poor woman endured many cruelties from her master and mistress, sometimes she was locked up, away from her nursing baby, for a whole day and night. When I had been in the family a few weeks, one of the plantation slaves was brought to town, by order of his master. It was near night when he arrived, and Dr. Flint ordered him to be taken to the work house, and tied up to the joist, so that his feet would just escape the ground. In that situation he was to wait till the doctor had taken his tea. I shall never forget that night. Never before, in my life, had I heard hundreds of blows fall, in succession, on a human being. His piteous groans, and his "O, pray don't, Massa," rang in my ear for months afterwards. There were many conjectures as to the cause of this terrible punishment. Some said master accused him of stealing corn, others said the slave had quarreled with his wife, in presence of the overseer, and had accused his master of being the father of her child. They were both black, and the child was very fair. I went into the work house next morning, and saw the cowhide still wet with blood, and the boards all covered with gore. The poor man lived, and continued to quarrel with his wife. A few months afterwards Dr. Flint handed them both over to a slave trader. The guilty man put their value into his pocket, and had the satisfaction of knowing that they were out of sight and hearing. When the mother was delivered into the trader's hands, she said, "You *promised* to treat me well." To which he replied, "You have let your tongue run too far, damn you!" She had forgotten that it was a crime for a slave to tell who was the father of her child. From others than the master persecution also comes in such cases. I once saw a young slave girl dying soon after the birth of a child nearly white. In her agony she cried out, "O Lord, come and take me!" Her mistress stood by, and mocked at her like an incarnate fiend. "You suffer, do you?" she exclaimed. "I am glad of it. You deserve it all, and, more too." The girl's mother said, "The baby is dead, thank God, and I hope my poor child will soon be in heaven, too." "Heaven!" retorted the mistress. "There is no such place for the like of her and her bastard."

The poor mother turned away, sobbing. Her dying daughter called her, feebly, and as she bent over her, I heard her say, "Don't grieve so, mother, God knows all about it, and *He* will have mercy upon me." Her sufferings, afterwards, became so intense, that her mistress felt unable to stay, but when she left the room, the scornful smile was still on her lips. Seven children called her mother. The poor black woman had but the one child, whose eyes she saw closing in death, while she thanked God for taking her away from the greater bitterness of life.

☐☐☐☐☐☐☐☐☐☐

Dr. Flint owned a fine residence in town, several farms, and about fifty slaves, besides hiring a number by the year. Hiring day at the South takes place on the 1st of January. On the 2nd, the slaves are expected to go to their new masters. On a farm, they work until the corn and cotton are laid. They then have two holidays. Some masters give them a good dinner under the trees. This over, they work until Christmas Eve. If no heavy charges are meantime brought against them, they are given four or five holidays, whichever the master or overseer may think proper. Then comes New Year's Eve, and they gather together their little alls, or more properly speaking, their little nothings, and wait anxiously for the dawning of day. At the appointed hour the grounds are thronged with men, women, and children, waiting, like criminals, to hear their doom pronounced. The slave is sure to know who is the most humane, or cruel master, within forty miles of him. It is easy to find out, on that day, who clothes and feeds his slaves well, for he is surrounded by a crowd, begging, "Please, Massa, hire me this year. I will work *very* hard, Massa." If a slave is unwilling to go with his new master, he is whipped, or locked up in jail, until he consents to go, and promises not to run away during the year. Should he chance to change his mind, thinking it justifiable to violate an extorted promise, woe unto him if he is caught! The whip is used till the blood flows at his feet, and his stiffened limbs are put in chains, to be dragged in the field for days and days! If he lives until the next year, perhaps the same man will hire him again, without even giving him an opportunity of going to the hiring ground. After those for hire are disposed of, those for sale are called up. O, you happy free women, contrast *your* New Year's Day with that of the poor bond woman! With you it is a pleasant season, and the light of the day is blessed. Friendly wishes meet you everywhere, and gifts are showered upon you. Even hearts that have been estranged from you soften at this season, and lips that have been silent echo back, "I wish you a Happy New Year." Children bring their little offerings, and raise their rosy lips for a caress. They are your own, and no hand but that of death can take them from you. But to the slave mother New Year's Day comes laden with peculiar sorrows. She sits on her cold cabin floor, watching the children who may all be torn from her the next morning, and often does she wish that she and they might die before the day dawns. She may be an ignorant creature, degraded by the system that has brutalized her from childhood, but she has a mother's instincts, and is capable of feeling a mother's agonies. On one of these sale days, I saw a mother lead seven children to the auction block. She knew that *some* of them would be taken from her, but they took *all*. The children were sold to a slave trader, and their mother was bought by a man in her own town. Before night her children were all far away. She begged the trader to tell her where he intended to take them, this he refused to do. How *could* he, when he knew he would sell them, one by one, wherever he could command the highest price? I met that mother in the street, and her wild, haggard face lives today in my mind. She wrung her hands in anguish, and exclaimed, "Gone! All gone! Why *don't* God kill me?" I had no words wherewith to comfort her. Instances of this kind are of daily, yeah, of hourly occurrence. Slaveholders have a method, peculiar to their institution, of getting rid of *old* slaves, whose lives have been worn out in their service. I knew an old woman, who for seventy years faithfully served her master. She had become almost helpless, from hard labor and disease. Her owners moved to Alabama, and the old black woman was left to be sold to anybody who would give twenty dollars for her.

☐☐☐☐☐☐☐☐☐☐☐

  Two years had passed since I entered Dr. Flint's family, and those years had brought much of the knowledge that comes from experience, though they had afforded little opportunity for any other kinds of knowledge. My grandmother had, as much as possible, been a mother to her orphan grandchildren. By perseverance and unwearied industry, she was now mistress of a snug little home, surrounded with the necessaries of life. She would have been happy could her children have shared them with her. There remained but three children and two grandchildren, all slaves. Most earnestly did she strive to make us feel that it was the will of God, that He had seen fit to place us under such circumstances, and though it seemed hard, we ought to pray for contentment. It was a beautiful faith, coming from a mother who could not call her children her own. But I, and Benjamin, her youngest boy, condemned it. We reasoned that it was much more the will of God that we should be situated as she was.

  We longed for a home like hers. There we always found sweet balsam for our troubles. She was so loving, so sympathizing! She always met us with a smile, and listened with patience to all our sorrows. She spoke so hopefully, that unconsciously the clouds gave place to sunshine. There was a grand big oven there, too, that baked bread and nice things for the town, and we knew there was always a choice bit in store for us. But, alas! Even the charms of the old oven failed to reconcile us to our hard lot. Benjamin was now a tall, handsome lad, strongly and gracefully made, and with a spirit too bold and daring for a slave. My brother William, now twelve years old, had the same aversion to the word master that he had when he was an urchin of seven years. I was his confidant. He came to me with all his troubles. I remember one instance in particular. It was on a lovely spring morning, and when I marked the sunlight dancing here and there, its beauty seemed to mock my sadness.

For my master, whose restless, craving, vicious nature roved about day and night, seeking whom to devour, had just left me, with stinging, scorching words, words that scathed ear and brain like fire. O, how I despised him! I thought how glad I should be, if some day when he walked the earth, it would open and swallow him up, and disencumber the world of a plague. When he told me that I was made for his use, made to obey his command in *everything*, that I was nothing but a slave, whose will must and should surrender to his, never before had my puny arm felt half so strong. So deeply was I absorbed in painful reflections afterwards, that I neither saw nor heard the entrance of anyone, till the voice of William sounded close beside me. "Linda," said he, "what makes you look so sad? I love you. O, Linda, isn't this a bad world? Everybody seems so cross and unhappy. I wish I had died when poor father did." I told him that everybody was *not* cross, or unhappy, that those who had pleasant homes, and kind friends, and who were not afraid to love them, were happy. But we, who were slave children, without father or mother, could not expect to be happy. We must be good, perhaps that would bring us contentment. "Yes," he said, "I try to be good, but what's the use? They are all the time troubling me." Then he proceeded to relate his afternoon's difficulty with young Master Nicholas.

It seemed that the brother of Master Nicholas had pleased himself with making up stories about William. Master Nicholas said he should be flogged, and he would do it. Whereupon he went to work, but William fought bravely, and the young master, finding he was getting the better of him, undertook to tie his hands behind him. He failed in that likewise. By dint of kicking and fisting, William came out of the skirmish none the worse for a few scratches. He continued to discourse on his young master's *meanness*, how he whipped the *little* boys, but was a perfect coward when a tussle ensued between him and white boys of his own size. On such occasions he always took to his legs.

William had other charges to make against him. One was his rubbing up pennies with quicksilver, and passing them off for quarters of a dollar on an old man who kept a fruit stall. William was often sent to buy fruit, and he earnestly inquired of me what he ought to do under such circumstances. I told him it was certainly wrong to deceive the old man, and that it was his duty to tell him of the impositions practiced by his young master. I assured him the old man would not be slow to comprehend the whole, and there the matter would end. William thought it might with the old man, but not with *him*. He said he did not mind the smart of the whip, but he did not like the *idea* of being whipped. While I advised him to be good and forgiving I was not unconscious of the beam in my own eye. It was the very knowledge of my own shortcomings that urged me to retain, if possible, some sparks of my brother's God-given nature. I had not lived fourteen years in slavery for nothing. I had felt, seen, and heard enough, to read the characters, and question the motives, of those around me. The war of my life had begun, and though one of God's most powerless creatures, I resolved never to be conquered. Alas, for me! If there was one pure, sunny spot for me, I believed it to be in Benjamin's heart, and in another's, whom I loved with all the ardor of a girl's first love. My owner knew of it, and sought in every way to render me miserable. He did not resort to corporal punishment, but to all the petty, tyrannical ways that human ingenuity could devise. I remember the first time I was punished. It was in the month of February.

My grandmother had taken my old shoes, and replaced them with a new pair. I needed them, for several inches of snow had fallen, and it still continued to fall. When I walked through Mrs. Flint's room, their creaking grated harshly on her refined nerves. She called me to her, and asked what I had about me that made such a horrid noise. I told her it was my new shoes. "Take them off," said she, "and if you put them on again, I'll throw them into the fire." I took them off, and my stockings also. She then sent me a long distance, on an errand. As I went through the snow, my bare feet tingled. That night I was very hoarse, and I went to bed thinking the next day would find me sick, perhaps dead. What was my grief on waking to find myself quite well! I had imagined if I died, or was laid up for some time, that my mistress would feel a twinge of remorse that she had so hated "the little imp," as she styled me. It was my ignorance of that mistress that gave rise to such extravagant imaginings.

Dr. Flint occasionally had high prices offered for me, but he always said, "She don't belong to me. She is my daughter's property, and I have no right to sell her." Good, honest man! My young mistress was still a child, and I could look for no protection from her. I loved her, and she returned my affection. I once heard her father allude to her attachment to me, and his wife promptly replied that it proceeded from fear. This put unpleasant doubts into my mind. Did the child feign what she did not feel? Or was her mother jealous of the mite of love she bestowed on me? I concluded it must be the latter. I said to myself, "Surely, little children are true." One afternoon I sat at my sewing, feeling unusual depression of spirits. My mistress had been accusing me of an offense, of which I assured her I was perfectly innocent, but I saw, by the contemptuous curl of her lip, that she believed I was telling a lie. I wondered for what wise purpose God was leading me through such thorny paths, and whether still darker days were in store for me. As I sat musing thus, the door opened softly, and William came in. "Well, brother," said I, "what is the matter this time?" "O Linda, Ben and his master have had a dreadful time!" said he. My first thought was that Benjamin was killed. "Don't be frightened, Linda," said William, "I will tell you all about it."

It appeared that Benjamin's master had sent for him, and he did not immediately obey the summons. When he did, his master was angry, and began to whip him. He resisted. Master and slave fought, and finally the master was thrown. Benjamin had cause to tremble, for he had thrown to the ground his master—one of the richest men in town. I anxiously awaited the result. That night I stole to my grandmother's house, and

Benjamin also stole thither from his master's. My grandmother had gone to spend a day or two with an old friend living in the country. "I have come," said Benjamin, "to tell you goodbye. I am going away." I inquired where. "To the North," he replied. I looked at him to see whether he was in earnest. I saw it all in his firm, set mouth. I implored him not to go, but he paid no heed to my words. He said he was no longer a boy, and every day made his yoke more galling. He had raised his hand against his master, and was to be publicly whipped for the offense. I reminded him of the poverty and hardships he must encounter among strangers.

    I told him he might be caught and brought back, and that was terrible to think of. He grew vexed, and asked if poverty and hardships with freedom, were not preferable to our treatment in slavery. "Linda," he continued, "we are dogs here, footballs, cattle, everything that's mean. No, I will not stay. Let them bring me back. We don't die but once." He was right, but it was hard to give him up. "Go," said I, "and break your mother's heart."

    I repented of my words ere they were out. "Linda," said he, speaking as I had not heard him speak that evening, "how *could* you say that? Poor mother! Be kind to her, Linda, and you, too, Cousin Fanny." Cousin Fanny was a friend who had lived some years with us. Farewells were exchanged, and the bright, kind boy, endeared to us by so many acts of love, vanished from our sight. It is not necessary to state how he made his escape. Suffice it to say, he was on his way to New York when a violent storm overtook the vessel. The captain said he must put into the nearest port. This alarmed Benjamin, who was aware that he would be advertised in every port near his own town. His embarrassment was noticed by the captain. To port they went.

    There the advertisement met the captain's eye. Benjamin so exactly answered its description, that the captain laid hold on him, and bound him in chains. The storm passed, and they proceeded to New York. Before reaching that port Benjamin managed to get off his chains and throw them overboard.

    He escaped from the vessel, but was pursued, captured, and carried back to his master. When my grandmother returned home and found her youngest child had fled, great was her sorrow, but, with characteristic piety, she said, "God's will be done." Each morning, she inquired if any news had been heard from her boy. Yes, news *was* heard. The master was rejoicing over a letter, announcing the capture of his human chattel. That day seems but as yesterday, so well do I remember it. I saw him led through the streets in chains, to jail. His face was ghastly pale, yet full of determination. He had begged one of the sailors to go to his mother's house and ask her not to meet him. He said the sight of her distress would take from him all self-control.

She yearned to see him, and she went, but she screened herself in the crowd, that it might be as her child had said. We were not allowed to visit him, but we had known the jailer for years, and he was a kindhearted man. At midnight he opened the jail door for my grandmother and myself to enter, in disguise. When we entered the cell not a sound broke, the stillness. "Benjamin, Benjamin!" whispered my grandmother. No answer. "Benjamin!" she again faltered. There was a jingle of chains. The moon had just risen, and cast an uncertain light through the bars of the window. We knelt down and took Benjamin's cold hands in ours. We did not speak. Sobs were heard, and Benjamin's lips were unsealed, for his mother was weeping on his neck.

How vividly does memory bring back that sad night! Mother and son talked together. He asked her pardon for the suffering he had caused her. She said she had nothing to forgive, she could not blame his desire for freedom. He told her that when he was captured, he broke away, and was about casting himself into the river, when thoughts of *her* came over him, and he desisted. She asked if he did not also think of God. I fancied I saw his face grow fierce in the moonlight. He answered, "No, I did not think of him. When a man is hunted like a wild beast he forgets there is a God, a heaven. He forgets everything in his struggle to get beyond the reach of the bloodhounds." "Don't talk so, Benjamin," said she. "Put your trust in God. Be humble, my child, and your master will forgive you." "Forgive me for *what*, mother? For not letting him treat me like a dog? No! I will never humble myself to him. I have worked for him for nothing all my life, and I am repaid with stripes and imprisonment. Here I will stay till I die, or till he sells me." The poor mother shuddered at his words. I think he felt it, for when he next spoke, his voice was calmer. "Don't fret about me, mother. I ain't worth it," said he. "I wish I had some of your goodness. You bear everything patiently, just as though you thought it was all right. I wish I could." She told him she had not always been so, once, she was like him, but when sore troubles came upon her, and she had no arm to lean upon, she learned to call on God, and he lightened her burdens. She besought him to do likewise. We overstayed our time, and were obliged to hurry from the jail. Benjamin had been imprisoned three weeks, when my grandmother went to intercede for him with his master. He was immovable. He said Benjamin should serve as an example to the rest of his slaves, he should be kept in jail till he was subdued, or be sold if he got but one dollar for him. However, he afterwards relented in some degree. The chains were taken off, and we were allowed to visit him. As his food was of the coarsest kind, we carried him as often as possible a warm supper, accompanied with some little luxury for the jailer.

Three months elapsed, and there was no prospect of release or of a purchaser. One day he was heard to sing and laugh. This piece of indecorum was told to his master, and the overseer was ordered to re-chain him. He was now confined in an apartment with other prisoners, who were covered with filthy rags. Benjamin was chained near them, and was soon covered with vermin. He worked at his chains till he succeeded in getting out of them. He passed them through the bars of the window, with a request that they should be taken to his master, and he should be informed that he was covered with vermin.

This audacity was punished with heavier chains, and prohibition of our visits. My grandmother continued to send him fresh changes of clothes. The old ones were burned up. The last night we saw him in jail his mother still begged him to send for his master, and beg his pardon. Neither persuasion nor argument could turn him from his purpose. He calmly answered, "I am waiting his time." Those chains were mournful to hear. Another three months passed, and Benjamin left his prison walls. We that loved him waited to bid him a long and last farewell. A slave trader had bought him. You remember, I told you what price he brought when ten years of age. Now he was more than twenty years old, and sold for three hundred dollars. The master had been blind to his own interest. Long confinement had made his face too pale, his form too thin, moreover, the trader had heard something of his character, and it did not strike him as suitable for a slave. He said he would give any price if the handsome lad was a girl. We thanked God that he was not. Could you have seen that mother clinging to her child, when they fastened the irons upon his wrists, could you have heard her heartrending groans, and seen her bloodshot eyes wander wildly from face to face, vainly pleading for mercy, could you have witnessed that scene as I saw it, you would exclaim, *slavery is damnable*. Benjamin, her youngest, her pet, was forever gone. She could not realize it. She had, had an interview with the trader for the purpose of ascertaining if Benjamin could be purchased. She was told it was impossible, as he had given bonds not to sell him till he was out of the state. He promised that he would not sell him till he reached New Orleans. With a strong arm and unvaried trust, my grandmother began her work of love. Benjamin must be free. If she succeeded, she knew they would still be separated, but the sacrifice was not too great. Day and night she labored.

    The trader's price would treble that he gave, but she was not discouraged. She employed a lawyer to write to a gentleman, whom she knew, in New Orleans. She begged him to interest himself for Benjamin, and he willingly favored her request. When he saw Benjamin, and stated his business, he thanked him, but said he preferred to wait a while before making the trader an offer. He knew he had tried to obtain a high price for him, and had invariably failed. This encouraged him to make another effort for freedom. So one morning, long before day, Benjamin was missing. He was riding over the blue billows, bound for Baltimore. For once his white face did him a kindly service. They had no suspicion that it belonged to a slave, otherwise, the law would have been followed out to the letter, and the *thing* rendered back to slavery. The brightest skies are often overshadowed by the darkest clouds. Benjamin was taken sick, and compelled to remain in Baltimore three weeks. His strength was slow in returning, and his desire to continue his journey seemed to retard his recovery. How could he get strength without air and exercise? He resolved to venture on a short walk. A bystreet was selected, where he thought himself secure of not being met by anyone that knew him, but a voice called out, "Halloo, Ben, my boy! What are you doing *here*?" His first impulse was to run, but his legs trembled so that he could not stir. He turned to confront his antagonist, and behold, there stood his old master's next door neighbor! He thought it was all over with him now, but it proved otherwise. That man was a miracle. He possessed a goodly number of slaves, and yet was not quite deaf to that mystic clock, whose ticking is rarely heard in the slaveholder's breast. "Ben, you are sick," said he. "Why, you look like a ghost. I guess I gave you something of a start. Never mind, Ben, I am not going to touch you. You had a pretty tough time of it, and you may go on your way rejoicing for all me. But I would advise you to get out of this place plaguy quick, for there are several gentlemen here from our town." He described the nearest and safest route to New York, and added, "I shall be glad to tell your mother I have seen you. Goodbye, Ben." Benjamin turned away, filled with gratitude, and surprised that the town he hated contained such a gem—a gem worthy of a purer setting. This gentleman was a Northerner by birth, and had married a Southern lady. On his return, he told my grandmother that he had seen her son, and of the service he had rendered him. Benjamin reached New York safely, and concluded to stop there until he had gained strength enough to proceed further. It happened that my grandmother's only remaining son had sailed for the same city on business for his mistress. Through God's Providence, the brothers met. You may be sure it was a happy meeting. "O Phil," exclaimed Benjamin, "I am here at last." Then he told him how near he came to dying almost in sight of free land, and how he prayed that he might live to get one breath of free air. He said life was worth something now, and it would be hard to die. In the old jail he had not valued it, once, he was tempted to destroy it, but something, he did not know what, had prevented him, perhaps it was fear.

    He had heard those who profess to be religious declare there was no heaven for self-murderers, and as his life had been pretty hot here, he did not desire a continuation of the same in another world. "If I die now," he exclaimed, "thank God, I shall die a free man!" He begged my Uncle Phillip not to return south, but stay and work with him, till they earned enough to buy those at home. His brother told him it would kill their mother if he deserted her in her trouble. She had pledged her house, and with difficulty had raised money to buy him. Would he be bought? "No, never!" he replied. "Do you suppose, Phil, when I have got so far out of their clutches, I will give them one red cent? No! And do you suppose I would turn mother out of her home in her old age? That I would let her pay all those hard-earned dollars for me, and never to see me? For you know she will stay south as long as her other children are slaves. What a good mother! Tell her to buy *you*, Phil. You have been a comfort to her, and I have been a trouble. And Linda, poor Linda, what'll become of her? Phil, you don't know what a life they lead her. She has told me something about it, and I wish old Flint was dead, or a better man. When I was in jail, he asked her if she didn't want *him* to ask my master to forgive me, and take me home again. She told him, no, that I didn't want to go back. He got mad, and said we were all alike. I never despised my own master half as much as I do that man. There is many a worse slaveholder than my master, but for all that I would not be his slave." While Benjamin was sick, he had parted with nearly all his clothes to pay necessary expenses. But he did not part with a little pin I fastened in his bosom when we parted. It was the most valuable thing I owned, and I thought none more worthy to wear it. He had it still. His brother furnished him with clothes, and gave him what money he had.

They parted with moistened eyes, and as Benjamin turned away, he said, "Phil, I part with all my kindred." And so it proved. We never heard from him again. Uncle Phillip came home, and the first words he uttered when he entered the house were, "Mother, Ben is free! I have seen him in New York." She stood looking at him with a bewildered air. "Mother, don't you believe it?" he said, laying his hand softly upon her shoulder.

She raised her hands, and exclaimed, "God be praised! Let us thank him." She dropped on her knees, and poured forth her heart in prayer. Then Phillip must sit down and repeat to her every word Benjamin had said. He told her all, only he forbore to mention how sick and pale her darling looked. Why should he distress her when she could do him no good? The brave old woman still toiled on, hoping to rescue some of her other children. After a while she succeeded in buying Phillip.

She paid eight hundred dollars, and came home with the precious document that secured his freedom. The happy mother and son sat together by the old hearthstone (flat stone) that night, telling how proud they were of each other, and how they would prove to the world that they could take care of themselves, as they had long taken care of others. We all concluded by saying, "He that is *willing* to be a slave, let him be a slave."

☐☐☐☐☐☐☐☐☐☐

During the first years of my service in Dr. Flint's family, I was accustomed to share some indulgences with the children of my mistress. Though this seemed to me no more than right, I was grateful for it, and tried to merit the kindness by the faithful discharge of my duties. But I now entered on my fifteenth year—a sad epoch in the life of a slave girl. My master began to whisper foul words in my ear. Young as I was, I could not remain ignorant of their import. I tried to treat them with indifference or contempt. The master's age, my extreme youth, and the fear that his conduct would be reported to my grandmother, made him bear this treatment for many months. He was a crafty man, and resorted to many means to accomplish his purposes.

Sometimes he had stormy, terrific ways, that made his victims tremble, sometimes he assumed a gentleness that he thought must surely subdue. Of the two, I preferred his stormy moods, although they left me trembling. He tried his utmost to corrupt the pure principles my grandmother had instilled. He peopled my young mind with unclean images, such as only a vile monster could think of. I turned from him with disgust and hatred. But he was my master. I was compelled to live under the same roof with him—where I saw a man forty years my senior daily violating the most sacred commandments of nature. He told me I was his property, that I must be subject to his will in all things. My soul revolted against the mean tyranny. But where could I turn for protection? No matter whether the slave girl be as black as ebony or as fair as her mistress. In either case, there is no shadow of law to protect her from insult, from violence, or even from death, all these are inflicted by fiends who bear the shape of men. The mistress, who ought to protect the helpless victim, has no other feelings towards her but those of jealousy and rage.

The degradation, the wrongs, the vices, that grow out of slavery, are more than I can describe. They are greater than you would willingly believe. Surely, if you credited one half the truths that are told you concerning the helpless millions suffering in this cruel bondage, you at the North would not help to tighten the yoke. You surely would refuse to do for the master, on your own soil, the mean and cruel work which trained bloodhounds and the lowest class of whites do for him at the South. Everywhere the years bring to all enough of sin and sorrow, but in slavery the very dawn of life is darkened by these shadows. Even the little child, who is accustomed to wait on her mistress and her children, will learn, before she is twelve years old, why it is that her mistress hates such and such a one among the slaves. Perhaps the child's own mother is among those hated ones. She listens to violent outbreaks of jealous passion, and cannot help understanding what is the cause. She will become prematurely knowing in evil things. Soon she will learn to tremble when she hears her master's footfall. She will be compelled to realize that she is no longer a child. If God has bestowed beauty upon her, it will prove her greatest curse. That which commands admiration in the white woman only hastens the degradation of the female slave. I know that some are too much brutalized by slavery to feel the humiliation of their position, but many slaves feel it most acutely, and shrink from the memory of it. I cannot tell how much I suffered in the presence of these wrongs, nor how I am still pained by the retrospect. My master met me at every turn, reminding me that I belonged to him, and swearing by heaven and earth that he would compel me to submit to him. If I went out for a breath of fresh air, after a day of unwearied toil, his footsteps dogged me. If I knelt by my mother's grave, his dark shadow fell on me even there. The light heart which nature had given me became heavy with sad forebodings. The other slaves in my master's house noticed the change. Many of them pitied me, but none dared to ask the cause. They had no need to inquire. They knew too well the guilty practices under that roof, and they were aware that to speak of them was an offense that never went unpunished. I longed for someone to confide in. I would have given the world to have laid my head on my grandmother's faithful bosom, and told her all my troubles. But Dr. Flint swore he would kill me, if I was not as silent as the grave.

Then, although my grandmother was all in all to me, I feared her as well as loved her. I had been accustomed to look up to her with a respect bordering upon awe. I was very young, and felt shamefaced about telling her such impure things, especially as I knew her to be very strict on such subjects.

Moreover, she was a woman of a high spirit. She was usually very quiet in her demeanor, but if her indignation was once roused, it was not very easily quelled. I had been told that she once chased a white gentleman with a loaded pistol, because he insulted one of her daughters. I dreaded the consequences of a violent outbreak, and both pride and fear kept me silent. But though I did not confide in my grandmother, and even evaded her vigilant watchfulness and inquiry, her presence in the neighborhood was some protection to me. Though she had been a slave, Dr. Flint was afraid of her. He dreaded her scorching rebukes. Moreover, she was known and patronized by many people, and he did not wish to have his villainy made public. It was lucky for me that I did not live on a distant plantation, but in a town not so large that the inhabitants were ignorant of each other's affairs. Bad as are the laws and customs in a slaveholding community, the doctor, as a professional man, deemed it prudent to keep up some outward show of decency. O, what days and nights of fear and sorrow that man caused me! Reader, it is not to awaken sympathy for myself that I am telling you truthfully what I suffered in slavery. I do it to kindle a flame of compassion in your hearts for my sisters who are still in bondage, suffering as I once suffered. I once saw two beautiful children playing together. One was a fair white child, the other was her slave, and also her sister. When I saw them embracing each other, and heard their joyous laughter, I turned sadly away from the lovely sight. I foresaw the inevitable blight that would fall on the little slave's heart. I knew how soon her laughter would be changed to sighs. The fair child grew up to be a still fairer woman. From childhood to womanhood her pathway was blooming with flowers, and overarched by a sunny sky. Scarcely one day of her life had been clouded when the sun rose on her happy bridal morning. How had those years dealt with her slave sister, the little playmate of her childhood? She, also, was very beautiful, but the flowers and sunshine of love were not for her. She drank the cup of sin, and shame, and misery, whereof her persecuted race are compelled to drink. In view of these things, why are ye silent, ye free men and women of the North? Why do your tongues falter in maintenance of the right? Would that I had more ability!

But my heart is so full, and my pen is so weak! There are noble men and women who plead for us, striving to help those who cannot help themselves. God bless them! God give them strength and courage to go on. God bless those, everywhere, who are laboring to advance the cause of humanity.

I would ten thousand times rather that my children should be the half-starved paupers of Ireland than to be the most pampered among the slaves of America. I would rather drudge out my life on a cotton plantation, till the grave opened to give me rest, than to live with an unprincipled master and a jealous mistress. The felon's home in a penitentiary is preferable. He may repent, and turn from the error of his ways, and so find peace, but it is not so with a favorite slave. She is not allowed to have any pride of character. It is deemed a crime in her to wish to be virtuous. Mrs. Flint possessed the key to her husband's character before I was born. She might have used this knowledge to counsel and to screen the young and the innocent among her slaves, but for them she had no sympathy. They were the objects of her constant suspicion and malevolence. She watched her husband with unceasing vigilance, but he was well-practiced in means to evade it. What he could not find opportunity to say in words he manifested in signs. He invented more than were ever thought of in a deaf and dumb asylum. I let them pass, as if I did not understand what he meant, and many were the curses and threats bestowed on me for my stupidity. One day he caught me teaching myself to write. He frowned, as if he was not well pleased, but I suppose he came to the conclusion that such an accomplishment might help to advance his favorite scheme.

Before long, notes were often slipped into my hand. I would return them, saying, "I can't read them, sir." "Can't you?" he replied, "then I must read them to you." He always finished the reading by asking, "Do you understand?" Sometimes he would complain of the heat of the tea room, and order his supper to be placed on a small table in the piazza. He would seat himself there with a well-satisfied smile, and tell me to stand by and brush away the flies. He would eat very slowly, pausing between the mouthfuls. These intervals were employed in describing the happiness I was so foolishly throwing away, and in threatening me with the penalty that finally awaited my stubborn disobedience. He boasted much of the forbearance he had exercised towards me, and reminded me that there was a limit to his patience. When I succeeded in avoiding opportunities for him to talk to me at home, I was ordered to come to his office, to do some errand. When there, I was obliged to stand and listen to such language as he saw fit to address to me. Sometimes I so openly expressed my contempt for him that he would become violently enraged, and I wondered why he did not strike me. Circumstanced as he was, he probably thought it was better policy to be forbearing. But the state of things grew worse and worse daily. In desperation I told him that I must and would apply to my grandmother for protection. He threatened me with death, and worse than death, if I made any complaint to her. Strange to say, I did not despair. I was naturally of a buoyant disposition, and always I had a hope of somehow getting out of his clutches. Like many a poor, simple slave before me, I trusted that some threads of joy would yet be woven into my dark destiny. I had entered my sixteenth year, and every day it became more apparent that my presence was intolerable to Mrs. Flint. Angry words frequently passed between her and her husband. He had never punished me himself, and he would not allow anybody else to punish me.

In that respect, she was never satisfied, but, in her angry moods, no terms were too vile for her to bestow upon me. Yet I, whom she detested so bitterly, had far more pity for her than he had, whose duty it was to make her life happy. I never wronged her, or wished to wrong her, and one word of kindness from her would have brought me to her feet. After repeated quarrels between the doctor and his wife, he announced his intention to take his youngest daughter, then four years old, to sleep in his apartment. It was necessary that a servant should sleep in the same room, to be on hand if the child stirred. I was selected for that office, and informed for what purpose that arrangement had been made. By managing to keep within sight of people, as much as possible, during the day time, I had hitherto succeeded in eluding my master, though a razor was often held to my throat to force me to change this line of policy. At night I slept by the side of my great aunt, where I felt safe. He was too prudent to come into her room. She was an old woman, and had been in the family many years. Moreover, as a married man, and a professional man, he deemed it necessary to save appearances in some degree. But he resolved to remove the obstacle in the way of his scheme, and he thought he had planned it so that he should evade suspicion. He was well-aware how much I prized my refuge by the side of my old aunt, and he determined to dispossess me of it. The first night the doctor had the little child in his room alone. The next morning, I was ordered to take my station as nurse the following night. A kind Providence interposed in my favor. During the day Mrs. Flint heard of this new arrangement, and a storm followed. I rejoiced to hear it rage. After a while my mistress sent for me to come to her room. Her first question was, "Did you know you were to sleep in the doctor's room?" "Yes, ma'am." "Who told you?" "My master." "Will you answer truly all the questions I ask?" "Yes, ma'am." "Tell me, then, as you hope to be forgiven, are you innocent of what I have accused you?" "I am." She handed me a Bible, and said, "Lay your hand on your heart, kiss this holy book, and swear before God that you tell me the truth." I took the oath she required, and I did it with a clear conscience. "You have taken God's holy word to testify your innocence," said she. "If you have deceived me, beware! Now take this stool, sit down, look me directly in the face, and tell me all that has passed between your master and you." I did as she ordered. As I went on with my account her color changed frequently, she wept, and sometimes groaned. She spoke in tones so sad, that I was touched by her grief. The tears came to my eyes, but I was soon convinced that her emotions arose from anger and wounded pride. She felt that her marriage vows were desecrated, her dignity insulted, but she had no compassion for the poor victim of her husband's perfidy. She pitied herself as a martyr, but she was incapable of feeling for the condition of shame and misery in which her unfortunate, helpless slave was placed. Yet perhaps she had some touch of feeling for me, for when the conference was ended, she spoke kindly, and promised to protect me. I should have been much comforted by this assurance if I could have had confidence in it, but my experiences in slavery had filled me with distrust. She was not a very refined woman, and had not much control over her passions. I was an object of her jealousy, and, consequently, of her hatred, and I knew I could not expect kindness or confidence from her under the circumstances in which I was placed. I could not blame her.

Slaveholder wives feel as other women would under similar circumstances. The fire of her temper kindled from small sparks, and now the flame became so intense that the doctor was obliged to give up his intended arrangement. I knew I had ignited the torch, and I expected to suffer for it afterwards, but I felt too thankful to my mistress for the timely aid she rendered me to care much about that. She now took me to sleep in a room adjoining her own. There I was an object of her especial care, though not of her especial comfort, for she spent many a sleepless night to watch over me. Sometimes I woke up, and found her bending over me. At other times she whispered in my ear, as though it was her husband who was speaking to me, and listened to hear what I would answer. If she startled me, on such occasions, she would glide stealthily away, and the next morning she would tell me I had been talking in my sleep, and ask who I was talking to. At last, I began to be fearful for my life.

It had been often threatened, and you can imagine, better than I can describe, what an unpleasant sensation it must produce to wake up in the dead of night and find a jealous woman bending over you. Terrible as this experience was, I had fears that it would give place to one more terrible. My mistress grew weary of her vigils, they did not prove satisfactory. She changed her tactics. She now tried the trick of accusing my master of crime, in my presence, and gave my name as the author of the accusation. To my utter astonishment, he replied, "I don't believe it, but if she did acknowledge it, you tortured her into exposing me." Tortured into exposing him! Truly, Satan had no difficulty in distinguishing the color of his soul! I understood his object in making this false representation. It was to show me that I gained nothing by seeking the protection of my mistress, that the power was still all in his own hands. I pitied Mrs. Flint. She was a second wife, many years the junior of her husband, and the hoary-headed miscreant was enough to try the patience of a wiser and better woman. She was completely foiled, and knew not how to proceed.

She would gladly have had me flogged for my supposed false oath, but, as I have already stated, the doctor never allowed anyone to whip me. The old sinner was politic. The application of the lash might have led to remarks that would have exposed him in the eyes of his children and grandchildren. How often did I rejoice that I lived in a town where all the inhabitants knew each other! If I had been on a remote plantation, or lost among the multitude of a crowded city, I should not be a living woman at this day. The secrets of slavery are concealed like those of the Inquisition. My master was, to my knowledge, the father of eleven slaves. But did the mothers dare to tell who was the father of their children? Did the other slaves dare to allude to it, except in whispers among themselves? No, indeed! They knew too well the terrible consequences. My grandmother could not avoid seeing things which excited her suspicions. She was uneasy about me, and tried various ways to buy me, but the never-changing answer was always repeated, "Linda does not belong to *me*. She is my daughter's property, and I have no legal right to sell her." The conscientious man! He was too scrupulous to *sell* me, but he had no scruples whatever about committing a much greater wrong against the helpless young girl placed under his guardianship, as his daughter's property. Sometimes my persecutor would ask me whether I would like to be sold. I told him I would rather be sold to anybody than to lead such a life as I did. On such occasions he would assume the air of a very injured individual, and reproach me for my ingratitude. "Did I not take you into the house, and make you the companion of my own children?" he would say. "Have I ever treated you like a Negro? I have never allowed you to be punished, not even to please your mistress. And this is the recompense I get, you ungrateful girl!"

I answered that he had reasons of his own for screening me from punishment, and that the course he pursued made my mistress hate me and persecute me. If I wept, he would say, "Poor child! Don't cry! Don't cry! I will make peace for you with your mistress. Only let me arrange matters in my own way. Poor, foolish girl! You don't know what is for your own good. I would cherish you. I would make a lady of you. Now go, and think of all I have promised you." I did think of it. Reader, I draw no imaginary pictures of Southern homes. I am telling you the plain truth. Yet when victims make their escape from this wild beast of slavery, Northerners consent to act the part of bloodhounds, and hunt the poor fugitive back into his den, "full of dead men's bones, and all uncleanness." Nay, more, they are not only willing, but proud, to give their daughters in marriage to slaveholders. The poor girls have romantic notions of a sunny clime (climate), and of the flowering vines that all the year round shade a happy home. To what disappointments are they destined! The young wife soon learns that the husband in whose hands she has placed her happiness pays no regard to his marriage vows. Children of every shade of complexion play with her own fair babies, and too well she knows that they are born unto him of his own household. Jealousy and hatred enter the flowery home, and it is ravaged of its loveliness. Southern women often marry a man knowing that he is the father of many little slaves. They do not trouble themselves about it. They regard such children as property, as marketable as the pigs on the plantation, and it is seldom that they do not make them aware of this by passing them into the slave trader's hands as soon as possible, and thus getting them out of their sight. I am glad to say there are some honorable exceptions. I have myself known two Southern wives who exhorted their husbands to free those slaves towards whom they stood in a "parental relation," and their request was granted.

These husbands blushed before the superior nobleness of their wives natures. Though they had only counseled them to do that which it was their duty to do, it commanded their respect, and rendered their conduct more exemplary. Concealment was at an end, and confidence took the place of distrust.

Though this bad institution deadens the moral sense, even in white women, to a fearful extent, it is not altogether extinct. I have heard Southern ladies say of Mr. Such a One, "He not only thinks it no disgrace to be the father of those little niggers, but he is not ashamed to call himself their master. I declare, such things ought not to be tolerated in any decent society!"

☐☐☐☐☐☐☐☐☐☐☐

Why does the slave ever love? Why allow the tendrils of the heart to twine around objects which may at any moment be wrenched away by the hand of violence? When separations come by the hand of death, the pious soul can bow in resignation, and say, "Not my will, but thine be done, O Lord!" But when the ruthless hand of man strikes the blow, regardless of the misery he causes, it is hard to be submissive. I did not reason thus when I was a young girl. Youth will be youth. I loved, and I indulged the hope that the dark clouds around me would turn out a bright lining. I forgot that in the land of my birth the shadows are too dense for light to penetrate. A land *"Where laughter is not mirth, nor thought the mind, nor words a language, nor even men mankind. Where cries reply to curses, shrieks to blows, and each is tortured in his separate hell."* There was in the neighborhood a young colored carpenter, a free-born man. We had been well acquainted in childhood, and frequently met together afterwards. We became mutually attached, and he proposed to marry me. I loved him with all the ardor of a young girl's first love. But when I reflected that I was a slave, and that the laws gave no sanction to the marriage of such, my heart sank within me. My lover wanted to buy me, but I knew that Dr. Flint was too willful and arbitrary a man to consent to that arrangement. From him, I was sure of experiencing all sorts of opposition, and I had nothing to hope from my mistress. She would have been delighted to have got rid of me, but not in that way. It would have relieved her mind of a burden if she could have seen me sold to some distant state, but if I was married near home I should be just as much in her husband's power as I had previously been—for the husband of a slave has no power to protect her. Moreover, my mistress, like many others, seemed to think that slaves had no right to any family ties of their own, that they were created merely to wait upon the family of the mistress. I once heard her abuse a young slave girl, who told her that a colored man wanted to make her his wife. "I will have you peeled and pickled, my lady," said she, "if I ever hear you mention that subject again. Do you suppose that I will have you tending *my* children with the children of that nigger?" The girl to whom she said this had a mulatto child, of course not acknowledged by its father. The poor black man who loved her would have been proud to acknowledge his helpless offspring. Many and anxious were the thoughts I revolved in my mind. I was at a loss what to do. Above all things, I was desirous to spare my lover the insults that had cut so deeply into my own soul. I talked with my grandmother about it, and partly told her my fears. I did not dare to tell her the worst. She had long suspected all was not right, and if I confirmed her suspicions I knew a storm would rise that would prove the overthrow of all my hopes. This love dream had been my support through many trials, and I could not bear to run the risk of having it suddenly dissipated. There was a lady in the neighborhood, a particular friend of Dr. Flint's, who often visited the house. I had a great respect for her, and she had always manifested a friendly interest in me. Grandmother thought she would have great influence with the doctor. I went to this lady, and told her my story.

 I told her I was aware that my lover's being a free-born man would prove a great objection, but he wanted to buy me, and if Dr. Flint would consent to that arrangement, I felt sure he would be willing to pay any reasonable price. She knew that Mrs. Flint disliked me, therefore, I ventured to suggest that perhaps my mistress would approve of my being sold, as that would rid her of me. The lady listened with kindly sympathy, and promised to do her utmost to promote my wishes. She had an interview with the doctor, and I believe she pleaded my cause earnestly, but it was all to no purpose. How I dreaded my master now! Every minute I expected to be summoned to his presence, but the day passed, and I heard nothing from him. The next morning, a message was brought to me, "Master wants you in his study." I found the door ajar, and I stood a moment gazing at the hateful man who claimed a right to rule me, body and soul. I entered, and tried to appear calm. I did not want him to know how my heart was bleeding. He looked fixedly at me, with an expression which seemed to say, "I have half a mind to kill you on the spot."

At last he broke the silence, and that was a relief to both of us. "So you want to be married, do you?" said he, "and to a free nigger." "Yes, sir." "Well, I'll soon convince you whether I am your master, or the nigger fellow you honor so highly. If you *must* have a husband, you may take up with one of my slaves."

What a situation I should be in, as the wife of one of *his* slaves, even if my heart had been interested! I replied, "Don't you suppose, sir, that a slave can have some preference about marrying? Do you suppose that all men are alike to her?" "Do you love this nigger?" said he, abruptly. "Yes, sir." "How dare you tell me so!" he exclaimed, in great wrath. After a slight pause, he added, "I supposed you thought more of yourself, that you felt above the insults of such puppies." I replied, "If he is a puppy I am a puppy, for we are both of the Negro race. It is right and honorable for us to love each other. The man you call a puppy never insulted me, sir, and he would not love me if he did not believe me to be a virtuous woman." He sprang upon me like a tiger, and gave me a stunning blow. It was the first time he had ever struck me, and fear did not enable me to control my anger. When I had recovered a little from the effects, I exclaimed, "You have struck me for answering you honestly. How I despise you!" There was silence for some minutes. Perhaps he was deciding what should be my punishment, or, perhaps, he wanted to give me time to reflect on what I had said, and to whom I had said it. Finally, he asked, "Do you know what you have said?" "Yes, sir, but your treatment drove me to it." "Do you know that I have a right to do as I like with you—that I can kill you, if I please?" "You have tried to kill me, and I wish you had, but you have no right to do as you like with me." "Silence!" he exclaimed, in a thundering voice. "By heavens, girl, you forget yourself too far! Are you mad? If you are, I will soon bring you to your senses. Do you think any other master would bear what I have borne from you this morning? Many masters would have killed you on the spot. How would you like to be sent to jail for your insolence?" "I know I have been disrespectful, sir," I replied, "but you drove me to it, I couldn't help it. As for the jail, there would be more peace for me there than there is here." "You deserve to go there," said he, "and to be under such treatment, that you would forget the meaning of the word *peace*. It would do you good. It would take some of your high notions out of you. But I am not ready to send you there yet, notwithstanding your ingratitude for all my kindness and forbearance. You have been the plague of my life. I have wanted to make you happy, and I have been repaid with the basest ingratitude, but though you have proved yourself incapable of appreciating my kindness, I will be lenient towards you, Linda. I will give you one more chance to redeem your character. If you behave yourself and do as I require, I will forgive you and treat you as I always have done, but if you disobey me, I will punish you as I would the meanest slave on my plantation. Never let me hear that fellow's name mentioned again. If I ever know of your speaking to him, I will cowhide you both, and if I catch him lurking about my premises, I will shoot him as soon as I would a dog. Do you hear what I say? I'll teach you a lesson about marriage and free niggers! Now go, and let this be the last time I have occasion to speak to you on this subject." Reader, did you ever hate? I hope not. I never did but once, and I trust I never shall again. Somebody has called it "the atmosphere of hell," and I believe it is so. For a fortnight the doctor did not speak to me.

He thought to mortify me, to make me feel that I had disgraced myself by receiving the honorable addresses of a respectable colored man, in preference to the base proposals of a white man. But though his lips disdained to address me, his eyes were very loquacious. No animal ever watched its prey more narrowly than he watched me. He knew that I could write, though he had failed to make me read his letters, and he was now troubled lest I should exchange letters with another man. After a while he became weary of silence, and I was sorry for it. One morning, as he passed through the hall, to leave the house, he contrived to thrust a note into my hand. I thought I had better read it, and spare myself the vexation of having him read it to me. It expressed regret for the blow he had given me, and reminded me that I myself was wholly to blame for it. He hoped I had become convinced of the injury I was doing myself by incurring his displeasure. He wrote that he had made up his mind to go to Louisiana, that he should take several slaves with him, and intended I should be one of the numbers. My mistress would remain where she was, therefore I should have nothing to fear from that quarter. If I merited kindness from him, he assured me that it would be lavishly bestowed. He begged me to think over the matter, and answer the following day. The next morning I was called to carry a pair of scissors to his room. I laid them on the table, with the letter beside them. He thought it was my answer, and did not call me back. I went as usual to attend my young mistress to and from school. He met me in the street, and ordered me to stop at his office on my way back. When I entered, he showed me his letter, and asked me why I had not answered it. I replied, "I am your daughter's property, and it is in your power to send me, or take me, wherever you please." He said he was very glad to find me so willing to go, and that we should start early in the autumn. He had a large practice in the town, and I rather thought he had made up the story merely to frighten me.

However that might be, I was determined that I would never go to Louisiana with him. Summer passed away, and early in the autumn Dr. Flint's eldest son was sent to Louisiana to examine the country, with a view to emigrating. That news did not disturb me. I knew very well that I should not be sent with *him*. That I had not been taken to the plantation before this time, was owing to the fact that his son was there. He was jealous of his son, and jealousy of the overseer had kept him from punishing me by sending me into the fields to work. Is it strange that I was not proud of these protectors? As for the overseer, he was a man for whom I had less respect than I had for a bloodhound. Young Mr. Flint did not bring back a favorable report of Louisiana, and I heard no more of that scheme. Soon after this, my lover met me at the corner of the street, and I stopped to speak to him.

Looking up, I saw my master watching us from his window. I hurried home, trembling with fear. I was sent for, immediately, to go to his room. He met me with a blow. "When is mistress to be married?" said he, in a sneering tone. A shower of oaths and imprecations followed. How thankful I was that my lover was a free man! That my tyrant had no power to flog him for speaking to me in the street! Again and again I revolved in my mind how all this would end. There was no hope that the doctor would consent to sell me on any terms. He had an iron will, and was determined to keep me, and to conquer me. My lover was an intelligent and religious man. Even if he could have obtained permission to marry me while I was a slave, the marriage would give him no power to protect me from my master. It would have made him miserable to witness the insults I should have been subjected to. And then, if we had children, I knew they must "follow the condition of the mother." What a terrible blight that would be on the heart of a free, intelligent father! For *his* sake, I felt that I ought not to link his fate with my own unhappy destiny. He was going to Savannah to see about a little property left him by an uncle, and hard as it was to bring my feelings to it, I earnestly entreated him not to come back. I advised him to go to the Free States, where his tongue would not be tied, and where his intelligence would be of more avail to him. He left me, still hoping the day would come when I could be bought. With me the lamp of hope had gone out. The dream of my girlhood was over. I felt lonely and desolate. Still I was not stripped of all.

I still had my good grandmother, and my affectionate brother. When he put his arms round my neck, and looked into my eyes, as if to read there the troubles I dared not tell, I felt that I still had something to love. But even that pleasant emotion was chilled by the reflection that he might be torn from me at any moment, by some sudden freak of my master. If he had known how we loved each other, I think he would have exulted in separating us. We often planned together how we could get to the North. But, as William remarked, such things are easier said than done. My movements were very closely watched, and we had no means of getting any money to defray our expenses. As for grandmother, she was strongly opposed to her children's undertaking any such project. She had not forgotten poor Benjamin's sufferings, and she was afraid that if another child tried to escape, he would have a similar or a worse fate. To me, nothing seemed more dreadful than my present life. I said to myself, "William *must* be free. He shall go to the North, and I will follow him." Many a slave sister has formed the same plans.

☐☐☐☐☐☐☐☐☐☐☐

Slaveholders pride themselves upon being honorable men, but if you were to hear the enormous lies they tell their slaves, you would have small respect for their veracity. I have spoken plain English. Pardon me. I cannot use a milder term. When they visit the North, and return home, they tell their slaves of the runaways they have seen, and describe them to be in the most deplorable condition. A slaveholder once told me that he had seen a runaway friend of mine in New York, and that she besought him to take her back to her master, for she was literally dying of starvation, that many days she had only one cold potato to eat, and at other times could get nothing at all. He said he refused to take her, because he knew her master would not thank him for bringing such a miserable wretch to his house. He ended by saying to me, "This is the punishment she brought on herself for running away from a kind master." This whole story was false. I afterwards stayed with that friend in New York, and found her in comfortable circumstances. She had never thought of such a thing as wishing to go back to slavery. Many of the slaves believe such stories, and think it is not worthwhile to exchange slavery for such a hard kind of freedom. It is difficult to persuade such that freedom could make them useful men, and enable them to protect their wives and children. If those heathen in our Christian land had as much teaching as some Hindus, they would think otherwise. They would know that liberty is more valuable than life. They would begin to understand their own capabilities, and exert themselves to become men and women. But while the Free States sustain a law which hurls fugitives back into slavery, how can the slaves resolve to become men? There are some who strive to protect wives and daughters from the insults of their masters, but those who have such sentiments have had advantages above the general mass of slaves. They have been partially civilized and Christianized by favorable circumstances. Some are bold enough to *utter* such sentiments to their masters. O, that there were more of them! Some poor creatures have been so brutalized by the lash that they will sneak out of the way to give their masters free access to their wives and daughters.

Do you think this proves the black man to belong to an inferior order of beings? What would *you* be, if you had been born and brought up a slave, with generations of slaves for ancestors? I admit that the black man is inferior. But what is it that makes him so? It is the ignorance in which white men compel him to live, it is the torturing whip that lashes manhood out of him, it is the fierce bloodhounds of the South, and the scarcely less cruel human bloodhounds of the North, who enforce the Fugitive Slave Law. *They* do the work. Southern gentlemen indulge in the most contemptuous expressions about the Yankees, while they, on their part, consent to do the vilest work for them, such as the ferocious bloodhounds and the despised Negro hunters are employed to do at home. When Southerners go to the North, they are proud to do them honor, but the Northern man is not welcome south of the Mason and Dixon line, unless he suppresses every thought and feeling at variance with their "peculiar institution." Nor is it enough to be silent. The masters are not pleased, unless they obtain a greater degree of subservience than that, and they are generally accommodated. Do they respect the Northerner for this? I trow (think) not. Even the slaves despise "a Northern man with Southern principles," and that is the class they generally see. When Northerners go to the South to reside they prove very apt scholars. They soon imbibe the sentiments and disposition of their neighbors, and generally go beyond their teachers. Of the two, they are proverbially the hardest masters. They seem to satisfy their consciences with the doctrine that God created the Africans to be slaves. What a libel upon the heavenly Father, who "made of one blood all nations of men!" And then who *are* Africans? Who can measure the amount of Anglo-Saxon blood coursing in the veins of American slaves? I have spoken of the pains slaveholders take to give their slaves a bad opinion of the North, but, notwithstanding this, intelligent slaves are aware that they have many friends in the Free States. Even the most ignorant have some confused notions about it. They knew that I could read, and I was often asked if I had seen anything in the newspapers about white folks over in the big North, who were trying to get their freedom for them. Some believe that the abolitionists have already made them free, and that it is established by law, but that their masters prevent the law from going into effect. One woman begged me to get a newspaper and read it over. She said her husband told her that the black people had sent word to the queen of America that they were all slaves, that she didn't believe it, and went to Washington City to see the president about it. They quarreled, she drew her sword upon him and swore that he should help her to make them all free.

That poor, ignorant woman thought that America was governed by a Queen, to whom the President was subordinate. I wish the President was subordinate to Queen Justice.

□□□□□□□□□□

There was a planter in the country, not far from us, whom I will call Mr. Litch. He was an ill-bred, uneducated man, but very wealthy. He had six hundred slaves, many of whom he did not know by sight. His extensive plantation was managed by well paid overseers. There was a jail and a whipping post on his grounds, and whatever cruelties were perpetrated there, they passed without comment. He was so effectually screened by his great wealth that he was called to no account for his crimes, not even for murder. Various were the punishments resorted to. A favorite one was to tie a rope round a man's body, and suspend him from the ground. A fire was kindled over him, from which was suspended a piece of fat pork. As this cooked, the scalding drops of fat continually fell on the bare flesh. On his own plantation, he required very strict obedience to the eighth commandment. But depredations on the neighbors were allowable, provided the culprit managed to evade detection or suspicion. If a neighbor brought a charge of theft against any of his slaves, he was browbeaten by the master, who assured him that his slaves had enough of everything at home, and had no inducement to steal. No sooner was the neighbor's back turned, than the accused was sought out, and whipped for his lack of discretion. If a slave stole from him even a pound of meat or a peck of corn, if detection followed, he was put in chains and imprisoned, and so kept till his form was attenuated by hunger and suffering. A freshet once bore his wine cellar and meat house miles away from the plantation. Some slaves followed, and secured bits of meat and bottles of wine. Two were detected, a ham and some liquor being found in their huts. They were summoned by their master. No words were used, but a club felled them to the ground. A rough box was their coffin, and their interment was a dog's burial. Nothing was said. Murder was so common on his plantation that he feared to be alone after nightfall. He might have believed in ghosts. His brother, if not equal in wealth, was at least equal in cruelty. His bloodhounds were well-trained. Their pen was spacious, and a terror to the slaves. They were let loose on a runaway, and, if they tracked him, they literally tore the flesh from his bones. When this slaveholder died, his shrieks and groans were so frightful that they appalled his own friends. His last words were, "I am going to hell, bury my money with me." After death his eyes remained open. To press the lids down, silver dollars were laid on them.

    These were buried with him. From this circumstance, a rumor went abroad that his coffin was filled with money. Three times his grave was opened, and his coffin taken out. The last time, his body was found on the ground, and a flock of buzzards were pecking at it. He was again interred, and a sentinel set over his grave. The perpetrators were never discovered. Cruelty is contagious in uncivilized communities. Mr. Conant, a neighbor of Mr. Litch, returned from town one evening in a partial state of intoxication. His body servant gave him some offense. He was divested of his clothes, except his shirt, whipped, and tied to a large tree in front of the house. It was a stormy night in winter. The wind blew bitterly cold, and the boughs of the old tree crackled under falling sleet. A member of the family, fearing he would freeze to death, begged that he might be taken down, but the master would not relent. He remained there three hours, and, when he was cut down, he was more dead than alive. Another slave, who stole a pig from this master, to appease his hunger, was terribly flogged. In desperation, he tried to run away. But at the end of two miles, he was so faint with loss of blood, he thought he was dying. He had a wife, and he longed to see her once more. Too sick to walk, he crept back that long distance on his hands and knees. When he reached his master's, it was night. He had not strength to rise and open the gate. He moaned, and tried to call for help. I had a friend living in the same family. At last his cry reached her. She went out and found the prostrate man at the gate. She ran back to the house for assistance, and two men returned with her. They carried him in, and laid him on the floor. The back of his shirt was one clot of blood. By means of lard, my friend loosened it from the raw flesh. She bandaged him, gave him cool drink, and left him to rest. The master said he deserved a hundred more lashes. When his own labor was stolen from him, he had stolen food to appease his hunger. This was his crime. Another neighbor was a Mrs. Wade. At no hour of the day was there cessation of the lash on her premises. Her labors began with the dawn, and did not cease till long after nightfall. The barn was her particular place of torture. There she lashed the slaves with the might of a man. An old slave of hers once said to me, "It is hell in missis's house. 'Pears I can never get out. Day and night I prays to die." The mistress died before the old woman, and, when dying, entreated her husband not to permit any one of her slaves to look on her after death. A slave who had nursed her children, and had still a child in her care, watched her chance, and stole with it in her arms to the room where lay her dead mistress. She gazed a while on her, then raised her hand and dealt two blows on her face, saying, as she did so, "The devil is got you *now*." She forgot that the child was looking on. She had just begun to talk, and she said to her father, "I did see ma, and mammy did strike ma, so," striking her own face with her little hand. The master was startled. He could not imagine how the nurse could obtain access to the room where the corpse lay, for he kept the door locked. He questioned her. She confessed that what the child had said was true, and told how she had procured the key. She was sold to Georgia. In my childhood I knew a valuable slave, named Charity, and loved her, as all children did. Her young mistress married, and took her to Louisiana. Her little boy, James, was sold to a good sort of master. He became involved in debt, and James was sold again to a wealthy slaveholder, noted for his cruelty.

With this man he grew up to manhood, receiving the treatment of a dog. After a severe whipping, to save himself from further infliction of the lash, with which he was threatened, he took to the woods. He was in a most miserable condition—cut by the cowskin, half-naked, half-starved, and without the means of procuring a crust of bread. Some weeks after his escape, he was captured, tied, and carried back to his master's plantation. This man considered punishment in his jail, on bread and water, after receiving hundreds of lashes, too mild for the poor slave's offense. Therefore he decided, after the overseer should have whipped him to his satisfaction, to have him placed between the screws of the cotton gin, to stay as long as he had been in the woods. This wretched creature was cut with the whip from his head to his feet, then washed with strong brine, to prevent the flesh from mortifying, and make it heal sooner than it otherwise would. He was then put into the cotton gin, which was screwed down, only allowing him room to turn on his side when he could not lie on his back. Every morning a slave was sent with a piece of bread and bowl of water, which were placed within reach of the poor fellow. The slave was charged, under penalty of severe punishment, not to speak to him. Four days passed, and the slave continued to carry the bread and water. On the second morning, he found the bread gone, but the water untouched. When he had been in the press four days and five nights, the slave informed his master that the water had not been used for four mornings, and that a horrible stench came from the gin house. The overseer was sent to examine into it. When the press was unscrewed, the dead body was found partly eaten by rats and vermin. Perhaps the rats that devoured his bread had gnawed him before life was extinct. Poor Charity! Grandmother and I often asked each other how her affectionate heart would bear the news, if she should ever hear of the murder of her son. We had known her husband, and knew that James was like him in manliness and intelligence. These were the qualities that made it so hard for him to be a plantation slave. They put him into a rough box, and buried him with less feeling than would have been manifested for an old house dog. Nobody asked any questions. He was a slave, and the feeling was that the master had a right to do what he pleased with his own property. And what did *he* care for the value of a slave? He had hundreds of them. When they had finished their daily toil, they must hurry to eat their little morsels, and be ready to extinguish their pine knots before nine o'clock, when the overseer went on his patrol rounds. He entered every cabin, to see that men and their wives had gone to bed together, lest the men, from over fatigue, should fall asleep in the chimney corner, and remain there till the morning horn called them to their daily task. Women are considered of no value, unless they continually increase their owner's stock. They are put on a par with animals. This same master shot a woman through the head, who had run away and been brought back to him. No one called him to account for it. If a slave resisted being whipped, the bloodhounds were unpacked, and set upon him, to tear his flesh from his bones. The master who did these things was highly-educated, and styled a perfect gentleman.

He also boasted the name and standing of a Christian, though Satan never had a truer follower. I could tell of more slaveholders as cruel as those I have described. They are not exceptions to the general rule. I do not say there are no humane slaveholders. Such characters do exist, notwithstanding the hardening influences around them. But they are "like angels visits—few and far between." I knew a young lady who was one of these rare specimens. She was an orphan, and inherited as slaves a woman and her six children. Their father was a free man. They had a comfortable home of their own, parents and children living together. The mother and eldest daughter served their mistress during the day, and at night returned to their dwelling, which was on the premises. The young lady was very pious, and there was some reality in her religion. She taught her slaves to lead pure lives, and wished them to enjoy the fruit of their own industry. *Her* religion was not a garb put on for Sunday, and laid aside till Sunday returned again. The eldest daughter of the slave mother was promised in marriage to a free man, and the day before the wedding this good mistress emancipated her, in order that her marriage might have the sanction of *law*. Report said that this young lady cherished an unrequited affection for a man who had resolved to marry for wealth. In the course of time a rich uncle of hers died. He left six thousand dollars to his two sons by a colored woman, and the remainder of his property to this orphan niece. The metal soon attracted the magnet. The lady and her weighty purse became his. She offered to manumit her slaves—telling them that her marriage might make unexpected changes in their destiny, and she wished to insure their happiness. They refused to take their freedom, saying that she had always been their best friend, and they could not be so happy anywhere as with her.

I was not surprised. I had often seen them in their comfortable home, and thought that the whole town did not contain a happier family. They had never felt slavery, and, when it was too late, they were convinced of its reality. When the new master claimed this family as his property, the father became furious, and went to his mistress for protection. "I can do nothing for you now, Harry," said she. "I no longer have the power I had a week ago. I have succeeded in obtaining the freedom of your wife, but I cannot obtain it for your children." The unhappy father swore that nobody should take his children from him.

He concealed them in the woods for some days, but they were discovered and taken. The father was put in jail, and the two oldest boys sold to Georgia. One little girl, too young to be of service to her master, was left with the wretched mother. The other three were carried to their master's plantation. The eldest soon became a mother, and, when the slaveholder's wife looked at the babe, she wept bitterly. She knew that her own husband had violated the purity she had so carefully inculcated.

She had a second child by her master, and then he sold her and his offspring to his brother. She bore two children to the brother, and was sold again. The next sister went crazy. The life she was compelled to lead drove her mad. The third one became the mother of five daughters. Before the birth of the fourth the pious mistress died. To the last, she rendered every kindness to the slaves that her unfortunate circumstances permitted. She passed away peacefully, glad to close her eyes on a life which had been made so wretched by the man she loved. This man squandered the fortune he had received, and sought to retrieve his affairs by a second marriage, but, having retired after a night of drunken debauch, he was found dead in the morning.

He was called a good master, for he fed and clothed his slaves better than most masters, and the lash was not heard on his plantation so frequently as on many others. Had it not been for slavery, he would have been a better man, and his wife a happier woman. No pen can give an adequate description of the all-pervading corruption produced by slavery. The slave girl is reared in an atmosphere of licentiousness and fear. The lash and the foul talk of her master and his sons are her teachers. When she is fourteen or fifteen, her owner, or his sons, or the overseer, or perhaps all of them, begin to bribe her with presents. If these fail to accomplish their purpose, she is whipped or starved into submission to their will. She may have had religious principles inculcated by some pious mother or grandmother, or some good mistress, she may have a lover, whose good opinion and peace of mind are dear to her heart, or the profligate men who have power over her may be exceedingly odious to her. But resistance is hopeless. *"The poor worm shall prove her contest vain. Life's little day shall pass, and she is gone!"* The slaveholder's sons are, of course, vitiated, even while boys, by the unclean influences everywhere around them. Nor do the master's daughters always escape. Severe retributions sometimes come upon him for the wrongs he does to the daughters of the slaves. The white daughters early hear their parents quarreling about some female slave. Their curiosity is excited, and they soon learn the cause. They are attended by the young slave girls whom their father has corrupted, and they hear such talk as should never meet youthful ears, or any other ears. They know that the women slaves are subject to their father's authority in all things, and in some cases they exercise the same authority over the men slaves. I have myself seen the master of such a household whose head was bowed down in shame, for it was known in the neighborhood that his daughter had selected one of the meanest slaves on his plantation to be the father of his first grandchild. She did not make her advances to her equals, nor even to her father's more intelligent servants. She selected the most brutalized, over whom her authority could be exercised with less fear of exposure. Her father, half frantic with rage, sought to revenge himself on the offending black man, but his daughter, foreseeing the storm that would arise, had given him free papers, and sent him out of the state. In such cases the infant is smothered, or sent where it is never seen by any who know its history. But if the white parent is the *father*, instead of the mother, the offspring are unblushingly reared for the market. If they are girls, I have indicated plainly enough what will be their inevitable destiny. You may believe what I say, for I write only that whereof I know. I was twenty-one years in that cage of obscene birds. I can testify, from my own experience and observation, that slavery is a curse to the whites as well as to the blacks. It makes the white fathers cruel and sensual, the sons violent and licentious, it contaminates the daughters, and makes the wives wretched. And as for the colored race, it needs an abler pen than mine to describe the extremity of their sufferings, the depth of their degradation. Yet few slaveholders seem to be aware of the widespread moral ruin occasioned by this wicked system. Their talk is of blighted cotton crops—not of the blight on their children's souls. If you want to be fully convinced of the abominations of slavery, go on a Southern plantation, and call yourself a Negro trader. Then there will be no concealment, and you will see and hear things that will seem to you impossible among human beings with immortal souls.

☐☐☐☐☐☐☐☐☐☐

After my lover went away, Dr. Flint contrived a new plan. He seemed to have an idea that my fear of my mistress was his greatest obstacle. In the blandest tones, he told me that he was going to build a small house for me, in a secluded place, four miles away from the town. I shuddered, but I was constrained to listen, while he talked of his intention to give me a home of my own, and to make a lady of me. Hitherto, I had escaped my dreaded fate, by being in the midst of people. My grandmother had already had high words with my master about me. She had told him pretty plainly what she thought of his character, and there was considerable gossip in the neighborhood about our affairs, to which the open-mouthed jealousy of Mrs. Flint contributed not a little. When my master said he was going to build a house for me, and that he could do it with little trouble and expense, I was in hopes something would happen to frustrate his scheme, but I soon heard that the house was actually begun.

I vowed before my Maker that I would never enter it. I had rather toil on the plantation from dawn till dark, I had rather live and die in jail, than drag on, from day to day, through such a living death. I was determined that the master, whom I so hated and loathed, who had blighted the prospects of my youth, and made my life a desert, should not, after my long struggle with him, succeed at last in trampling his victim under his feet. I would do anything, everything, for the sake—of defeating him. What *could* I do? I thought and thought, till I became desperate, and made a plunge into the abyss. And now, reader, I come to a period in my unhappy life, which I would gladly forget if I could. The remembrance fills me with sorrow and shame. It pains me to tell you of it, but I have promised to tell you the truth, and I will do it honestly, let it cost me what it may. I will not try to screen myself behind the plea of compulsion from a master, for it was not so. Neither can I plead ignorance or thoughtlessness.

For years, my master had done his utmost to pollute my mind with foul images, and to destroy the pure principles inculcated by my grandmother, and the good mistress of my childhood. The influences of slavery had, had the same effect on me that they had on other young girls, they had made me prematurely knowing, concerning the evil ways of the world. I knew what I did, and I did it with deliberate calculation. But, O, ye happy women, whose purity has been sheltered from childhood, who have been free to choose the objects of your affection, whose homes are protected by law, do not judge the poor desolate slave girl too severely. If slavery had been abolished, I, also, could have married the man of my choice, I could have had a home shielded by the laws, and I should have been spared the painful task of confessing what I am now about to relate, but all my prospects had been blighted by slavery. I wanted to keep myself pure, and, under the most adverse circumstances, I tried hard to preserve my self-respect, but I was struggling alone in the powerful grasp of the demon slavery, and the monster proved too strong for me. I felt as if I was forsaken by God and man, as if all my efforts must be frustrated, and I became reckless in my despair. I have told you that Dr. Flint's persecutions and his wife's jealousy had given rise to some gossip in the neighborhood. Among others, it chanced that a white unmarried gentleman had obtained some knowledge of the circumstances in which I was placed. He knew my grandmother, and often spoke to me in the street. He became interested for me, and asked questions about my master, which I answered in part. He expressed a great deal of sympathy, and a wish to aid me. He constantly sought opportunities to see me, and wrote to me frequently. I was a poor slave girl, only fifteen years old. So much attention from a superior person was, of course, flattering, for human nature is the same in all. I also felt grateful for his sympathy, and encouraged by his kind words. It seemed to me a great thing to have such a friend. By degrees, a more tender feeling crept into my heart.

He was an educated and eloquent gentleman, too eloquent, alas, for the poor slave girl who trusted in him. Of course I saw whither all this was tending. I knew the impassable gulf between us, but to be an object of interest to a man who is not married, and who is not her master, is agreeable to the pride and feelings of a slave, if her miserable situation has left her any pride or sentiment. It seems less degrading to give one's self, than to submit to compulsion. There is something akin to freedom in having a lover who has no control over you, except that which he gains by kindness and attachment. A master may treat you as rudely as he pleases, and you dare not speak, moreover, the wrong does not seem so great with an unmarried man, as with one who has a wife to be made unhappy. There may be sophistry in all this, but the condition of a slave confuses all principles of morality, and, in fact, renders the practice of them impossible. When I found that my master had actually begun to build the lonely cottage, other feelings mixed with those I have described. Revenge, and calculations of interest, were added to flattered vanity and sincere gratitude for kindness.

I knew nothing would enrage Dr. Flint so much as to know that I favored another, and it was something to triumph over my tyrant even in that small way. I thought he would revenge himself by selling me, and I was sure my friend, Mr. Sands, would buy me. He was a man of more generosity and feeling than my master, and I thought my freedom could be easily obtained from him. The crisis of my fate now came so near that I was desperate. I shuddered to think of being the mother of children that should be owned by my old tyrant. I knew that as soon as a new fancy took him, his victims were sold far off to get rid of them, especially if they had children. I had seen several women sold, with his babies at the breast. He never allowed his offspring by slaves to remain long in sight of himself and his wife. Of a man who was not my master I could ask to have my children well-supported, and in this case, I felt confident I should obtain the boon. I also felt quite sure that they would be made free. With all these thoughts revolving in my mind, and seeing no other way of escaping the doom I so much dreaded, I made a headlong plunge. Pity me, and pardon me, O virtuous reader! You never knew what it is to be a slave, to be entirely unprotected by law or custom, to have the laws reduce you to the condition of a chattel, entirely subject to the will of another. You never exhausted your ingenuity in avoiding the snares, and eluding the power of a hated tyrant, you never shuddered at the sound of his footsteps, and trembled within hearing of his voice. I know I did wrong. No one can feel it more sensibly than I do. The painful and humiliating memory will haunt me to my dying day. Still, in looking back, calmly, on the events of my life, I feel that the slave woman ought not to be judged by the same standard as others. The months passed on. I had many unhappy hours. I secretly mourned over the sorrow I was bringing on my grandmother, who had so tried to shield me from harm. I knew that I was the greatest comfort of her old age, and that it was a source of pride to her that I had not degraded myself, like most of the slaves. I wanted to confess to her that I was no longer worthy of her love, but I could not utter the dreaded words. As for Dr. Flint, I had a feeling of satisfaction and triumph in the thought of telling *him*. From time to time he told me of his intended arrangements, and I was silent. At last, he came and told me the cottage was completed, and ordered me to go to it. I told him I would never enter it. He said, "I have heard enough of such talk as that. You shall go, if you are carried by force, and you shall remain there." I replied, "I will never go there. In a few months I shall be a mother." He stood and looked at me in dumb amazement, and left the house without a word. I thought I should be happy in my triumph over him. But now that the truth was out, and my relatives would hear of it, I felt wretched. Humble as were their circumstances, they had pride in my good character. Now, how could I look them in the face? My self-respect was gone! I had resolved that I would be virtuous, though I was a slave.

I had said, "Let the storm beat! I will brave it till I die." And now, how humiliated I felt! I went to my grandmother. My lips moved to make confession, but the words stuck in my throat. I sat down in the shade of a tree at her door and began to sew. I think she saw something unusual was the matter with me. The mother of slaves is very watchful. She knows there is no security for her children. After they have entered their teens she lives in daily expectation of trouble. This leads to many questions. If the girl is of a sensitive nature, timidity keeps her from answering truthfully, and this well-meant course has a tendency to drive her from maternal counsels. Presently, in came my mistress, like a mad woman, and accused me concerning her husband.

My grandmother, whose suspicions had been previously awakened, believed what she said. She exclaimed, "O Linda! Has it come to this? I had rather see you dead than to see you as you now are. You are a disgrace to your dead mother." She tore from my fingers my mother's wedding ring and her silver thimble. "Go away!" she exclaimed, "and never come to my house, again." Her reproaches fell so hot and heavy, that they left me no chance to answer. Bitter tears, such as the eyes never shed but once, were my only answer. I rose from my seat, but fell back again, sobbing. She did not speak to me, but the tears were running down her furrowed cheeks, and they scorched me like fire. She had always been so kind to me! *So* kind! How I longed to throw myself at her feet, and tell her all the truth! But she had ordered me to go, and never to come there again. After a few minutes, I mustered strength, and started to obey her. With what feelings did I now close that little gate, which I used to open with such an eager hand in my childhood! It closed upon me with a sound I never heard before. Where could I go? I was afraid to return to my master's. I walked on recklessly, not caring where I went, or what would become of me. When I had gone four or five miles, fatigue compelled me to stop. I sat down on the stump of an old tree. The stars were shining through the boughs above me. How they mocked me, with their bright, calm light! The hours passed by, and as I sat there alone a chilliness and deadly sickness came over me. I sank on the ground. My mind was full of horrid thoughts. I prayed to die, but the prayer was not answered. At last, with great effort I roused myself, and walked some distance further, to the house of a woman who had been a friend of my mother.

When I told her why I was there, she spoke soothingly to me, but I could not be comforted. I thought I could bear my shame if I could only be reconciled to my grandmother. I longed to open my heart to her. I thought if she could know the real state of the case, and all I had been bearing for years, she would perhaps judge me less harshly. My friend advised me to send for her. I did so, but days of agonizing suspense passed before she came. Had she utterly forsaken me? No. She came at last. I knelt before her, and told her the things that had poisoned my life, how long I had been persecuted, that I saw no way of escape, and in an hour of extremity I had become desperate. She listened in silence. I told her I would bear anything and do anything, if in time I had hopes of obtaining her forgiveness. I begged of her to pity me, for my dead mother's sake. And she did pity me.

She did not say, "I forgive you," but she looked at me lovingly, with her eyes full of tears. She laid her old hand gently on my head, and murmured, "Poor child! Poor child!"

☐☐☐☐☐☐☐☐☐☐

I returned to my good grandmother's house. She had an interview with Mr. Sands. When she asked him why he could not have left her one ewe lamb—whether there were not plenty of slaves who did not care about character—he made no answer, but he spoke kind and encouraging words. He promised to care for my child, and to buy me, be the conditions what they might. I had not seen Dr. Flint for five days. I had never seen him since I made the avowal to him. He talked of the disgrace I had brought on myself, how I had sinned against my master, and mortified my old grandmother. He intimated that if I had accepted his proposals, he, as a physician, could have saved me from exposure. He even condescended to pity me. Could he have offered wormwood more bitter? He, whose persecutions had been the cause of my sin! "Linda," said he, "though you have been criminal towards me, I feel for you, and I can pardon you if you obey my wishes. Tell me whether the fellow you wanted to marry is the father of your child. If you deceive me, you shall feel the fires of hell." I did not feel as proud as had done. My strongest weapon with him was gone. I was lowered in my own estimation, and had resolved to bear his abuse in silence. But when he spoke contemptuously of the lover who had always treated me honorably, when I remembered that but for *him* I might have been a virtuous, free, and happy wife, I lost my patience. "I have sinned against God and myself," I replied, "but not against you." He clinched his teeth, and muttered, "Curse you!"

    He came towards me, with ill-suppressed rage, and exclaimed, "You obstinate girl! I could grind your bones to powder! You have thrown yourself away on some worthless rascal. You are weak-minded, and have been easily persuaded by those who don't care a straw for you. The future will settle accounts between us. You are blinded now, but hereafter you will be convinced that your master was your best friend. My lenity towards you is a proof of it. I might have punished you in many ways. I might have had you whipped till you fell dead under the lash. But I wanted you to live, I would have bettered your condition. Others cannot do it. You are my slave. Your mistress, disgusted by your conduct, forbids you to return to the house, therefore I leave you here for the present, but I shall see you often. I will call tomorrow." He came with frowning brows, that showed a dissatisfied state of mind. After asking about my health, he inquired whether my board was paid, and who visited me. He then went on to say that he had neglected his duty, that as a physician there were certain things that he ought to have explained to me. Then followed talk such as would have made the most shameless blush. He ordered me to stand up before him. I obeyed. "I command you," said he, "to tell me whether the father of your child is white or black." I hesitated. "Answer me this instant!" he exclaimed. I did answer. He sprang upon me like a wolf, and grabbed my arm as if he would have broken it.

"Do you love him?" said he, in a hissing tone. "I am thankful that I do not despise him," I replied. He raised his hand to strike me, but it fell again. I don't know what arrested the blow. He sat down, with lips tightly compressed. At last he spoke. "I came here," said he, "to make you a friendly proposition, but your ingratitude chafes me beyond endurance. You turn aside all my good intentions towards you. I don't know what it is that keeps me from killing you." Again he rose, as if he had a mind to strike me. But he resumed. "On one condition I will forgive your insolence and crime. You must henceforth have no communication of any kind with the father of your child. You must not ask anything from him, or receive anything from him. I will take care of you and your child. You had better promise this at once, and not wait till you are deserted by him. This is the last act of mercy I shall show towards you." I said something about being unwilling to have my child supported by a man who had cursed it and me also. He rejoined, that a woman who had sunk to my level had no right to expect anything else. He asked, for the last time, would I accept his kindness? I answered that I would not. "Very well," said he, "then take the consequences of your wayward course. Never look to me for help. You are my slave, and shall always be my slave. I will never sell you, that you may depend upon." Hope died away in my heart as he closed the door after him. I had calculated that in his rage he would sell me to a slave trader, and I knew the father of my child was on the watch to buy me. About this time my Uncle Phillip was expected to return from a voyage. The day before his departure I had officiated as bridesmaid to a young friend. My heart was then ill at ease, but my smiling countenance did not betray it. Only a year had passed, but what fearful changes it had wrought.

My heart had grown gray in misery. Lives that flash in sunshine, and lives that are born in tears, receive their hue from circumstances. None of us know what a year may bring forth. I felt no joy when they told me my uncle had come. He wanted to see me, though he knew what had happened. I shrank from him at first, but at last consented that he should come to my room. He received me as he always had done. O, how my heart smote me when I felt his tears on my burning cheeks! The words of my grandmother came to my mind—"Perhaps your mother and father are taken from the evil days to come." My disappointed heart could now praise God that it was so. But why, thought I, did my relatives ever cherish hopes for me? What was there to save me from the usual fate of slave girls? Many more beautiful and more intelligent than I had experienced a similar fate, or a far worse one. How could they hope that I should escape? My uncle's stay was short, and I was not sorry for it. I was too ill in mind and body to enjoy my friends as I had done. For some weeks I was unable to leave my bed. I could not have any doctor but my master, and I would not have him sent for. At last, alarmed by my increasing illness, they sent for him. I was very weak and nervous, and as soon as he entered the room, I began to scream. They told him my state was very critical. He had no wish to hasten me out of the world, and he withdrew. When my babe was born, they said it was premature. It weighed only four pounds, but God let it live. I heard the doctor say I could not survive till morning. I had often prayed for death, but now I did not want to die, unless my child could die too. Many weeks passed before I was able to leave my bed. I was a mere wreck of my former self. For a year there was scarcely a day when I was free from chills and fever.

 My babe also was sickly. His little limbs were often racked with pain. Dr. Flint continued his visits, to look after my health, and he did not fail to remind me that my child was an addition to his stock of slaves. I felt too feeble to dispute with him, and listened to his remarks in silence. His visits were less frequent, but his busy spirit could not remain quiet. He employed my brother in his office, and he was made the medium of frequent notes and messages to me. William was a bright lad, and of much use to the doctor. He had learned to put up medicines, to leech, cup, and bleed. He had taught himself to read and spell. I was proud of my brother, and the old doctor suspected as much. One day, when I had not seen him for several weeks, I heard his steps approaching the door. I dreaded the encounter, and hid myself. He inquired for me, of course, but I was nowhere to be found. He went to his office, and dispatched William with a note. The color mounted to my brother's face when he gave it to me, and he said, "Don't you hate me, Linda, for bringing you these things?" I told him I could not blame him, he was a slave, and obliged to obey his master's will. The note ordered me to come to his office. I went. He demanded to know where I was when he called. I told him I was at home. He flew into a passion, and said he knew better. Then he launched out upon his usual themes—my crimes against him, and my ingratitude for his forbearance. The laws were laid down to me anew, and I was dismissed. I felt humiliated that my brother should stand by, and listen to such language as would be addressed only to a slave. Poor boy! He was powerless to defend me, but I saw the tears, which he vainly strove to keep back.

  This manifestation of feeling irritated the doctor. William could do nothing to please him. One morning he did not arrive at the office so early as usual, and that circumstance afforded his master an opportunity to vent his spleen. He was put in jail. The next day my brother sent a trader to the doctor, with a request to be sold. His master was greatly incensed at what he called his insolence. He said he had put him there to reflect upon his bad conduct, and he certainly was not giving any evidence of repentance. For two days he harassed himself to find somebody to do his office work, but everything went wrong without William. He was released, and ordered to take his old stand, with many threats, if he was not careful about his future behavior. As the months passed on, my boy improved in health. When he was a year old, they called him beautiful. The little vine was taking deep root in my existence, though its clinging fondness excited a mixture of love and pain. When I was most sorely oppressed I found a solace in his smiles. I loved to watch his infant slumbers, but always there was a dark cloud over my enjoyment. I could never forget that he was a slave. Sometimes I wished that he might die in infancy. God tried me. My darling became very ill. The bright eyes grew dull, and the little feet and hands were so icy cold that I thought death had already touched them. I had prayed for his death, but never so earnestly as I now prayed for his life, and my prayer was heard. Alas, what mockery it is for a slave mother to try to pray back her dying child to life!

Death is better than slavery. It was a sad thought that I had no name to give my child. His father caressed him and treated him kindly, whenever he had a chance to see him.

He was not unwilling that he should bear his name, but he had no legal claim to it, and if I had bestowed it upon him, my master would have regarded it as a new crime, a new piece of insolence, and would, perhaps, revenge it on the boy. O, the serpent of slavery has many and poisonous fangs!

Not far from this time Nat Turner's insurrection broke out, and the news threw our town into great commotion. Strange that they should be alarmed, when their slaves were so "contented and happy!" But so it was. It was always the custom to have a muster every year. On that occasion every white man shouldered his musket. The citizens and the so-called country gentlemen wore military uniforms. The poor whites took their places in the ranks in everyday dress, some without shoes, some without hats. This grand occasion had already passed, and when the slaves were told there was to be another muster, they were surprised and rejoiced. Poor creatures! They thought it was going to be a holiday. I was informed of the true state of affairs, and imparted it to the few I could trust. Most gladly would I have proclaimed it to every slave, but I dared not. All could not be relied on. Mighty is the power of the torturing lash. By sunrise, people were pouring in from every quarter within twenty miles of the town. I knew the houses were to be searched, and I expected it would be done by country bullies and the poor whites. I knew nothing annoyed them so much as to see colored people living in comfort and respectability, so I made arrangements for them with especial care. I arranged everything in my grandmother's house as neatly as possible. I put white quilts on the beds, and decorated some of the rooms with flowers. When all was arranged, I sat down at the window to watch. Far as my eye could reach, it rested on a motley crowd of soldiers. Drums and fifes were discoursing martial music. The men were divided into companies of sixteen, each headed by a captain. Orders were given, and the wild scouts rushed in every direction, wherever a colored face was to be found. It was a grand opportunity for the low whites, who had no Negroes of their own to scourge. They exulted in such a chance to exercise a little brief authority, and show their subserviency to the slaveholders, not reflecting that the power which trampled on the colored people also kept themselves in poverty, ignorance, and moral degradation. Those who never witnessed such scenes can hardly believe what I know was inflicted at this time on innocent men, women, and children, against whom there was not the slightest ground for suspicion. Colored people and slaves who lived in remote parts of the town suffered in an especial manner. In some cases the searchers scattered powder and shot among their clothes, and then sent other parties to find them, and bring them forward as proof that they were plotting insurrection. Everywhere men, women, and children were whipped till the blood stood in puddles at their feet. Some received five hundred lashes, others were tied hands and feet, and tortured with a bucking paddle, which blisters the skin terribly. The dwellings of the colored people, unless they happened to be protected by some influential white person, who was nigh at hand, were robbed of clothing and everything else the marauders thought worth carrying away. All day long these unfeeling wretches went round, like a troop of demons, terrifying and tormenting the helpless. At night, they formed themselves into patrol bands, and went wherever they chose among the colored people, acting out their brutal will. Many women hid themselves in woods and swamps, to keep out of their way. If any of the husbands or fathers told of these outrages, they were tied up to the public whipping post, and cruelly scourged for telling lies about white men. The consternation was universal. No two people that had the slightest tinge of color in their faces dared to be seen talking together. I entertained no positive fears about our household, because we were in the midst of white families who would protect us. We were ready to receive the soldiers whenever they came. It was not long before we heard the tramp of feet and the sound of voices. The door was rudely pushed open, and in, they tumbled, like a pack of hungry wolves. They snatched at everything within their reach. Every box, trunk, closet, and corner underwent a thorough examination. A box in one of the drawers containing some silver change was eagerly pounced upon.

When I stepped forward to take it from them, one of the soldiers turned and said angrily, "What d'ye foller us fur? D'ye s'pose white folks is come to steal?" I replied, "You have come to search, but you have searched that box, and I will take it, if you please." At that moment I saw a white gentleman who was friendly to us, and I called to him, and asked him to have the goodness to come in and stay till the search was over. He readily complied. His entrance into the house brought in the captain of the company, whose business it was to guard the outside of the house, and see that none of the inmates left it. This officer was Mr. Litch, the wealthy slaveholder whom I mentioned, in the account of neighboring planters, as being notorious for his cruelty. He felt above soiling his hands with the search. He merely gave orders, and, if a bit of writing was discovered, it was carried to him by his ignorant followers, who were unable to read. My grandmother had a large trunk of bedding and table cloths. When that was opened, there was a great shout of surprise, and one exclaimed, "Where'd the damned niggers git all dis sheet an' table clarf?" My grandmother, emboldened by the presence of our white protector, said, "You may be sure we didn't pilfer 'em from *your* houses." "Look here, mammy," said a grim-looking fellow without any coat, "you seem to feel mighty gran' 'cause you got all them 'ere fixens. White folks oughter have 'em all." His remarks were interrupted by a chorus of voices shouting, "We's got 'em! We's got 'em! Dis 'ere yaller gal's got letters!" There was a general rush for the supposed letter, which, upon examination, proved to be some verses written to me by a friend. In packing away my things, I had overlooked them. When their captain informed them of their contents, they seemed much disappointed. He inquired of me who wrote them. I told him it was one of my friends. "Can you read them?" he asked. When I told him I could, he swore, and raved, and tore the paper into bits. "Bring me all your letters!" said he, in a commanding tone. I told him I had none. "Don't be afraid," he continued, in an insinuating way. "Bring them all to me. Nobody shall do you any harm." Seeing I did not move to obey him, his pleasant tone changed to oaths and threats. "Who writes to you? Half-free niggers?" inquired he. I replied, "O, no, most of my letters are from white people. Some request me to burn them after they are read, and some I destroy without reading." An exclamation of surprise from some of the company put a stop to our conversation. Some silver spoons which ornamented an old-fashioned buffet had just been discovered. My grandmother was in the habit of preserving fruit for many ladies in the town, and of preparing suppers for parties, consequently she had many jars of preserves. The closet that contained these was next invaded, and the contents tasted.

One of them, who was helping himself freely, tapped his neighbor on the shoulder, and said, "Wal done! Don't wonder de niggers want to kill all de white folks, when dey live on 'sarves." (preserves). I stretched out my hand to take the jar, saying, "You were not sent here to search for sweetmeats." "And what *were* we sent for?" said the captain, bristling up to me. I evaded the question. The search of the house was completed, and nothing found to condemn us. They next proceeded to the garden, and knocked about every bush and vine, with no better success. The captain called his men together, and, after a short consultation, the order to march was given. As they passed out of the gate, the captain turned back, and pronounced a malediction (curse) on the house. He said it ought to be burned to the ground, and each of its inmates receive thirty-nine lashes. We came out of this affair very fortunately, not losing anything except some wearing apparel. Towards evening the turbulence increased. The soldiers, stimulated by drink, committed still greater cruelties. Shrieks and shouts continually rent the air. Not daring to go to the door, I peeped under the window curtain. I saw a mob dragging along a number of colored people, each white man, with his musket upraised, threatening instant death if they did not stop their shrieks. Among the prisoners was a respectable old colored minister. They had found a few parcels of shot in his house, which his wife had for years used to balance her scales. For this they were going to shoot him on Court House Green. What a spectacle was that for a civilized country! A rabble, staggering under intoxication, assuming to be the administrators of justice! The better class of the community exerted their influence to save the innocent, persecuted people, and in several instances they succeeded, by keeping them shut up in jail till the excitement abated. At last the white citizens found that their own property was not safe from the lawless rabble they had summoned to protect them. They rallied the drunken swarm, drove them back into the country, and set a guard over the town. The next day, the town patrols were commissioned to search colored people that lived out of the city, and the most shocking outrages were committed with perfect impunity. Every day for a fortnight, if I looked out, I saw horsemen with some poor panting Negro tied to their saddles, and compelled by the lash to keep up with their speed, till they arrived at the jail yard. Those who had been whipped too unmercifully to walk were washed with brine, tossed into a cart, and carried to jail. One black man, who had not fortitude to endure scourging, promised to give information about the conspiracy. But it turned out that he knew nothing at all. He had not even heard the name of Nat Turner.

    The poor fellow had, however, made up a story, which augmented his own sufferings and those of the colored people. The day patrol continued for some weeks, and at sundown a night guard was substituted. Nothing at all was proved against the colored people, bond or free. The wrath of the slaveholders was somewhat appeased by the capture of Nat Turner. The imprisoned were released. The slaves were sent to their masters, and the free were permitted to return to their ravaged homes. Visiting was strictly forbidden on the plantations.

The slaves begged the privilege of again meeting at their little church in the woods, with their burying ground around it. It was built by the colored people, and they had no higher happiness than to meet there and sing hymns together, and pour out their hearts in spontaneous prayer. Their request was denied, and the church was demolished. They were permitted to attend the white churches, a certain portion of the galleries being appropriated to their use. There, when everybody else had partaken of the communion, and the benediction had been pronounced, the minister said, "Come down, now, my colored friends." They obeyed the summons, and partook of the bread and wine, in commemoration of the meek and lowly Jesus, who said, "God is your Father, and all ye are brethren."

☐☐☐☐☐☐☐☐☐☐

After the alarm caused by Nat Turner's insurrection had subsided, the slaveholders came to the conclusion that it would be well to give the slaves enough of religious instruction to keep them from murdering their masters. The Episcopal clergyman offered to hold a separate service on Sundays for their benefit. His colored members were very few, and also very respectable—a fact which I presume had some weight with him. The difficulty was to decide on a suitable place for them to worship.

The Methodist and Baptist churches admitted them in the afternoon, but their carpets and cushions were not so costly as those at the Episcopal church. It was at last decided that they should meet at the house of a free colored man, who was a member. I was invited to attend, because I could read.

Sunday evening came, and, trusting to the cover of night, I ventured out. I rarely ventured out by daylight, for I always went with fear, expecting at every turn to encounter Dr. Flint, who was sure to turn me back, or order me to his office to inquire where I got my bonnet, or some other article of dress. When the

Reverend Mr. Pike came, there were some twenty persons present. The reverend gentleman knelt in prayer, then seated himself, and requested all present, who could read, to open their books, while he gave out the portions he wished them to repeat or respond to. His text was, "Servants, be obedient to them that are your masters according to the flesh, with fear and trembling, in singleness of your heart, as unto Christ." Pious Mr. Pike brushed up his hair till it stood upright, and, in deep, solemn tones, began, "Hearken, ye servants! Give strict heed unto my words. You are rebellious sinners. Your hearts are filled with all manner of evil. Tis the devil who tempts you. God is angry with you, and will surely punish you, if you don't forsake your wicked ways. You that live in town are eye servants behind your master's back. Instead of serving your masters faithfully, which is pleasing in the sight of your heavenly Master, you are idle, and shirk your work. God sees you. You tell lies. God hears you. Instead of being engaged in worshipping him, you are hidden away somewhere, feasting on your master's substance, tossing coffee grounds with some wicked fortune teller, or cutting cards with another old hag. Your masters may not find you out, but God sees you, and will punish you. O, the depravity of your hearts! When your master's work is done, are you quietly together, thinking of the goodness of God to such sinful creatures? No, you are quarrelling, and tying up little bags of roots to bury under the doorsteps to poison each other with. God sees you. You men steal away to every grog shop to sell your master's corn, that you may buy rum to drink. God sees you. You sneak into the back streets, or among the bushes, to pitch coppers. Although your masters may not find you out, God sees you, and he will punish you. You must forsake your sinful ways, and be faithful servants. Obey your old master and your young master—your old mistress and your young mistress. If you disobey your earthly master, you offend your heavenly Master. You must obey God's commandments. When you go from here, don't stop at the corners of the streets to talk, but go directly home, and let your master and mistress see that you have come." The benediction was pronounced. We went home, highly amused at brother Pike's gospel teaching, and we determined to hear him again. I went the next Sabbath evening, and heard pretty much a repetition of the last discourse. At the close of the meeting, Mr. Pike informed us that he found it very inconvenient to meet at the friend's house, and he should be glad to see us, every Sunday evening, at his own kitchen. I went home with the feeling that I had heard the Reverend Mr. Pike for the last time. Some of his members repaired to his house, and found that the kitchen sported two tallow candles, the first time, I am sure, since its present occupant owned it, for the servants never had anything but pine knots. It was so long before the reverend gentleman descended from his comfortable parlor that the slaves left, and went to enjoy a Methodist shout. They never seem so happy as when shouting and singing at religious meetings.

Many of them are sincere, and nearer to the gate of heaven than sanctimonious Mr. Pike, and other long-faced Christians, who see wounded Samaritans, and pass by on the other side. The slaves generally compose their own songs and hymns, and they do not trouble their heads much about the measure. They often sing the following verses, *"Old Satan is one busy ole man, he rolls dem blocks all in my way, but Jesus is my bosom friend, he rolls dem blocks away. If I had died when I was young, den how my stammering tongue would have sung, but I am ole, and now I stand a narrow chance for to tread dat heavenly land."* I well remember one occasion when I attended a Methodist class meeting. I went with a burdened spirit, and happened to sit next a poor, bereaved mother, whose heart was still heavier than mine. The class leader was the town constable—a man who bought and sold slaves, who whipped his brethren and sisters of the church at the public whipping post, in jail or out of jail. He was ready to perform that Christian office anywhere for fifty cents. This white-faced, black-hearted brother came near us, and said to the stricken woman, "Sister, can't you tell us how the Lord deals with your soul? Do you love him as you did formerly?"

She rose to her feet, and said, in piteous tones, "My Lord and Master, help me! My load is more than I can bear. God has hid himself from me, and I am left in darkness and misery." Then, striking her breast, she continued, "I can't tell you what is in here! They've got all my children. Last week they took the last one. God only knows where they've sold her. They let me have her sixteen years, and then—O! O! Pray for her brothers and sisters! I've got nothing to live for now. God make my time short!" She sat down, quivering in every limb. I saw that constable class leader become crimson in the face with suppressed laughter, while he held up his handkerchief, that those who were weeping for the poor woman's calamity might not see his merriment. Then, with assumed gravity, he said to the bereaved mother, "Sister, pray to the Lord that every dispensation of his divine will may be sanctified to the good of your poor needy soul!" The congregation struck up a hymn, and sung as though they were as free as the birds that warbled round us, *"Ole Satan thought he had a mighty aim, he missed my soul, and caught my sins. Cry Amen, cry Amen, cry Amen to God! He took my sins upon his back, went muttering and grumbling down to hell. Cry Amen, cry Amen, cry Amen to God! Ole Satan's church is here below. Up to God's free church I hope to go. Cry Amen, cry Amen, cry Amen to God!"* Precious are such moments to the poor slaves. If you were to hear them at such times, you might think they were happy. But can that hour of singing and shouting sustain them through the dreary week, toiling without wages, under constant dread of the lash? The Episcopal clergyman, who, ever since my earliest recollection, had been a sort of god among the slaveholders, concluded, as his family was large, that he must go where money was more abundant. A very different clergyman took his place. The change was very agreeable to the colored people, who said, "God has sent us a good man this time." They loved him, and their children followed him for a smile or a kind word. Even the slaveholders felt his influence. He brought to the rectory five slaves. His wife taught them to read and write, and to be useful to her and themselves. As soon as he was settled, he turned his attention to the needy slaves around him. He urged upon his parishioners the duty of having a meeting expressly for them every Sunday, with a sermon adapted to their comprehension. After much argument and importunity, it was finally agreed that they might occupy the gallery of the church on Sunday evenings. Many colored people, hitherto unaccustomed to attend church, now gladly went to hear the gospel preached. The sermons were simple, and they understood them. Moreover, it was the first time they had ever been addressed as human beings. It was not long before his white parishioners began to be dissatisfied.

He was accused of preaching better sermons to the Negroes than he did to them. He honestly confessed that he bestowed more pains upon those sermons than upon any others, for the slaves were reared in such ignorance that it was a difficult task to adapt himself to their comprehension. Dissensions arose in the parish. Some wanted he should preach to them in the evening, and to the slaves in the afternoon. In the midst of these disputes, his wife died, after a very short illness. Her slaves gathered round her dying bed in great sorrow. She said, "I have tried to do you good and promote your happiness, and if I have failed, it has not been for want of interest in your welfare. Do not weep for me, but prepare for the new duties that lie before you. I leave you all free. May we meet in a better world." Her liberated slaves were sent away, with funds to establish them comfortably. The colored people will long bless the memory of that truly Christian woman. Soon after her death her husband preached his farewell sermon, and many tears were shed at his departure. Several years after, he passed through our town and preached to his former congregation. In his afternoon sermon he addressed the colored people. "My friends," said he, "it affords me great happiness to have an opportunity of speaking to you again. For two years I have been striving to do something for the colored people of my own parish, but nothing is yet accomplished. I have not even preached a sermon to them. Try to live according to the word of God, my friends. Your skin is darker than mine, but God judges men by their hearts, not by the color of their skins." This was strange doctrine from a Southern pulpit. It was very offensive to slaveholders. They said he and his wife had made fools of their slaves, and that he preached like a fool to the Negroes. I knew an old black man, whose piety and child-like trust in God were beautiful to witness. At fifty-three years old he joined the Baptist church. He had a most earnest desire to learn to read. He thought he should know how to serve God better if he could only read the Bible. He came to me, and begged me to teach him. He said he could not pay me, for he had no money, but he would bring me nice fruit when the season for it came. I asked him if he didn't know it was contrary to law, and that slaves were whipped and imprisoned for teaching each other to read. This brought the tears into his eyes. "Don't be troubled, Uncle Fred," said I. "I have no thoughts of refusing to teach you. I only told you of the law, that you might know the danger, and be on your guard." He thought he could plan to come three times a week without it being suspected. I selected a quiet nook, where no intruder was likely to penetrate, and there I taught him his A-B-C. Considering his age, his progress was astonishing. As soon as he could spell in two syllables he wanted to spell out words in the Bible. The happy smile that illuminated his face put joy into my heart.

After spelling out a few words, he paused, and said, "Honey, it 'pears when I can read dis good book I shall be nearer to God. White man is got all de sense. He can larn easy. It ain't easy for ole black man like me. I only wants to read dis book, dat I may know how to live, den I hab no fear 'bout dying." I tried to encourage him by speaking of the rapid progress he had made. "Hab patience, child," he replied. "I larns slow." I had no need of patience. His gratitude, and the happiness I imparted, were more than a recompense for all my trouble. At the end of six months he had read through the New Testament, and could find any text in it. One day, when he had recited unusually well, I said, "Uncle Fred, how do you manage to get your lessons so well?" "Lord bress you, chile," he replied. "You nebber gibs me a lesson dat I don't pray to God to help me to understan' what I spells and what I reads. And he *does* help me, chile. Bress his holy name!"

There are thousands, who, like good Uncle Fred, are thirsting for the water of life, but the law forbids it, and the churches withhold it. They send the Bible to heathen abroad, and neglect the heathen at home. I am glad that missionaries go out to the dark corners of the earth, but I ask them not to overlook the dark corners at home. Talk to American slaveholders as you talk to savages in Africa. Tell *them* it is wrong to traffic in men. Tell them it is sinful to sell their own children, and atrocious to violate their own daughters. Tell them that all men are brethren, and that man has no right to shut out the light of knowledge from his brother. Tell them they are answerable to God for sealing up the Fountain of Life from souls that are thirsting for it.

There are men who would gladly undertake such missionary work as this, but, alas! Their number is small. They are hated by the South, and would be driven from its soil, or dragged to prison to die, as others have been before them. The field is ripe for the harvest, and awaits the reapers. Perhaps the great grandchildren of Uncle Fred may have freely imparted to them the divine treasures, which he sought by stealth, at the risk of the prison and the scourge. Are doctors of divinity blind, or are they hypocrites? I suppose some are the one, and some the other, but I think if they felt the interest in the poor and the lowly, that they ought to feel, they would not be so *easily* blinded. A clergyman who goes to the South, for the first time, has usually some feeling, however vague, that slavery is wrong. The slaveholder suspects this, and plays his game accordingly. He makes himself as agreeable as possible, talks on theology, and other kindred topics. The reverend gentleman* is asked to invoke a blessing on a table loaded with luxuries. After dinner he walks round the premises, and sees the beautiful groves and flowering vines, and the comfortable huts of favored household slaves. The Southerner invites him to talk with these slaves. He asks them if they want to be free, and they say, "O, no, Massa." This is sufficient to satisfy him. He comes home to publish *A South Side View of Slavery*, and to complain of the exaggerations of abolitionists. He assures people that he has been to the South and seen slavery for himself, that it is a beautiful "patriarchal institution," that the slaves don't want their freedom, that they have hallelujah meetings, and other religious privileges. What does *he* know of the half-starved wretches toiling from dawn till dark on the plantations? Of mothers shrieking for their children, torn from their arms by slave traders? Of young girls dragged down into moral filth? Of pools of blood around the whipping post? Of hounds trained to tear human flesh? Of men screwed into cotton gins to die? The slaveholder showed him none of these things, and the slaves dared not tell of them if he had asked them. There is a great difference between Christianity and religion at the South. If a man goes to the communion table, and pays money into the treasury of the church, no matter if it be the price of blood, he is called religious. If a pastor has offspring by a woman not his wife, the church dismisses him, if she is a white woman, but if she is colored, it does not hinder his continuing to be their good shepherd. When I was told that Dr. Flint had joined the Episcopal church, I was much surprised. I supposed that religion had a purifying effect on the character of men, but the worst persecutions I endured from him were after he was a communicant. The conversation of the doctor, the day after he had been confirmed, certainly gave *me* no indication that he had "renounced the devil and all his works." In answer to some of his usual talk, I reminded him that he had just joined the church.

"Yes, Linda," said he. "It was proper for me to do so. I am getting in years, and my position in society requires it, and it puts an end to all the damned slang. You would do well to join the church, too, Linda." "There are sinners enough in it already," rejoined I. "If I could be allowed to live like a Christian, I should be glad." "You can do what I require, and if you are faithful to me, you will be as virtuous as my wife," he replied. I answered that the Bible didn't say so. His voice became hoarse with rage. "How dare you preach to me about your infernal Bible!" he exclaimed. "What right have you, who are my Negro, to talk to me about what you would like, and what you wouldn't like? I am your master, and you shall obey me." No wonder the slaves sing, *"Ole Satan's church is here below, up to God's free church I hope to go."*

*The "reverend gentleman" mentioned by Jacobs was Nehemiah Adams who wrote an account (1854) of his visit to the South and what he saw while there. The problems with his account was that he was shown what slave owners he encountered wanted him to see and told what they wanted him to hear. Like Amelia Murray's book two years later, this "memoir" by Adams was complete fiction, whether it was intentional or not isn't known. It should also be noted Nehemiah Adams was an avowed racist who believed white people were superior to black people despite calling himself an abolitionist. That fact alone is very telling with how easily Adams could be misled by plantation owners. Needless to say, today his so-called "memoir" has a loyal following among readers of white supremacy trash—which shouldn't be surprising to anyone.

☐☐☐☐☐☐☐☐☐☐

  I had not returned to my master's house since the birth of my child. The old man raved to have me thus removed from his immediate power, but his wife vowed, by all that was good and great, she would kill me if I came back, and he did not doubt her word. Sometimes he would stay away for a season. Then he would come and renew the old threadbare discourse about his forbearance and my ingratitude. He labored, most unnecessarily, to convince me that I had lowered myself. The venomous old reprobate had no need of descanting on that theme. I felt humiliated enough. My unconscious babe was the ever-present witness of my shame. I listened with silent contempt when he talked about my having forfeited *his* good opinion, but I shed bitter tears that I was no longer worthy of being respected by the good and pure. Alas! Slavery still held me in its poisonous grasp. There was no chance for me to be respectable. There was no prospect of being able to lead a better life. Sometimes, when my master found that I still refused to accept what he called his kind offers, he would threaten to sell my child. "Perhaps that will humble you," said he. Humble *me*! Was I not already in the dust? But his threat lacerated my heart. I knew the law gave him power to fulfill it, for slaveholders have been cunning enough to enact that "the child shall follow the condition of the *mother*," not of the *father*, thus taking care that licentiousness shall not interfere with avarice. This reflection made me clasp my innocent babe all the more firmly to my heart. Horrid visions passed through my mind when I thought of his liability to fall into the slave trader's hands. I wept over him, and said, "O my child! Perhaps they will leave you in some cold cabin to die, and then throw you into a hole, as if you were a dog." When Dr. Flint learned that I was again to be a mother, he was exasperated beyond measure.

He rushed from the house, and returned with a pair of shears. I had a fine head of hair, and he often railed about my pride of arranging it nicely. He cut every hair close to my head, storming and swearing all the time. I replied to some of his abuse, and he struck me. Some months before, he had pitched me downstairs in a fit of passion, and the injury I received was so serious that I was unable to turn myself in bed for many days.

He then said, "Linda, I swear by God I will never raise my hand against you again," but I knew that he would forget his promise. After he discovered my situation, he was like a restless spirit from the pit. He came every day, and I was subjected to such insults as no pen can describe. I would not describe them if I could, they were too low, too revolting. I tried to keep them from my grandmother's knowledge as much as I could. I knew she had enough to sadden her life, without having my troubles to bear. When she saw the doctor treat me with violence, and heard him utter oaths terrible enough to palsy a man's tongue, she could not always hold her peace. It was natural and mother-like that she should try to defend me, but it only made matters worse.

When they told me my newborn babe was a girl, my heart was heavier than it had ever been before. Slavery is terrible for men, but it is far more terrible for women. Superadded to the burden common to all, *they* have wrongs, and sufferings, and mortifications peculiarly their own. Dr. Flint had sworn that he would make me suffer, to my last day, for this new crime against *him*, as he called it, and as long as he had me in his power he kept his word. On the fourth day after the birth of my babe, he entered my room suddenly, and commanded me to rise and bring my baby to him. The nurse who took care of me had gone out of the room to prepare some nourishment, and I was alone. There was no alternative. I rose, took up my babe, and crossed the room to where he sat. "Now stand there," said he, "till I tell you to go back!" My child bore a strong resemblance to her father, and to the deceased Mrs. Sands, her grandmother. He noticed this, and while I stood before him, trembling with weakness, he heaped upon me and my little one every vile epithet he could think of. Even the grandmother in her grave did not escape his curses.

In the midst of his vituperations I fainted at his feet. This recalled him to his senses. He took the baby from my arms, laid it on the bed, dashed cold water in my face, took me up, and shook me violently, to restore my consciousness before anyone entered the room. Just then my grandmother came in, and he hurried out of the house. I suffered in consequence of this treatment, but I begged my friends to let me die, rather than send for the doctor. There was nothing I dreaded so much as his presence.

My life was spared, and I was glad for the sake of my little ones. Had it not been for these ties to life, I should have been glad to be released by death, though I had lived only nineteen years. Always it gave me a pang that my children had no lawful claim to a name. Their father offered his, but, if I had wished to accept the offer, I dared not while my master lived. Moreover, I knew it would not be accepted at their baptism. A Christian name they were at least entitled to, and we resolved to call my boy for our dear good Benjamin, who had gone far away from us.

My grandmother belonged to the church, and she was very desirous of having the children christened. I knew Dr. Flint would forbid it, and I did not venture to attempt it. But chance favored me. He was called to visit a patient out of town, and was obliged to be absent during Sunday. "Now is the time," said my grandmother, "we will take the children to church, and have them christened." When I entered the church, recollections of my mother came over me, and I felt subdued in spirit. There she had presented me for baptism, without any reason to feel ashamed. She had been married, and had such legal rights as slavery allows to a slave. The vows had at least been sacred to *her*, and she had never violated them. I was glad she was not alive, to know under what different circumstances her grandchildren were presented for baptism. Why had my lot been so different from my mother's? *Her* master had died when she was a child, and she remained with her mistress till she married. She was never in the power of any master, and thus she escaped one class of the evils that generally fall upon slaves. When my baby was about to be christened, the former mistress of my father stepped up to me, and proposed to give it her Christian name. To this I added the surname of my father, who had himself no legal right to it, for my grandfather on the paternal side was a white gentleman. What tangled skeins are the genealogies of slavery. I loved my father, but it mortified me to be obliged to bestow his name on my children. When we left the church, my father's old mistress invited me to go home with her. She clasped a gold chain round my baby's neck. I thanked her for this kindness, but I did not like the emblem. I wanted no chain to be fastened on my daughter, not even if its links were of gold. How earnestly I prayed that she might never feel the weight of slavery's chain, whose iron entereth into the soul.

□□□□□□□□□□

My children grew finely, and Dr. Flint would often say to me, with an exulting smile, "These brats will bring me a handsome sum of money one of these days." I thought to myself that, God being my helper, they should never pass into his hands. It seemed to me I would rather see them killed than have them given up to his power. The money for the freedom of myself and my children could be obtained, but I derived no advantage from that circumstance. Dr. Flint loved money, but he loved power more. After much discussion, my friends resolved on making another trial. There was a slaveholder about to leave for Texas, and he was commissioned to buy me. He was to begin with nine hundred dollars, and go up to twelve. My master refused his offers. "Sir," said he, "she don't belong to me. She is my daughter's property, and I have no right to sell her. I mistrust that you come from her paramour. If so, you may tell him that he cannot buy her for any money, neither can he buy her children." The doctor came to see me the next day, and my heart beat quicker as he entered. I never had seen the old man tread with so majestic a step. He seated himself and looked at me with withering scorn. My children had learned to be afraid of him. The little one would shut her eyes and hide her face on my shoulder whenever she saw him, and Benny, who was now nearly five years old, often inquired, "What makes that bad man come here so many times? Does he want to hurt us?" I would clasp the dear boy in my arms, trusting that he would be free before he was old enough to solve the problem. And now, as the doctor sat there so grim and silent, the child left his play and came and nestled up by me. At last my tormentor spoke. "So you are left in disgust, are you?" said he. "It is no more than I expected. You remember I told you years ago that you would be treated so. So he is tired of you? Ha! Ha! Ha! The virtuous madam don't like to hear about it, does she? Ha! Ha! Ha!" There was a sting in his calling me virtuous madam. I no longer had the power of answering him as I had formerly done. He continued, "So it seems you are trying to get up another intrigue. Your new paramour came to me, and offered to buy you, but you may be assured you will not succeed. You are mine, and you shall be mine for life. There lives no human being that can take you out of slavery. I would have done it, but you rejected my kind offer." I told him I did not wish to get up any intrigue, that I had never seen the man who offered to buy me. "Do you tell me I lie?" exclaimed he, dragging me from my chair. "Will you say again that you never saw that man?" I answered, "I do say so." He clinched my arm with a volley of oaths. Ben began to scream, and I told him to go to his grandmother. "Don't you stir a step, you little wretch!" said he. The child drew nearer to me, and put his arms round me, as if he wanted to protect me.

  This was too much for my enraged master. He caught him up and hurled him across the room. I thought he was dead, and rushed towards him to take him up. "Not yet!" exclaimed the doctor. "Let him lie there till he comes to." "Let me go! Let me go!" I screamed, "or I will raise the whole house." I struggled and got away, but he clinched me again. Somebody opened the door, and he released me. I picked up my insensible child, and when I turned my tormentor was gone. Anxiously I bent over the little form, so pale and still, and when the brown eyes at last opened, I don't know whether I was very happy. All the doctor's former persecutions were renewed. He came morning, noon, and night. No jealous lover ever watched a rival more closely than he watched me and the unknown slaveholder, with whom he accused me of wishing to get up an intrigue. When my grandmother was out of the way he searched every room to find him. In one of his visits, he happened to find a young girl, whom he had sold to a trader a few days previous. His statement was, that he sold her because she, had been too familiar with the overseer. She had had a bitter life with him, and was glad to be sold. She had no mother, and no near ties. She had been torn from all her family years before. A few friends had entered into bonds for her safety, if the trader would allow her to spend with them the time that intervened between her sale and the gathering up of his human stock. Such a favor was rarely granted. It saved the trader the expense of board and jail fees, and though the amount was small, it was a weighty consideration in a slave trader's mind. Dr. Flint always had an aversion to meeting slaves after he had sold them. He ordered Rose out of the house, but he was no longer her master, and she took no notice of him.

 For once the crushed Rose was the conqueror. His gray eyes flashed angrily upon her, but that was the extent of his power. "How came this girl here?" he exclaimed. "What right had you to allow it, when you knew I had sold her?" I answered "This is my grandmother's house, and Rose came to see her. I have no right to turn anybody out of doors, that comes here for honest purposes." He gave me the blow that would have fallen upon Rose if she had still been his slave. My grandmother's attention had been attracted by loud voices, and she entered in time to see a second blow dealt. She was not a woman to let such an outrage, in her own house, go unrebuked. The doctor undertook to explain that I had been insolent. Her indignant feelings rose higher and higher, and finally boiled over in words. "Get out of my house!" she exclaimed. "Go home, and take care of your wife and children, and you will have enough to do, without watching my family." He threw the birth of my children in her face, and accused her of sanctioning the life I was leading. She told him I was living with her by compulsion of his wife, that he needn't accuse her, for he was the one to blame, he was the one who had caused all the trouble. She grew more and more excited as she went on. "I tell you what, Dr. Flint," said she, "you ain't got many more years to live, and you'd better be saying your prayers. It will take 'em all, and more too, to wash the dirt off your soul."

"Do you know whom you are talking to?" he exclaimed. She replied, "Yes, I know very well who I am talking to." He left the house in a great rage. I looked at my grandmother. Our eyes met. Their angry expression had passed away, but she looked sorrowful and weary—weary of incessant strife. I wondered that it did not lessen her love for me, but if it did she never showed it. She was always kind, always ready to sympathize with my troubles. There might have been peace and contentment in that humble home if it had not been for the demon slavery. The winter passed undisturbed by the doctor. The beautiful spring came, and when nature resumes her loveliness, the human soul is apt to revive also. My drooping hopes came to life again with the flowers. I was dreaming of freedom again, more for my children's sake than my own. I planned and I planned. Obstacles hit against plans. There seemed no way of overcoming them, and yet I hoped. Back came the wily doctor. I was not at home when he called. A friend had invited me to a small party, and to gratify her I went. To my great consternation, a messenger came in haste to say that Dr. Flint was at my grandmother's, and insisted on seeing me. They did not tell him where I was, or he would have come and raised a disturbance in my friend's house. They sent me a dark wrapper, I threw it on and hurried home. My speed did not save me, the doctor had gone away in anger. I dreaded the morning, but I could not delay it, it came, warm and bright.

At an early hour the doctor came and asked me where I had been last night. I told him. He did not believe me, and sent to my friend's house to ascertain the facts. He came in the afternoon to assure me he was satisfied that I had spoken the truth. He seemed to be in a facetious mood, and I expected some jeers were coming. "I suppose you need some recreation," said he, "but I am surprised at your being there, among those Negroes. It was not the place for *you*. Are you *allowed* to visit such people?" I understood this covert fling at the white gentleman who was my friend, but I merely replied, "I went to visit my friends, and any company they keep is good enough for me." He went on to say, "I have seen very little of you of late, but my interest in you is unchanged. When I said I would have no more mercy on you I was rash. I recall my words. Linda, you desire freedom for yourself and your children, and you can obtain it only through me. If you agree to what I am about to propose, you and they shall be free. There must be no communication of any kind between you and their father. I will procure a cottage, where you and the children can live together. Your labor shall be light, such as sewing for my family. Think what is offered you, Linda—a home and freedom! Let the past be forgotten. If I have been harsh with you at times, your willfulness drove me to it. You know I exact obedience from my own children, and I consider you as yet a child." He paused for an answer, but I remained silent. "Why don't you speak?" said he. "What more do you wait for?" "Nothing, sir." "Then you accept my offer?" "No, sir." His anger was ready to break loose, but he succeeded in curbing it, and replied, "You have answered without thought. But I must let you know there are two sides to my proposition, if you reject the bright side, you will be obliged to take the dark one. You must either accept my offer, or you and your children shall be sent to your young master's plantation, there to remain till your young mistress is married, and your children shall fare like the rest of the Negro children. I give you a week to consider of it." He was shrewd, but I knew he was not to be trusted. I told him I was ready to give my answer now. "I will not receive it now," he replied. "You act too much from impulse. Remember that you and your children can be free a week from today if you choose." On what a monstrous chance hung the destiny of my children? I knew that my master's offer was a snare, and that if I entered it escape would be impossible. As for his promise, I knew him so well that I was sure if he gave me free papers, they would be so managed as to have no legal value. The alternative was inevitable. I resolved to go to the plantation. But then I thought how completely I should be in his power, and the prospect was appalling. Even if I should kneel before him, and implore him to spare me, for the sake of my children, I knew he would spurn me with his foot, and my weakness would be his triumph. Before the week expired, I heard that young Mr. Flint was about to be married to a lady of his own stamp. I foresaw the position I should occupy in his establishment. I had once been sent to the plantation for punishment, and fear of the son had induced the father to recall me very soon. My mind was made up, I was resolved that I would foil my master and save my children, or I would perish in the attempt. I kept my plans to myself, I knew that friends would try to dissuade me from them, and I would not wound their feelings by rejecting their advice. On the decisive day the doctor came, and said he hoped I had made a wise choice.

"I am ready to go to the plantation, sir," I replied. "Have you thought how important your decision is to your children?" said he. I told him I had. "Very well. Go to the plantation, and my curse go with you," he replied. "Your boy shall be put to work, and he shall soon be sold, and your girl shall be raised for the purpose of selling well. Go your own ways!" He left the room with curses, not to be repeated. As I stood rooted to the spot, my grandmother came and said, "Linda, child, what did you tell him?" I answered that I was going to the plantation. "*Must* you go?" said she. "Can't something be done to stop it?" I told her it was useless to try, but she begged me not to give up. She said she would go to the doctor, and remind him how long and how faithfully she had served in the family, and how she had taken her own baby from her breast to nourish his wife. She would tell him I had been out of the family so long they would not miss me, that she would pay them for my time, and the money would procure a woman who had more strength for the situation than I had. I begged her not to go, but she persisted in saying, "He will listen to *me*, Linda." She went, and was treated as I expected. He coolly listened to what she said, but denied her request. He told her that what he did was for my good, that my feelings were entirely above my situation, and that on the plantation I would receive treatment that was suitable to my behavior. My grandmother was much cast down. I had my secret hopes, but I must fight my battle alone. I had a woman's pride, and a mother's love for my children, and I resolved that out of the darkness of this hour a brighter dawn should rise for them. My master had power and law on his side, I had a determined will. There is might in each.

☐☐☐☐☐☐☐☐☐☐

Early the next morning I left my grandmother's with my youngest child. My boy was ill, and left him behind. I had many sad thoughts as the old wagon jolted on. Hitherto, I had suffered alone, now, my little one was to be treated as a slave. As we drew near the great house, I thought of the time when I was formerly sent there out of revenge. I wondered for what purpose I was now sent. I could not tell. I resolved to obey orders so far as duty required, but within myself, I determined to make my stay as short as possible. Mr. Flint was waiting to receive us, and told me to follow him up stairs to receive orders for the day. My little Ellen was left below in the kitchen. It was a change for her, who had always been so carefully tended. My young master said she might amuse herself in the yard. This was kind of him, since the child was hateful to his sight. My task was to fit up the house for the reception of the bride. In the midst of sheets, tablecloths, towels, drapery, and carpeting, my head was as busy planning, as were my fingers with the needle. At noon I was allowed to go to Ellen. She had sobbed herself to sleep. I heard Mr. Flint say to a neighbor, "I've got her down here, and I'll soon take the town notions out of her head. My father is partly to blame for her nonsense. He ought to have broke her in long ago." The remark was made within my hearing, and it would have been quite as manly to have made it to my face. He *had* said things to my face which might, or might not, have surprised his neighbor if he had known of them. He was "a chip of the old block." I resolved to give him no cause to accuse me of being too much of a lady, so far as work was concerned. I worked day and night, with wretchedness before me. When lay down beside my child, I felt how much easier it would be to see her die than to see her master beat her about, as I daily saw him beat other little ones. The spirit of the mothers was so crushed by the lash, that they stood by, without courage to remonstrate. How much more must I suffer, before I should be "broke in" to that degree? I wished to appear as contented as possible. Sometimes I had an opportunity to send a few lines home, and this brought up recollections that made it difficult, for a time, to seem calm and indifferent to my lot.

Notwithstanding my efforts, I saw that Mr. Flint regarded me with a suspicious eye. Ellen broke down under the trials of her new life. Separated from me, with no one to look after her, she wandered about, and in a few days cried herself sick. One day, she sat under the window where I was at work, crying that weary cry which makes a mother's heart bleed. I was obliged to steel myself to bear it. After a while it ceased. I looked out, and she was gone. As it was near noon, I ventured to go down in search of her. The great house was raised two feet above the ground. I looked under it, and saw her about midway, fast asleep. I crept under and drew her out. As I held her in my arms, I thought how well it would be for her if she never waked up, and I uttered my thought aloud. I was startled to hear someone say, "Did you speak to me?" I looked up, and saw Mr. Flint standing beside me. He said nothing further, but turned, frowning, away. That night he sent Ellen a biscuit and a cup of sweetened milk. This generosity surprised me. I learned afterwards, that in the afternoon he had killed a large snake, which crept from under the house, and I supposed that incident had prompted his unusual kindness. The next morning the old cart was loaded with shingles for town. I put Ellen into it, and sent her to her grandmother. Mr. Flint said I ought to have asked his permission. I told him the child was sick, and required attention which I had no time to give. He let it pass for he was aware that I had accomplished much work in a little time. I had been three weeks on the plantation, when I planned a visit home. It must be at night, after everybody was in bed. I was six miles from town, and the road was very dreary. I was to go with a young man, who, I knew, often stole to town to see his mother. One night, when all was quiet, we started. Fear gave speed to our steps, and we were not long in performing the journey. I arrived at my grandmother's. Her bedroom was on the first floor, and the window was open, the weather being warm. I spoke to her and she awoke. She let me in and closed the window, lest some late passerby should see me. A light was brought, and the whole household gathered round me, some smiling and some crying. I went to look at my children, and thanked God for their happy sleep. The tears fell as I leaned over them. As I moved to leave, Benny stirred. I turned back, and whispered, "Mother is here." After digging at his eyes with his little fist, they opened, and he sat up in bed, looking at me curiously. Having satisfied himself that it was I, he exclaimed, "O mother! You ain't dead, are you? They didn't cut off your head at the plantation, did they?" My time was up too soon, and my guide was waiting for me. I laid Benny back in his bed, and dried his tears by a promise to come again soon. Rapidly we retraced our steps back to the plantation. About halfway we were met by a company of four patrols. Luckily we heard their horse's hoofs before they came in sight, and we had time to hide behind a large tree. They passed, hallooing and shouting in a manner that indicated a recent carousal. How thankful we were that they had not their dogs with them! We hastened our footsteps, and when we arrived on the plantation we heard the sound of the hand mill. The slaves were grinding their corn. We were safely in the house before the horn summoned them to their labor. I divided my little parcel of food with my guide, knowing that he had lost the chance of grinding his corn, and must toil all day in the field.

    Mr. Flint often took an inspection of the house, to see that no one was idle. The entire management of the work was trusted to me because he knew nothing about it, and rather than hire a superintendent he contented himself with my arrangements. He had often urged upon his father the necessity of having me at the plantation to take charge of his affairs, and make clothes for the slaves, but the old man knew him too well to consent to that arrangement. When I had been working a month at the plantation, the great aunt of Mr. Flint came to make him visit.

This was the good old lady who paid fifty dollars for my grandmother, for the purpose of making her free, when she stood on the auction block. My grandmother loved this old lady, whom we all called Miss Fanny. She often came to take tea with us. On such occasions the table was spread with a snow white cloth, and the china cups and silver spoons were taken from the old fashioned buffet. There were hot muffins, tea rusks (sweet toast), and delicious sweetmeats. My grandmother kept two cows, and the fresh cream was Miss Fanny's delight. She invariably declared that it was the best in town. The old ladies had cozy times together. They would work and chat, and sometimes, while talking over old times, their spectacles would get dim with tears, and would have to be taken off and wiped. When Miss Fanny bade us goodbye, her bag was filled with grandmother's best cakes, and she was urged to come again soon. There had been a time when Dr. Flint's wife came to take tea with us, and when her children were also sent to have a feast of "Aunt Marthy's" nice cooking. But after I became an object of her jealousy and spite, she was angry with grandmother for giving a shelter to me and my children. She would not even speak to her in the street. This wounded my grandmother's feelings, for she could not retain ill will against the woman whom she had nourished with her milk when a babe. The doctor's wife would gladly have prevented our intercourse with Miss Fanny if she could have done it, but fortunately she was not dependent on the bounty of the Flints. She had enough to be independent, and that is more than can ever be gained from charity, however lavish it maybe. Miss Fanny was endeared to me by many recollections, and I was rejoiced to see her at the plantation. The warmth of her large, loyal heart made the house seem pleasanter while she was in it. She stayed a week, and I had many talks with her. She said her principal object in coming was to see how I was treated, and whether anything could be done for me. She inquired whether she could help me in any way. I told her I believed not. She condoled with me in her own peculiar way, saying she wished that I and all my grandmother's family were at rest in our graves, for not until then should she feel any peace about us. The good old soul did not dream that I was planning to bestow peace upon her, with regard to myself and my children, not by death, but by securing our freedom. Again and again I had traversed those dreary twelve miles, to and from the town, and all the way, I was meditating upon some means of escape for myself and my children.

My friends had made every effort that ingenuity could devise to effect our purchase, but all their plans had proved abortive. Dr. Flint was suspicious, and determined not to loosen his grasp upon us. I could have made my escape alone, but it was more for my helpless children than for myself that I longed for freedom. Though the boon would have been precious to me, above all price, I would not have taken it at the expense of leaving them in slavery. Every trial I endured, every sacrifice I made for their sakes, drew them closer to my heart, and gave me fresh courage to beat back the dark waves that rolled and rolled over me in a seemingly endless night of storms. The six weeks were nearly completed, when Mr. Flint's bride was expected to take possession of her new home. The arrangements were all completed, and Mr. Flint said I had done well. He expected to leave home on Saturday, and return with his bride the following Wednesday. After receiving various orders from him, I ventured to ask permission to spend Sunday in town. It was granted, for which favor I was thankful. It was the first I had ever asked of him, and I intended it should be the last. It needed more than one night to accomplish the project I had in view, but the whole of Sunday would give me an opportunity. I spent the Sabbath with my grandmother. A calmer, more beautiful day never came down out of heaven. To me it was a day of conflicting emotions.

Perhaps it was the last day I should ever spend under that dear, old sheltering roof. Perhaps these were the last talks I should ever have with the faithful old friend of my whole life! Perhaps it was the last time I and my children should be together! Well, better so, I thought, than that they should be slaves. I knew the doom that awaited my fair baby in slavery, and I determined to save her from it, or perish in the attempt. I went to make this vow at the graves of my poor parents, in the burying ground of the slaves. "There the wicked cease from troubling, and there the weary be at rest. There the prisoners rest together, they hear not the voice of the oppressor, the servant is free from his master." I knelt by the graves of my parents, and thanked God, as I had often done before, that they had not lived to witness my trials, or to mourn over my sins. I had received my mother's blessing when she died, and in many an hour of tribulation I had seemed to hear her voice, sometimes chiding me, sometimes whispering loving words into my wounded heart. I have shed many and bitter tears, to think that when I am gone from my children they cannot remember me with such entire satisfaction as I remembered my mother. The graveyard was in the woods, and twilight was coming on. Nothing broke the death-like stillness except the occasional twitter of a bird. My spirit was overawed by the solemnity of the scene. For more than ten years I had frequented this spot, but never had it seemed to me so sacred as now.

A black stump, at the head of my mother's grave, was all that remained of a tree my father had planted. His grave was marked by a small wooden board, bearing his name, the letters of which were nearly obliterated. I knelt down and kissed them, and poured forth a prayer to God for guidance and support in the perilous step I was about to take. As I passed the wreck of the old meeting house, where, before Nat Turner's time, the slaves had been allowed to meet for worship, I seemed to hear my father's voice come from it, bidding me not to tarry till I reached freedom or the grave. I rushed on with renovated hopes. My trust in God had been strengthened by that prayer among the graves. My plan was to conceal myself at the house of a friend, and remain there a few weeks till the search was over. My hope was that the doctor would get discouraged, and, for fear of losing my value, and also of subsequently finding my children among the missing, he would consent to sell us, and I knew somebody would buy us. I had done all in my power to make my children comfortable during the time I expected to be separated from them. I was packing my things, when grandmother came into the room, and asked what I was doing. "I am putting my things in order," I replied. I tried to look and speak cheerfully, but her watchful eye detected something beneath the surface. She drew me towards her, and asked me to sit down. She looked earnestly at me, and said, "Linda, do you want to kill your old grandmother? Do you mean to leave your little, helpless children? I am old now, and cannot do for your babies as I once did for you." I replied, that if I went away, perhaps their father would be able to secure their freedom. "Ah, my child," said she, "don't trust too much to him. Stand by your own children, and suffer with them till death. Nobody respects a mother who forsakes her children, and if you leave them, you will never have a happy moment. If you go, you will make me miserable the short time I have to live. You would be taken and brought back, and your sufferings would be dreadful. Remember poor Benjamin. Do give it up, Linda. Try to bear a little longer. Things may turn out better than we expect." My courage failed me, in view of the sorrow I should bring on that faithful, loving old heart. I promised that I would try longer, and that I would take nothing out of her house without her knowledge. Whenever the children climbed on my knee, or laid their heads on my lap, she would say, "Poor little souls! What would you do without a mother? She don't love you as I do." And she would hug them to her own bosom, as if to reproach me for my want of affection, but she knew all the while that I loved them better than my life.

I slept with her that night, and it was the last time. The memory of it haunted me for many a year. On Monday I returned to the plantation, and busied myself with preparations for the important day. Wednesday came. It was a beautiful day, and the faces of the slaves were as bright as the sunshine.

The poor creatures were merry. They were expecting little presents from the bride, and hoping for better times under her administration. I had no such hopes for them. I knew that the young wives of slaveholders often thought their authority and importance would be best established and maintained by cruelty, and what I had heard of young Mrs. Flint gave me no reason to expect that her rule over them would be less severe than that of the master and overseer. Truly, the colored race are the most cheerful and forgiving people on the face of the earth. That their masters sleep in safety is owing to their superabundance of heart, and yet they look upon their sufferings with less pity than they would bestow on those of a horse or a dog. I stood at the door with others to receive the bridegroom and bride. She was a handsome, delicate-looking girl, and her face flushed with emotion at sight of her new home. I thought it likely that visions of a happy future were rising before her. It made me sad, for I knew how soon clouds would come over her sunshine.

She examined every part of the house, and told me she was delighted with the arrangements I had made. I was afraid old Mrs. Flint had tried to prejudice her against me, and I did my best to please her. All passed off smoothly for me until dinner time arrived. I did not mind the embarrassment of waiting on a dinner party, for the first time in my life, half so much as I did the meeting with Dr. Flint and his wife, who would be among the guests. It was a mystery to me why Mrs. Flint had not made her appearance at the plantation during all the time I was putting the house in order. I had not met her, face to face, for five years, and I had no wish to see her now. She was a praying woman, and, doubtless, considered my present position a special answer to her prayers. Nothing could please her better than to see me humbled and trampled upon. I was just where she would have me—in the power of a hard, unprincipled master. She did not speak to me when she took her seat at table, but her satisfied, triumphant smile, when I handed her plate, was more eloquent than words. The old doctor was not so quiet in his demonstrations. He ordered me here and there, and spoke with peculiar emphasis when he said "your *mistress*." I was drilled like a disgraced soldier. When all was over, and the last key turned, I sought my pillow, thankful that God had appointed a season of rest for the weary. The next day my new mistress began her housekeeping. I was not exactly appointed maid of all work, but I was to do whatever I was told. Monday evening came. It was always a busy time.

On that night the slaves received their weekly allowance of food. Three pounds of meat, a peck of corn, and perhaps a dozen herring were allowed to each man. Women received a pound and a half of meat, a peck of corn, and the same number of herring. Children over twelve years old had half the allowance of the women. The meat was cut and weighed by the foreman of the field hands, and piled on planks before the meat house. Then the second foreman went behind the building, and when the first foreman called out, "Who takes this piece of meat?" he answered by calling somebody's name. This method was resorted to as a means of preventing partiality in distributing the meat.

The young mistress came out to see how things were done on her plantation, and she soon gave a specimen of her character. Among those in waiting for their allowance was a very old slave, who had faithfully served the Flint family through three generations. When he hobbled up to get his bit of meat, the mistress said he was too old to have any allowance, that when niggers were too old to work, they ought to be fed on grass. Poor old man! He suffered much before he found rest in the grave. My mistress and I got along very well together. At the end of a week, old Mrs. Flint made us another visit, and was closeted a long time with her daughter-in-law. I had my suspicions what was the subject of the conference. The old doctor's wife had been informed that I could leave the plantation on one condition, and she was very desirous to keep me there. If she had trusted me, as I deserved to be trusted by her, she would have had no fears of my accepting that condition. When she entered her carriage to return home, she said to young Mrs. Flint, "Don't neglect to send for them as quick as possible." My heart was on the watch all the time, and I at once concluded that she spoke of my children.

The doctor came the next day, and as I entered the room to spread the tea table, I heard him say, "Don't wait any longer. Send for them tomorrow." I saw through the plan. They thought my children being there would fetter me to the spot, and that it was a good place to break us all into abject submission to our lot as slaves. After the doctor left, a gentleman called, who had always manifested friendly feelings towards my grandmother and her family. Mr. Flint carried him over the plantation to show him the results of labor performed by men and women who were unpaid, miserably clothed, and half-famished. The cotton crop was all they thought of. It was duly admired, and the gentleman returned with specimens to show his friends. I was ordered to carry water to wash his hands. As did so, he said, "Linda, how do you like your new home?" I told him I liked it as well as I expected. He replied, "They don't think you are contented, and tomorrow they are going to bring your children to be with you. I am sorry for you, Linda. I hope they will treat you kindly." I hurried from the room, unable to thank him. My suspicions were correct. My children were to be brought to the plantation to be "broke in."

To this day I feel grateful to the gentleman who gave me this timely information. It nerved me to immediate action.

▫▫▫▫▫▫▫▫▫▫

Mr. Flint was hard pushed for house servants, and rather than lose me he had restrained his malice. I did my work faithfully, though not, of course, with a willing mind. They were evidently afraid I should leave them. Mr. Flint wished that I should sleep in the great house instead of the servants quarters. His wife agreed to the proposition, but said I mustn't bring my bed into the house, because it would scatter feathers on her carpet. I knew when I went there that they would never think of such a thing as furnishing a bed of any kind for me and my little one. I therefore carried my own bed, and now I was forbidden to use it.

I did as I was ordered. But now that I was certain my children were to be put in their power, in order to give them a stronger hold on me, I resolved to leave them that night. I remembered the grief this step would bring upon my dear old grandmother, and nothing less than the freedom of my children would have induced me to disregard her advice. I went about my evening work with trembling steps. Mr. Flint twice called from his chamber door to inquire why the house was not locked up. I replied that I had not done my work. "You have had time enough to do it," said he. "Take care how you answer me!" I shut all the windows, locked all the doors, and went up to the third story, to wait till midnight. How long those hours seemed, and how fervently I prayed that God would not forsake me in this hour of utmost need! I was about to risk everything on the throw of a die, and if I failed, O what would become of me and my poor children? They would be made to suffer for my fault. At half past twelve I stole softly downstairs. I stopped on the second floor, thinking I heard a noise. I felt my way down into the parlor, and looked out of the window. The night was so intensely dark that I could see nothing. I raised the window very softly and jumped out.

  Large drops of rain were falling, and the darkness bewildered me. I dropped on my knees, and breathed a short prayer to God for guidance and protection. I groped my way to the road, and rushed towards the town with almost lightning speed. I arrived at my grandmother's house, but dared not see her. She would say, "Linda, you are killing me," and I knew that would unnerve me. I tapped softly at the window of a room, occupied by a woman, who had lived in the house several years. I knew she was a faithful friend, and could be trusted with my secret. I tapped several times before she heard me. At last she raised the window, and I whispered, "Sally, I have run away. Let me in, quick." She opened the door softly, and said in low tones, "For God's sake, don't. Your grandmother is trying to buy you and de chillern. Mr. Sands was here last week. He tole her he was going away on business, but he wanted her to go ahead about buying you and de chillern, and he would help her all he could. Don't run away, Linda. Your grandmother is all bowed down wid trouble now." I replied, "Sally, they are going to carry my children to the plantation tomorrow, and they will never sell them to anybody so long as they have me in their power. Now, would you advise me to go back?" "No, chile, no," answered she. "When dey finds you is gone, dey won't want de plague ob de chillern, but where is you going to hide? Dey knows ebery inch ob dis house." I told her I had a hiding place, and that was all it was best for her to know. I asked her to go into my room as soon as it was light, and take all my clothes out of my trunk, and pack them in hers, for I knew Mr. Flint and the constable would be there early to search my room. I feared the sight of my children would be too much for my full heart, but I could not go out into the uncertain future without one last look. I bent over the bed where lay my little Benny and baby Ellen. Poor little ones! Fatherless and motherless! Memories of their father came over me. He wanted to be kind to them, but they were not all to him, as they were to my womanly heart. I knelt and prayed for the innocent little sleepers. I kissed them lightly, and turned away. As I was about to open the street door, Sally laid her hand on my shoulder, and said, "Linda, is you gwine all alone? Let me call your uncle." "No, Sally," I replied, "I want no one to be brought into trouble on my account." I went forth into the darkness and rain. I ran on till I came to the house of the friend who was to conceal me.

Early the next morning Mr. Flint was at my grandmother's inquiring for me. She told him she had not seen me, and supposed I was at the plantation. He watched her face narrowly, and said, "Don't you know anything about her running off?" She assured him that she did not. He went onto say, "Last night she ran off without the least provocation. We had treated her very kindly. My wife liked her. She will soon be found and brought back. Are her children with you?" When told that they were, he said, "I am very glad to hear that. If they are here, she cannot be far off. If I find out that any of my niggers have had anything to do with this damned business, I'll give 'em five hundred lashes." As he started to go to his father's, he turned round and added persuasively, "Let her be brought back, and she shall have her children to live with her." The tidings made the old doctor rave and storm at a furious rate. It was a busy day for them. My grandmother's house was searched from top to bottom. As my trunk was empty, they concluded I had taken my clothes with me. Before ten o'clock every vessel northward bound was thoroughly examined, and the law against harboring fugitives was read to all on board. At night a watch was set over the town. Knowing how distressed my grandmother would be, I wanted to send her a message, but it could not be done. Everyone who went in or out of her house was closely watched. The doctor said he would take my children, unless she became responsible for them, which of course she willingly did. The next day was spent in searching.

Before night, the following advertisement was posted at every corner, and in every public place for miles round.

$300 Reward! Ran away from the subscriber, an intelligent, bright, mulatto girl, named Linda, 21 years of age. Five feet four inches high. Dark eyes, and black hair inclined to curl, but it can be made straight. Has a decayed spot on a front tooth. She can read and write, and in all probability will try to get to the Free States. All persons are forbidden, under penalty of the law, to harbor or employ said slave. $150 will be given to whoever takes her in the state, and $300 if taken out of the state and delivered to me, or lodged in jail.

☐☐☐☐☐☐☐☐☐☐☐

The search for me was kept up with more perseverance than I had anticipated. I began to think that escape was impossible. I was in great anxiety lest I should implicate the friend who harbored me. I knew the consequences would be frightful, and much as I dreaded being caught, even that seemed better than causing an innocent person to suffer for kindness to me.

A week had passed in terrible suspense, when my pursuers came into such close vicinity that I concluded they had tracked me to my hiding place. I flew out of the house, and concealed myself in a thicket of bushes. There I remained in an agony of fear for two hours. Suddenly, a reptile of some kind seized my leg. In my fright, I struck a blow which loosened its hold, but I could not tell whether I had killed it, it was so dark, I could not see what it was, I only knew it was something cold and slimy. The pain I felt soon indicated that the bite was poisonous. I was compelled to leave my place of concealment, and I groped my way back into the house. The pain had become intense, and my friend was startled by my look of anguish. I asked her to prepare a poultice of warm ashes and vinegar, and I applied it to my leg, which was already much swollen. The application gave me some relief, but the swelling did not abate. The dread of being disabled was greater than the physical pain I endured. My friend asked an old woman, who doctored among the slaves, what was good for the bite of a snake or a lizard. She told her to steep a dozen coppers in vinegar, overnight, and apply the cankered vinegar to the inflamed part. I had succeeded in cautiously conveying some messages to my relatives. They were harshly threatened, and despairing of my having a chance to escape, they advised me to return to my master, ask his forgiveness, and let him make an example of me. But such counsel had no influence with me. When I started upon this hazardous undertaking, I had resolved that, come what would, there should be no turning back. "Give me liberty, or give me death," was my motto. When my friend contrived to make known to my relatives the painful situation I had been in for twenty-four hours, they said no more about my going back to my master. Something must be done, and that speedily, but where to turn for help, they knew not. God in his mercy raised up "a friend in need." Among the ladies who were acquainted with my grandmother, was one who had known her from childhood, and always been very friendly to her. She had also known my mother and her children, and felt interested for them. At this crisis of affairs she called to see my grandmother, as she not unfrequently did. She observed the sad and troubled expression of her face, and asked if she knew where Linda was, and whether she was safe. My grandmother shook her head, without answering. "Come, Aunt Martha," said the kind lady, "tell me all about it. Perhaps I can do something to help you." The husband of this lady held many slaves, and bought and sold slaves. She also held a number in her own name, but she treated them kindly, and would never allow any of them to be sold. She was unlike the majority of slaveholder wives. My grandmother looked earnestly at her. Something in the expression of her face said "Trust me!" and she did trust her. She listened attentively to the details of my story, and sat thinking for a while. At last she said, "Aunt Martha, I pity you both. If you think there is any chance of Linda's getting to the Free States, I will conceal her for a time. But first you must solemnly promise that my name shall never be mentioned. If such a thing should become known, it would ruin me and my family. No one in my house must know of it, except the cook. She is so faithful that I would trust my own life with her, and I know she likes Linda. It is a great risk, but I trust no harm will come of it. Get word to Linda to be ready as soon as it is dark, before the patrols are out. I will send the housemaids on errands, and Betty shall go to meet Linda." The place where we were to meet was designated and agreed upon. My grandmother was unable to thank the lady for this noble deed, overcome by her emotions, she sank on her knees and sobbed like a child.

    I received a message to leave my friend's house at such an hour, and go to a certain place where a friend would be waiting for me. As a matter of prudence no names were mentioned. I had no means of conjecturing who I was to meet, or where I was going. I did not like to move thus blindfolded, but I had no choice. It would not do for me to remain where I was. I disguised myself, summoned up courage to meet the worst, and went to the appointed place. My friend Betty was there, she was the last person I expected to see. We hurried along in silence. The pain in my leg was so intense that it seemed as if I should drop, but fear gave me strength. We reached the house and entered unobserved. Her first words were. "Honey, now you is safe. Dem devils ain't coming to search *dis* house. When I get you into missis's safe place, I will bring some nice hot supper. I specs you need it after all dis skeering." Betty's vocation led her to think eating the most important thing in life. She did not realize that my heart was too full for me to care much about supper. The mistress came to meet us, and led me upstairs to a small room over her own sleeping apartment. "You will be safe here, Linda," said she, "I keep this room to store away things that are out of use. The girls are not accustomed to be sent to it, and they will not suspect anything unless they hear some noise. I always keep it locked, and Betty shall take care of the key. But you must be very careful, for my sake as well as your own, and you must never tell my secret, for it would ruin me and my family. I will keep the girls busy in the morning, that Betty may have a chance to bring your breakfast, but it will not do for her to come to you again till night. I will come to see you sometimes. Keep up your courage. I hope this state of things will not last long." Betty came with the "nice hot supper," and the mistress hastened downstairs to keep things straight till she returned. How my heart overflowed with gratitude! Words choked in my throat, but I could have kissed the feet of my benefactress. For that deed of Christian womanhood, may God forever bless her! I went to sleep that night with the feeling that I was for the present the most fortunate slave in town. Morning came and filled my little cell with light. I thanked the heavenly Father for this safe retreat. Opposite my window was a pile of feather beds. On the top of these I could lie perfectly concealed, and command a view of the street through which Dr. Flint passed to his office. Anxious as I was, I felt a gleam of satisfaction when I saw him. Thus far I had outwitted him, and I triumphed over it. Who can blame slaves for being cunning? They are constantly compelled to resort to it. It is the only weapon of the weak and oppressed against the strength of their tyrants.

I was daily hoping to hear that my master had sold my children, for I knew who was on the watch to buy them. But Dr. Flint cared even more for revenge than he did for money. My brother William, and the good aunt who had served in his family twenty years, and my little Benny, and Ellen, who was a little over two years old, were thrust into jail, as a means of compelling my relatives to give some information about me. He swore my grandmother should never see one of them again till I was brought back. They kept these facts from me for several days.

When I heard that my little ones were in a loathsome jail, my first impulse was to go to them. I was encountering dangers for the sake of freeing them, and must I be the cause of their death? The thought was agonizing. My benefactress tried to soothe me by telling me that my aunt would take good care of the children while they remained in jail. But it added to my pain to think that the good old aunt, who had always been so kind to her sister's orphan children, should be shut up in prison for no other crime than loving them. I suppose my friends feared a reckless movement on my part, knowing, as they did, that my life was bound up in my children. I received a note from my brother William. It was scarcely legible, and ran thus. "Wherever you are, dear sister, I beg of you not to come here. We are all much better off than you are. If you come, you will ruin us all. They would force you to tell where you had been, or they would kill you. Take the advice of your friends, if not for the sake of me and your children, at least for the sake of those you would ruin." Poor William! He also must suffer for being my brother. I took his advice and kept quiet. My aunt was taken out of jail at the end of a month, because Mrs. Flint could not spare her any longer. She was tired of being her own housekeeper. It was quite too fatiguing to order her dinner and eat it too. My children remained in jail, where brother William did all he could for their comfort. Betty went to see them sometimes, and brought me tidings. She was not permitted to enter the jail, but William would hold them up to the grated window while she chatted with them. When she repeated their prattle, and told me how they wanted to see their ma, my tears would flow. Old Betty would exclaim, "Lors, chile! What's you crying 'bout? Dem young uns vil kill you dead. Don't be so chick'n hearted! If you does, you vil nebber git thro' dis world." Good old soul! She had gone through the world childless. She had never had little ones to clasp their arms round her neck, she had never seen their soft eyes looking into hers, no sweet little voices had called her mother, she had never pressed her own infants to her heart, with the feeling that even in fetters (chains) there was something to live for. How could she realize my feelings? Betty's husband loved children dearly, and wondered why God had denied them to him. He expressed great sorrow when he came to Betty with the tidings that Ellen had been taken out of jail and carried to Dr. Flint's. She had the measles a short time before they carried her to jail, and the disease had left her eyes affected. The doctor had taken her home to attend to them. My children had always been afraid of the doctor and his wife. They had never been inside of their house. Poor little Ellen cried all day to be carried back to prison. The instincts of childhood are true. She knew she was loved in the jail. Her screams and sobs annoyed Mrs. Flint. Before night she called one of the slaves, and said, "Here, Bill, carry this brat back to the jail. I can't stand her noise. If she would be quiet I should like to keep the little minx. She would make a handy waiting maid for my daughter by and by. But if she stayed here, with her white face, I suppose I should either kill her or spoil her. I hope the doctor will sell them as far as wind and water can carry them. As for their mother, her ladyship will find out yet what she gets by running away. She hasn't so much feeling for her children as a cow has for its calf. If she had, she would have come back long ago, to get them out of jail, and save all this expense and trouble. The good-for-nothing hussy! When she is caught, she shall stay in jail, in irons, for one six months, and then be sold to a sugar plantation. I shall see her broke in yet. What do you stand there for, Bill? Why don't you go off with the brat? Mind, now, that you don't let any of the niggers speak to her in the street!" When these remarks were reported to me, I smiled at Mrs. Flint's saying that she should either kill my child or spoil her. I thought to myself there was very little danger of the latter. I have always considered it as one of God's special Providences that Ellen screamed till she was carried back to jail.

  That same night Dr. Flint was called to a patient, and did not return till near morning. Passing my grandmother's, he saw a light in the house, and thought to himself, "Perhaps this has something to do with Linda." He knocked, and the door was opened. "What calls you up so early?" said he. "I saw your light, and I thought I would just stop and tell you that I have found out where Linda is. I know where to put my hands on her, and I shall have her before twelve o'clock." When he had turned away, my grandmother and my uncle looked anxiously at each other. They did not know whether or not it was merely one of the doctor's tricks to frighten them. In their uncertainty, they thought it was best to have a message conveyed to my friend Betty. Unwilling to alarm her mistress, Betty resolved to dispose of me herself. She came to me, and told me to rise and dress quickly. We hurried downstairs, and across the yard, into the kitchen. She locked the door, and lifted up a plank in the floor. A buffalo skin and a bit of carpet were spread for me to lie on, and a quilt thrown over me. "Stay dar," said she, "till I sees if dey know 'bout you. Dey say dey vil put thar hans on you afore twelve o'clock. If dey *did* know whar you are, dey won't know *now*. Dey'll be disapinted dis time. Dat's all I got to say. If dey comes rummaging 'mong *my* tings, dey'll get one bressed sarssin from dis 'ere nigger." In my shallow bed I had but just room enough to bring my hands to my face to keep the dust out of my eyes, for Betty walked over me twenty times in an hour, passing from the dresser to the fireplace. When she was alone, I could hear her pronouncing anathemas over Dr. Flint and all his tribe, every now and then saying, with a chuckling laugh, "Dis nigger's too cute for 'em dis time." When the housemaids were about, she had sly ways of drawing them out, that I might hear what they would say. She would repeat stories she had heard about my being in this, or that, or the other place. To which they would answer, that I was not fool enough to be staying round there, that I was in Philadelphia or New York before this time. When all were abed and asleep, Betty raised the plank, and said, "Come out, chile, come out. Dey don't know nottin 'bout you. 'Twas only white folks lies, to skeer de niggers." Some days after this adventure I had a much worse fright.

    As I sat very still in my retreat above stairs, cheerful visions floated through my mind. I thought Dr. Flint would soon get discouraged, and would be willing to sell my children, when he lost all hopes of making them the means of my discovery. I knew who was ready to buy them. Suddenly I heard a voice that chilled my blood. The sound was too familiar to me, it had been too dreadful, for me not to recognize at once my old master.

He was in the house, and I at once concluded he had come to seize me. I looked round in terror. There was no way of escape. The voice receded. I supposed the constable was with him, and they were searching the house. In my alarm I did not forget the trouble I was bringing on my generous benefactress. It seemed as if I were born to bring sorrow on all who befriended me, and that was the bitterest drop in the bitter cup of my life. After a while I heard approaching footsteps, the key was turned in my door. I braced myself against the wall to keep from falling.

I ventured to look up, and there stood my kind benefactress alone. I was too much overcome to speak, and sunk down upon the floor. "I thought you would hear your master's voice," she said, "and knowing you would be terrified, I came to tell you there is nothing to fear. You may even indulge in a laugh at the old gentleman's expense. He is so sure you are in New York, that he came to borrow five hundred dollars to go in pursuit of you. My sister had some money to loan on interest. He has obtained it, and proposes to start for New York tonight. So, for the present, you see you are safe. The doctor will merely lighten his pocket hunting after the bird he has left behind."

□□□□□□□□□□

The doctor came back from New York, of course without accomplishing his purpose. He had expended considerable money, and was rather disheartened. My brother and the children had now been in jail two months, and that also was some expense. My friends thought it was a favorable time to work on his discouraged feelings. Mr. Sands sent a speculator to offer him nine hundred dollars for my brother William, and eight hundred for the two children. These were high prices, as slaves were then selling, but the offer was rejected. If it had been merely a question of money, the doctor would have sold any boy of Benny's age for two hundred dollars, but he could not bear to give up the power of revenge. But he was hard pressed for money, and he revolved the matter in his mind. He knew that if he could keep Ellen till she was fifteen, he could sell her for a high price, but I presume he reflected that she might die, or might be stolen away. At all events, he came to the conclusion that he had better accept the slave trader's offer. Meeting him in the street, he inquired when he would leave town. "Today, at ten o'clock," he replied. "Ah, do you go so soon?" said the doctor, "I have been reflecting upon your proposition, and I have concluded to let you have the three Negroes if you will say nineteen hundred dollars." After some parley, the trader agreed to his terms. He wanted the bill of sale drawn up and signed immediately, as he had a great deal to attend to during the short time he remained in town. The doctor went to the jail and told William he would take him back into his service if he would promise to behave himself, but he replied that he would rather be sold. "And you *shall* be sold, you ungrateful rascal!" exclaimed the doctor. In less than an hour the money was paid, the papers were signed, sealed, and delivered, and my brother and children were in the hands of the trader. It was a hurried transaction, and after it was over, the doctor's characteristic caution returned. He went back to the speculator, and said, "Sir, I have come to lay you under obligations of a thousand dollars not to sell any of those Negroes in this state."

"You come too late," replied the trader, "our bargain is closed." He had, in fact, already sold them to Mr. Sands, but he did not mention it. The doctor required him to put irons on "that rascal, Bill," and to pass through the back streets when he took his gang out of town. The trader was privately instructed to concede to his wishes. My good old aunt went to the jail to bid the children goodbye, supposing them to be the speculator's property, and that she should never see them again. As she held Benny in her lap, he said, "Aunt Nancy, I want to show you something." He led her to the door and showed her a long row of marks, saying, "Uncle Will taught me to count. I have made a mark for every day I have been here, and it is sixty days. It is a long time, and the speculator is going to take me and Ellen away. He's a bad man. It's wrong for him to take grandmother's children. I want to go to my mother." My grandmother was told that the children would be restored to her, but she was requested to act as if they were really to be sent away. Accordingly, she made up a bundle of clothes and went to the jail. When she arrived, she found William handcuffed among the gang, and the children in the trader's cart. The scene seemed too much like reality. She was afraid there might have been some deception or mistake. She fainted, and was carried home. When the wagon stopped at the hotel, several gentlemen came out and proposed to purchase William, but the trader refused their offers, without stating that he was already sold. And now came the trying hour for that drove of human beings, driven away like cattle, to be sold they knew not where. Husbands were torn from wives, parents from children, never to look upon each other again this side the grave. There was wringing of hands and cries of despair.

Dr. Flint had the supreme satisfaction of seeing the wagon leave town, and Mrs. Flint had the gratification of supposing that my children were going "as far as wind and water would carry them." According to agreement, my uncle followed the wagon some miles, until they came to an old farmhouse. There the trader took the irons from William, and as he did so, he said, "You are a damned clever fellow. I should like to own you myself. Them gentlemen that wanted to buy you said you was a bright, honest chap, and I must git you a good home. I guess your old master will swear tomorrow, and call himself an old fool for selling the children. I reckon he'll never git their mammy back agin. I expect she's made tracks for the North. Goodbye, old boy. Remember, I have done you a good turn. You must thank me by coaxing all the pretty gals to go with me next fall. That's going to be my last trip. This trading in niggers is a bad business for a fellow that's got any heart. Move on, you fellows!" And the gang went on, God alone knows where. Much as I despise and detest the class of slave traders, whom I regard as the vilest wretches on earth, I must do this man the justice to say that he seemed to have some feeling. He took a fancy to William in the jail, and wanted to buy him. When he heard the story of my children, he was willing to aid them in getting out of Dr. Flint's power, even without charging the customary fee. My uncle procured a wagon and carried

William and the children back to town. Great was the joy in my grandmother's house! The curtains were closed, and the candles lighted. The happy grandmother cuddled the little ones to her bosom. They hugged her, and kissed her, and clapped their hands, and shouted. She knelt down and poured forth one of her heartfelt prayers of thanksgiving to God. The father was present for a while, and though such a "parental relation" as existed between him and my children takes slight hold of the hearts or consciences of slaveholders, it must be that he experienced some moments of pure joy in witnessing the happiness he had imparted. I had no share in the rejoicings of that evening.

The events of the day had not come to my knowledge. And now I will tell you something that happened to me, though you will, perhaps, think it illustrates the superstition of slaves. I sat in my usual place on the floor near the window, where I could hear much that was said in the street without being seen. The family had retired for the night, and all was still. I sat there thinking of my children, when I heard a low strain of music.

A band of serenaders were under the window, playing "home, sweet home." I listened till the sounds did not seem like music, but like the moaning of children. It seemed as if my heart would burst. I rose from my sitting posture, and knelt. A streak of moonlight was on the floor before me, and in the midst of it appeared the forms of my two children. They vanished, but I had seen them distinctly. Some will call it a dream, others a vision.

I know not how to account for it, but it made a strong impression on my mind, and I felt certain something had happened to my little ones. I had not seen Betty since morning. Now I heard her softly turning the key. As soon as she entered, I clung to her, and begged her to let me know whether my children were dead, or whether they were sold, for I had seen their spirits in my room, and I was sure something had happened to them. "Lor, chile," said she, putting her arms round me, "you's got de highsterics. I'll sleep wid you tonight, 'cause you'll make a noise and ruin missis. Something has stirred you up mightily. When you is done cryin, I'll talk wid you. De chillern is well, and mighty happy. I seed 'em myself. Does dat satisfy you? Dar, chile, be still! Somebody vill hear you." I tried to obey her. She lay down, and was soon sound asleep, but no sleep would come to my eyelids. At dawn, Betty was up and off to the kitchen. The hours passed on, and the vision of the night kept constantly recurring to my thoughts. After a while I heard the voices of two women in the entry. In one of them I recognized the housemaid. The other said to her, "Did you know Linda Brent's children was sold to the speculator yesterday. They say ole Massa Flint was mighty glad to see 'em drove out of town, but they say they've come back agin. I'spect it's all their daddy's doings. They say he's bought William too. Lor! How it will take hold of ole Massa Flint! I'm going roun' to Aunt Marthy's to see 'bout it." I bit my lips till the blood came to keep from crying out. Were my children with their grandmother, or had the speculator carried them off? The suspense was dreadful. Would Betty *never* come, and tell me the truth about it? At last she came, and I eagerly repeated what I had overheard. Her face was one broad, bright smile. "Lor, you foolish ting!" said she. "I'se gwine to tell you all 'bout it. De gals is eating thar breakfast, and missus tole me to let her tell you, but, poor creeter! T'aint right to keep you waitin,' and I'se gwine to tell you. Brudder, chillern, all is bought by de daddy! I'se laugh more dan nuff, tinking 'bout ole Massa Flint. Lor, how he *vill* swar! He's got ketched dis time, anyhow, but I must be getting out o' dis, or dem gals vill come and ketch *me*." Betty went off laughing, and I said to myself, "Can it be true that my children are free? I have not suffered for them in vain. Thank God!" Great surprise was expressed when it was known that my children had returned to their grandmother's. The news spread through the town, and many a kind word was bestowed on the little ones. Dr. Flint went to my grandmother's to ascertain who was the owner of my children, and she informed him. "I expected as much," said he. "I am glad to hear it. I have had news from Linda lately, and I shall soon have her. You need never expect to see *her* free. She shall be my slave as long as I live, and when I am dead she shall be the slave of my children. If I ever find out that you or Phillip had anything to do with her running off I'll kill him. And if I meet William in the street, and he presumes to look at me, I'll flog him within an inch of his life. Keep those brats out of my sight!"

As he turned to leave, my grandmother said something to remind him of his own doings. He looked back upon her, as if he would have been glad to strike her to the ground. I had my season of joy and thanksgiving. It was the first time since my childhood that I had experienced any real happiness. I heard of the old doctor's threats, but they no longer had the same power to trouble me. The darkest cloud that hung over my life had rolled away. Whatever slavery might do to me, it could not shackle my children. If I fell a sacrifice, my little ones were saved. It was well for me that my simple heart believed all that had been promised for their welfare. It is always better to trust than to doubt.

☐☐☐☐☐☐☐☐☐☐

The doctor, more exasperated than ever, again tried to revenge himself on my relatives. He arrested Uncle Phillip on the charge of having aided my flight. He was carried before a court, and swore truly that he knew nothing of my intention to escape, and that he had not seen me since I left my master's plantation. The doctor then demanded that he should give bail for five hundred dollars that he would have nothing to do with me. Several gentlemen offered to be security for him, but Mr. Sands told him he had better go back to jail, and he would see that he came out without giving bail. The news of his arrest was carried to my grandmother, who conveyed it to Betty. In the kindness of her heart, she again stowed me away under the floor, and as she walked back and forth, in the performance of her culinary duties, she talked apparently to herself, but with the intention that I should hear what was going on. I hoped that my uncle's imprisonment would last but few days, still I was anxious.

I thought it likely Dr. Flint would do his utmost to taunt and insult him, and I was afraid my uncle might lose control of himself, and retort in some way that would be construed into a punishable offense, and I was well-aware that in court his word would not be taken against any white man's. The search for me was renewed. Something had excited suspicions that I was in the vicinity. They searched the house I was in. I heard their steps and their voices. At night, when all were asleep, Betty came to release me from my place of confinement. The fright I had undergone, the constrained posture, and the dampness of the ground, made me ill for several days. My uncle was soon after taken out of prison, but the movements of all my relatives, and of all our friends, were very closely watched. We all saw that I could not remain where I was much longer. I had already stayed longer than was intended, and I knew my presence must be a source of perpetual anxiety to my kind benefactress. During this time, my friends had laid many plans for my escape, but the extreme vigilance of my persecutors made it impossible to carry them into effect. One morning I was much startled by hearing somebody trying to get into my room. Several keys were tried, but none fitted. I instantly conjectured it was one of the housemaids, and I concluded she must either have heard some noise in the room, or have noticed the entrance of Betty. When my friend came, at her usual time, I told her what had happened. "I knows who it was," said she. "'Pend upon it, 'twas dat Jenny. Dat nigger allers got de debble in her." I suggested that she might have seen or heard something that excited her curiosity. "Tut! Tut! Chile!" exclaimed Betty, "she ain't seen notin,' nor hearn notin.' She only 'spects someting. Dat's all. She wants to fine out who hab cut and make my gownd. But she won't nebber know. Dat's sartin. I'll git missis to fix her." I reflected a moment, and said, "Betty, I must leave here tonight." A "Do as you tink best, poor chile," she replied. "I'se mighty 'fraid dat 'ere nigger vill pop on you sometime." She reported the incident to her mistress, and received orders to keep Jenny busy in the kitchen till she could see my Uncle Phillip. He told her he would send a friend for me that very evening. She told him she hoped I was going to the North, for it was very dangerous for me to remain anywhere in the vicinity. Alas, it was not an easy thing, for one in my situation, to go to the North. In order to leave the coast quite clear for me, she went into the country to spend the day with her brother, and took Jenny with her. She was afraid to come and bid me goodbye, but she left a kind message with Betty. I heard her carriage roll from the door, and I never again saw her who had so generously befriended the poor, trembling fugitive! Though she was a slaveholder, to this day my heart blesses her! I had not the slightest idea where I was going. Betty brought me a suit of sailor's clothes—jacket, trowsers, and tarpaulin hat. She gave me a small bundle, saying I might need it where I was going. In cheery tones, she exclaimed, "I'se *so* glad you is gwine to free parts! Don't forget ole Betty. P'raps I'll come 'long by and by." I tried to tell her how grateful I felt for all her kindness, but she interrupted me. "I don't want no tanks, honey. I'se glad I could help you, and I hope de good Lord vill open de path for you. I'se gwine wid you to de lower gate. Put your hands in your pockets, and walk rickety, like de sailors." I performed to her satisfaction. At the gate I found Peter, a young colored man, waiting for me. I had known him for years. He had been an apprentice to my father, and had always borne a good character. I was not afraid to trust to him. Betty bade me a hurried goodbye, and we walked off. "Take courage, Linda," said my friend Peter. "I've got a dagger, and no man shall take you from me, unless he passes over my dead body." It was a long time since I had taken a walk out of doors, and the fresh air revived me. It was also pleasant to hear a human voice speaking to me above a whisper. I passed several people whom I knew, but they did not recognize me in my disguise. I prayed internally that, for Peter's sake, as well as my own, nothing might occur to bring out his dagger. We walked on till we came to the wharf. My Aunt Nancy's husband was a seafaring man, and it had been deemed necessary to let him into our secret. He took me into his boat, rowed out to a vessel not far distant, and hoisted me on board. We three were the only occupants of the vessel. I now ventured to ask what they proposed to do with me. They said I was to remain on board till near dawn, and then they would hide me in Snaky Swamp, till my Uncle Phillip had prepared a place of concealment for me. If the vessel had been bound North, it would have been of no avail to me, for it would certainly have been searched. About four o'clock, we were again seated in the boat, and rowed three miles to the swamp. My fear of snakes had been increased by the venomous bite I had received, and I dreaded to enter this hiding place.

But I was in no situation to choose, and I gratefully accepted the best that my poor, persecuted friends could do for me. Peter landed first, and with a large knife cut a path through bamboos and briers of all descriptions. He came back, took me in his arms, and carried me to a seat made among the bamboos. Before we reached it, we were covered with hundreds of mosquitoes. In an hour's time they had so poisoned my flesh that I was a pitiful sight to behold. As the light increased, I saw snake after snake crawling round us. I had been accustomed to the sight of snakes all my life, but these were larger than any I had ever seen. To this day I shudder when I remember that morning.

As evening approached, the number of snakes increased so much that we were continually obliged to thrash them with sticks to keep them from crawling over us. The bamboos were so high and so thick that it was impossible to see beyond a very short distance. Just before it became dark we procured a seat nearer to the entrance of the swamp, being fearful of losing our way back to the boat. It was not long before we heard the paddle of oars, and the low whistle, which had been agreed upon as a signal. We made haste to enter the boat, and were rowed back to the vessel. I passed a wretched night, for the heat of the swamp, the mosquitoes, and the constant terror of snakes, had brought on a burning fever. I had just dropped asleep, when they came and told me it was time to go back to that horrid swamp. I could scarcely summon courage to rise. But even those large, venomous snakes were less dreadful to my imagination than the white men in that community called civilized. This time Peter took a quantity of tobacco to burn, to keep off the mosquitoes it produced the desired effect on them, but gave me nausea and severe headache. At dark we returned to the vessel. I had been so sick during the day, that Peter declared I should go home that night, if the devil himself was on patrol. They told me a place of concealment had been provided for me at my grandmother's. I could not imagine how it was possible to hide me in her house, every nook and corner of which was known to the Flint family. They told me to wait and see. We were rowed ashore, and went boldly through the streets, to my grandmother's. I wore my sailor's clothes, and had blackened my face with charcoal.

I passed several people whom I knew. The father of my children came so near that I brushed against his arm, but he had no idea who it was. "You must make the most of this walk," said my friend Peter, "for you may not have another very—soon." I thought his voice sounded sad. It was kind of him to conceal from me what a dismal hole was to be my home for a long, long time.

□□□□□□□□□□

A small shed had been added to my grandmother's house years ago. Some boards were laid across the joists at the top, and between these boards and the roof was a very small garret, never occupied by anything but rats and mice. It was a pent roof, covered with nothing but shingles, according to the Southern custom for such buildings. The garret was only nine feet long and seven wide. The highest part was three feet high, and sloped down abruptly to the loose board floor. There was no admission for either light or air. My Uncle Phillip, who was a carpenter, had very skillfully made a concealed trapdoor, which communicated with the storeroom. He had been doing this while I was waiting in the swamp. The storeroom opened upon a piazza. To this hole I was conveyed as soon as I entered the house. The air was stifling, the darkness total. A bed had been spread on the floor. I could sleep quite comfortably on one side, but the slope was so sudden that I could not turn on the other without hitting the roof.

The rats and mice ran over my bed, but I was weary, and I slept such sleep as the wretched may, when a tempest has passed over them. Morning came. I knew it only by the noises I heard, for in my small den day and night were all the same. I suffered for air even more than for light. But I was not comfortless. I heard the voices of my children. There was joy and there was sadness in the sound. It made my tears flow. How I longed to speak to them! I was eager to look on their faces, but there was no hole, no crack, through which I could peep. This continued darkness was oppressive. It seemed horrible to sit or lie in a cramped position day after day, without one gleam of light. Yet I would have chosen this, rather than my lot as a slave, though white people considered it an easy one, and it was so compared with the fate of others. I was never cruelly overworked. I was never lacerated with the whip from head to foot. I was never so beaten and bruised that I could not turn from one side to the other. I never had my heel strings cut to prevent my running away. I was never chained to a log and forced to drag it about, while I toiled in the fields from morning till night. I was never branded with hot iron, or torn by bloodhounds. On the contrary, I had always been kindly treated, and tenderly eared for, until I came into the hands of Dr. Flint. I had never wished for freedom till then. But though my life in slavery was comparatively devoid of hardships, God pity the woman who is compelled to lead such a life! My food was passed up to me through the trapdoor my uncle had contrived, and my grandmother, my Uncle Phillip, and Aunt Nancy would seize such opportunities as they could, to mount up there and chat with me at the opening. But of course this was not safe in the daytime. It must all be done in darkness. It was impossible for me to move in an erect position, but I crawled about my den for exercise. One day I hit my head against something, and found it was a gimlet. My uncle had left it sticking there when he made the trapdoor.

    I was as rejoiced as *Robinson Crusoe* could have been at finding such a treasure. It put a lucky thought into my head. I said to myself, "Now I will have some light. Now I will see my children." I did not dare to begin my work during the daytime, for fear of attracting attention. But I groped round, and having found the side next to the street, where I could frequently see my children, I stuck the gimlet in and waited for evening. I bored three rows of holes, one above another, then I bored out the interstices between. I thus succeeded in making one hole about an inch long and an inch broad. I sat by it till late into the night, to enjoy the little whiff of air that floated in. In the morning I watched for my children. The first person I saw in the street was Dr. Flint. I had a shuddering, superstitious feeling that it was a bad omen. Several familiar faces passed by. At last I heard the merry laugh of children, and presently two sweet little faces were looking up at me, as though they knew I was there, and were conscious of the joy they imparted. How I longed to *tell* them I was there! My condition was now a little improved. But for weeks I was tormented by hundreds of little red insects, fine as a needle's point, that pierced through my skin, and produced an intolerable burning. The good grandmother gave me herb teas and cooling medicines, and finally I got rid of them.

    The heat of my den was intense, for nothing but thin shingles protected me from the scorching summer's sun. But I had my consolations. Through my peeping hole I could watch the children, and when they were near enough, I could hear their talk. Aunt Nancy brought me all the news she could hear at Dr. Flint's. From her I learned that the doctor had written to New York to a colored woman, who had been born and raised in our neighborhood, and had breathed his contaminating atmosphere. He offered her a reward if she could find out anything about me. I know not what was the nature of her reply, but he soon after started for New York in haste, saying to his family that he had business of importance to transact. I peeped at him as he passed on his way to the steamboat. It was a satisfaction to have miles of land and water between us, even for a little while, and it was a still greater satisfaction to know that he believed me to be in the Free States. My little den seemed less dreary than it had done. He returned, as he did from his former journey to New York, without obtaining any satisfactory information. When he passed our house next morning, Benny was standing at the gate. He had heard them say that he had gone to find me, and he called out, "Dr. Flint, did you bring my mother home? I want to see her." The doctor stamped his foot at him in a rage, and exclaimed, "Get out of the way, you little damned rascal! If you don't, I'll cut off your head." Benny ran terrified into the house, saying, "You can't put me in jail again. I don't belong to you now." It was well that the wind carried the words away from the doctor's ear.

I told my grandmother of it, when we had our next conference at the trapdoor, and begged of her not to allow the children to be impertinent to the irascible old man.

Autumn came, with a pleasant abatement of heat. My eyes had become accustomed to the dim light, and by holding my book or work in a certain position near the aperture I contrived to read and sew. That was a great relief to the tedious monotony of my life. But when winter came, the cold penetrated through the thin shingle roof, and I was dreadfully chilled. The winters there are not so long, or so severe, as in northern latitudes, but the houses are not built to shelter from cold, and my little den was peculiarly comfortless. The kind grandmother brought me bed clothes and warm drinks. Often I was obliged to lie in bed all day to keep comfortable, but with all my precautions, my shoulders and feet were frostbitten. O, those long, gloomy days, with no object for my eye to rest upon, and no thoughts to occupy my mind, except the dreary past and the uncertain future! I was thankful when there came a day sufficiently mild for me to wrap myself up and sit at the loophole to watch the passersby. Southerners have the habit of stopping and talking in the streets, and I heard many conversations not intended to meet my ears. I heard slave hunters planning how to catch some poor fugitive. Several times I heard allusions to Dr. Flint, myself, and the history of my children, who, perhaps, were playing near the gate. One would say, "I wouldn't move my little finger to catch her, as old Flint's property." Another would say, "I'll catch *any* nigger for the reward. A man ought to have what belongs to him, *even* if he *is* a damned brute." The opinion was often expressed that I was in the Free States. Very rarely did anyone suggest that I might be in the vicinity. Had the least suspicion rested on my grandmother's house, it would have been burned to the ground.

But it was the last place they thought of. Yet there was no place, where slavery existed, that could have afforded me so good a place of concealment. Dr. Flint and his family repeatedly tried to coax and bribe my children to tell something they had heard said about me. One day the doctor took them into a shop, and offered them some bright little silver pieces and gay handkerchiefs if they would tell where their mother was. Ellen shrank away from him, and would not speak, but Benny spoke up and said, "Dr. Flint, I don't know where my mother is. I guess she's in New York, and when you go there again, I wish you'd ask her to come home, for I want to see her, but if you put her in jail or tell her you'll cut her head off, I'll tell her to go right back."

□□□□□□□□□□

Christmas was approaching. Grandmother brought me materials, and I busied myself making some new garments and little playthings for my children. Were it not that hiring day is near at hand, and many families are fearfully looking forward to the probability of separation in a few days, Christmas might be a happy season for the poor slaves. Even slave mothers try to gladden the hearts of their little ones on that occasion. Benny and Ellen had their Christmas stockings filled. Their imprisoned mother could not have the privilege of witnessing their surprise and joy. But I had the pleasure of peeping at them as they went into the street with their new suits on. I heard Benny ask a little playmate whether Santa Claus brought him anything. "Yes," replied the boy, "but Santa Claus ain't a real man. It's the children's mothers that put things into the stockings." "No, that can't be," replied Benny, "for Santa Claus brought Ellen and me these new clothes, and my mother has been gone this long time." How I longed to tell him that his mother made those garments, and that many a tear fell on them while she worked! Every child rises early on Christmas morning to see the Johnkannaus.

Without them, Christmas would be shorn of its greatest attraction. They consist of companies of slaves from the plantations, generally of the lower class. Two athletic men, in calico wrappers, have a net thrown over them, covered with all manner of bright-colored stripes. Cow tails are fastened to their backs, and their heads are decorated with horns. A box, covered with sheepskin, is called the gumbo box. A dozen beat on this, while others strike triangles and jawbones, to which bands of dancers keep time. For a month previous they are composing songs, which are sung on this occasion. These companies, of a hundred each, turn out early in the morning, and are allowed to go round till twelve o'clock, begging for contributions. Not a door is left unvisited where there is the least chance of obtaining a penny or a glass of rum. They do not drink while they are out, but carry the rum home in jugs, to have a carousal. These Christmas donations frequently amount to twenty or thirty dollars.

It is seldom that any white man or child refuses to give them a trifle. If he does, they regale his ears with the following song, "*Poor Massa, so dey say, down in de heel, so dey say, got no money, so dey say, not one shillin, so dey say, God a'mighty bress you, so dey say.*" Christmas is a day of feasting, both with white and colored people. Slaves, who are lucky enough to have a few shillings, are sure to spend them for good eating, and many a turkey and pig is captured, without saying, "By your leave, sir." Those who cannot obtain these, cook a 'possum, or a raccoon, from which savory dishes can be made. My grandmother raised poultry and pigs for sale, and it was her established custom to have both a turkey and a pig roasted for Christmas dinner.

On this occasion, I was warned to keep extremely quiet, because two guests had been invited. One was the town constable, and the other was a free colored man, who tried to pass himself off for white, and who was always ready to do any mean work for the sake of currying favor with white people. My grandmother had a motive for inviting them. She managed to take them all over the house. All the rooms on the lower floor were thrown open for them to pass in and out, and after dinner, they were invited upstairs to look at a fine mockingbird my uncle had just brought home. There, too, the rooms were all thrown open, that they might look in. When I heard them talking on the piazza, my heart almost stood still. I knew this colored man had spent many nights hunting for me. Everybody knew he had the blood of a slave father in his veins, but for the sake of passing himself off for white, he was ready to kiss the slaveholders feet. How I despised him! As for the constable, he wore no false colors. The duties of his office were despicable, but he was superior to his companion, inasmuch as he did not pretend to be what he was not. Any white man, who could raise money enough to buy a slave, would have considered himself degraded by being a constable, but the office enabled its possessor to exercise authority. If he found any slave out after nine o'clock, he could whip him as much as he liked, and that was a privilege to be coveted. When the guests were ready to depart, my grandmother gave them some pudding, as a present for their wives. Through my peephole I saw them go out of the gate, and I was glad when it closed after them. So passed the first Christmas in my den.

☐☐☐☐☐☐☐☐☐☐

When spring returned, and I took in the little patch of green the aperture commanded, I asked myself how many more summers and winters I must be condemned to spend thus. I longed to draw in a plentiful draught of fresh air, to stretch my cramped limbs, to have room to stand erect, to feel the earth under my feet again. My relatives were constantly on the lookout for a chance of escape, but none offered that seemed practicable, and even tolerably safe. The hot summer came again, and made the turpentine drop from the thin roof over my head.

During the long nights I was restless for want of air, and I had no room to toss and turn. There was but one compensation, the atmosphere was so stifled that even mosquitoes would not condescend to buzz in it. With all my detestation of Dr. Flint, I could hardly wish him a worse punishment, either in this world or that which is to come, than to suffer what I suffered in one single summer. Yet the laws allowed *him* to be out in the free air, while I, guiltless of crime, was pent up here, as the only means of avoiding the cruelties the laws allowed him to inflict upon me! I don't know what kept life within me. Again and again, I thought I should die before long, but I saw the leaves of another autumn whirl through the air, and felt the touch of another winter.

In summer the most terrible thunderstorms were acceptable, for the rain came through the roof, and I rolled up my bed that it might cool the hot boards under it. Later in the season, storms sometimes wet my clothes through and through, and that was not comfortable when the air grew chilly. Moderate storms I could keep out by filling the chinks with oakum. But uncomfortable as my situation was, I had glimpses of things out of doors, which made me thankful for my wretched hiding place. One day I saw a slave pass our gate, muttering, "It's his own, and he can kill it if he will." My grandmother told me that woman's history. Her mistress had that day seen her baby for the first time, and in the lineaments of its fair face she saw a likeness to her husband. She turned the bondwoman and her child out of doors, and forbade her ever to return. The slave went to her master, and told him what had happened. He promised to talk with her mistress, and make it all right. The next day she and her baby were sold to a Georgia trader. Another time I saw a woman rush wildly by, pursued by two men. She was a slave, the wet nurse of her mistress's children. For some trifling offense her mistress ordered her to be stripped and whipped. To escape the degradation and the torture, she rushed to the river, jumped in, and ended her wrongs in death. Senator Brown, of Mississippi, could not be ignorant of many such facts as these, for they are of frequent occurrence in every Southern State. Yet he stood up in the Congress of the United States, and declared that slavery was "a great moral, social, and political blessing, a blessing to the master, and a blessing to the slave!" I suffered much more during the second winter than I did during the first. My limbs were benumbed by inaction, and the cold filled them with cramp. I had a very painful sensation of coldness in my head, even my face and tongue stiffened, and I lost the power of speech. Of course it was impossible, under the circumstances, to summon any physician.

My brother William came and did all he could for me. Uncle Phillip also watched tenderly over me, and poor grandmother crept up and down to inquire whether there were any signs of returning life. I was restored to consciousness by the dashing of cold water in my face, and found myself leaning against my brother's arm, while he bent over me with streaming eyes. He afterwards told me he thought I was dying, for I had been in an unconscious state sixteen hours. I next became delirious, and was in great danger of betraying myself and my friends. To prevent this, they stupefied me with drugs. I remained in bed six weeks, weary in body and sick at heart. How to get medical advice was the question. William finally went to a Thompsonian doctor, and described himself as having all my pains and aches. He returned with herbs, roots, and ointment. He was especially charged to rub on the ointment by a fire, but how could a fire be made in my little den? Charcoal in a furnace was tried, but there was no outlet for the gas, and it nearly cost me my life. Afterwards coals, already kindled, were brought up in an iron pan, and placed on bricks. I was so weak, and it was so long since I had enjoyed the warmth of fire, that those few coals actually made me weep. I think the medicines did me some good, but my recovery was very slow. Dark thoughts passed through my mind as I lay there day after day. I tried to be thankful for my little cell, dismal as it was, and even to love it, as part of the price I had paid for the redemption of my children. Sometimes I thought God was a compassionate Father, who would forgive my sins for the sake of my sufferings. At other times, it seemed to me there was no justice or mercy in the divine government. I asked why the curse of slavery was permitted to exist, and why I had been so persecuted and wronged from youth upward. These things took the shape of mystery, which is to this day not so clear to my soul as I trust it will be hereafter. In the midst of my illness, grandmother broke down under the weight of anxiety and toil. The idea of losing her, who had always been my best friend and a mother to my children, was the sorest trial I had yet had. O, how earnestly I prayed that she might recover! How hard it seemed, that I could not tend upon her, who had so long and so tenderly watched over me! One day the screams of a child nerved me with strength to crawl to my peeping hole, and I saw my son covered with blood. A fierce dog, usually kept chained, had seized and bitten him. A doctor was sent for, and I heard the groans and screams of my child while the wounds were being sewed up.

O, what torture to a mother's heart, to listen to this and be unable to go to him! But childhood is like a day in spring, alternately shower and sunshine. Before night Benny was bright and lively, threatening the destruction of the dog, and great was his delight when the doctor told him the next day that the dog had bitten another boy and been shot. Benny recovered from his wounds, but it was long before he could walk. When my grandmother's illness became known, many ladies, who were her customers, called to bring her some little comforts, and to inquire whether she had everything she wanted. Aunt Nancy one night asked permission to watch with her sick mother, and Mrs. Flint replied, "I don't see any need of your going. I can't spare you."

But when she found other ladies in the neighborhood were so attentive, not wishing to be outdone in Christian charity, she also sallied forth, in magnificent condescension, and stood by the bedside of her who had loved her in her infancy, and who had been repaid by such grievous wrongs. She seemed surprised to find her so ill, and scolded Uncle Phillip for not sending for Dr. Flint. She herself sent for him immediately, and he came. Secure as I was in my retreat, I should have been terrified if I had known he was so near me. He pronounced my grandmother in a very critical situation, and said if her attending physician wished it, he would visit her. Nobody wished to have him coming to the house at all hours, and we were not disposed to give him a chance to make out a long bill. As Mrs. Flint went out, Sally told her the reason Benny was lame was, that a dog had bitten him. "I'm glad of it," replied she. "I wish he had killed him. It would be good news to send to his mother. *Her* day will come. The dogs will grab *her* yet." With these Christian words she and her husband departed, and, to my great satisfaction, returned no more.

I heard from Uncle Phillip, with feelings of unspeakable joy and gratitude, that the crisis was passed and grandmother would live. I could now say from my heart, "God is merciful. He has spared me the anguish of feeling that I caused her death."

The summer had nearly ended, when Dr. Flint made a third visit to New York, in search of me. Two candidates were running for Congress, and he returned in season to vote. The father of my children was the Whig candidate. The doctor had hitherto been a staunch Whig, but now he exerted all his energies for the defeat of Mr. Sands. He invited large parties of men to dine in the shade of his trees, and supplied them with plenty of rum and brandy. If any poor fellow drowned his wits in the bowl, and, in the openness of his convivial heart, proclaimed that he did not mean to vote the Democratic ticket, he was shoved into the street without ceremony. The doctor expended his liquor in vain. Mr. Sands was elected, an event which occasioned me some anxious thoughts. He had not emancipated my children, and if he should die they would be at the mercy of his heirs.

Two little voices, that frequently met my ear, seemed to plead with me not to let their father depart without striving to make their freedom secure. Years had passed since I had spoken to him. I had not even seen him since the night I passed him, unrecognized, in my disguise of a sailor. I supposed he would call before he left, to say something to my grandmother concerning the children, and I resolved what course to take. The day before his departure for Washington I made arrangements, towards evening, to get from my hiding place into the storeroom below.

I found myself so stiff and clumsy that it was with great difficulty I could hitch from one resting place to another. When I reached the storeroom my ankles gave way under me, and I sank exhausted on the floor. It seemed as if I could never use my limbs again. But the purpose I had in view roused all the strength I had. I crawled on my hands and knees to the window, and, screened behind a barrel, I waited for his coming. The clock struck nine, and I knew the steamboat would leave between ten and eleven. My hopes were failing. But presently I heard his voice, saying to someone, "Wait for me a moment. I wish to see Aunt Martha." When he came out, as he passed the window, I said, "Stop one moment, and let me speak for my children." He started, hesitated, and then passed on, and went out of the gate. I closed the shutter I had partially opened, and sank down behind the barrel. I had suffered much, but seldom had I experienced a keener pang than I then felt. Had my children, then, become of so little consequence to him? And had he so little feeling for their wretched mother that he would not listen a moment while she pleaded for them? Painful memories were so busy within me, that I forgot I had not hooked the shutter, till I heard someone opening it. I looked up. He had come back. "Who called me?" said he, in a low tone. "I did," I replied. "Oh, Linda," said he, "I knew your voice, but I was afraid to answer, lest my friend should hear me. Why do you come here? Is it possible you risk yourself in this house? They are mad to allow it. I shall expect to hear that you are all ruined." I did not wish to implicate him, by letting him know my place of concealment, so I merely said, "I thought you would come to bid grandmother goodbye, and so I came here to speak a few words to you about emancipating my children. Many changes may take place during the six months you are gone to Washington, and it does not seem right for you to expose them to the risk of such changes. I want nothing for myself, all I ask is, that you will free my children, or authorize some friend to do it, before you go." He promised he would do it, and also expressed a readiness to make any arrangements whereby I could be purchased. I heard footsteps approaching, and closed the shutter hastily. I wanted to crawl back to my den, without letting the family know what I had done, for I knew they would deem it very imprudent. But he stepped back into the house, to tell my grandmother that he had spoken with me at the storeroom window, and to beg of her not to allow me to remain in the house overnight. He said it was the height of madness for me to be there, that we should certainly all be ruined. Luckily, he was in too much of a hurry to wait for a reply, or the dear old woman would surely have told him all. I tried to go back to my den, but found it more difficult to go up than I had to come down. Now that my mission was fulfilled, the little strength that had supported me through it was gone, and I sank helpless on the floor. My grandmother, alarmed at the risk I had run, came into the storeroom in the dark, and locked the door behind her. "Linda," she whispered, "where are you?" "I am here by the window," I replied. "I *couldn't* have him go away without emancipating the children. Who knows what may happen?" "Come, come, child," said she, "it won't do for you to stay here another minute. You've done wrong, but I can't blame you, poor thing!" I told her I could not return without assistance, and she must call my uncle. Uncle Phillip came, and pity prevented him from scolding me. He carried me back to my dungeon, laid me tenderly on the bed, gave me some medicine, and asked me if there was anything more he could do. Then he went away, and I was left with my own thoughts—starless as the midnight darkness around me. My friends feared I should become a cripple for life, and I was so weary of my long imprisonment that, had it not been for the hope of serving my children, I should have been thankful to die, but, for their sakes, I was willing to bear on.

□□□□□□□□□□

Dr. Flint had not given me up. Every now and then he would say to my grandmother that I would yet come back, and voluntarily surrender myself, and that when I did, I could be purchased by my relatives, or anyone who wished to buy me. I knew his cunning nature too well not to perceive that this was a trap laid for me, and so all my friends understood it. I resolved to match my cunning against his cunning. In order to make him believe that I was in New York, I resolved to write him a letter dated from that place. I sent for my friend Peter, and asked him if he knew any trustworthy seafaring person, who would carry such a letter to New York, and put it in the post office there. He said he knew one that he would trust with his own life to the ends of the world. I reminded him that it was a hazardous thing for him to undertake. He said he knew it, but he was willing to do anything to help me. I expressed a wish for a New York paper, to ascertain the names of some of the streets. He ran his hand into his pocket and said, "Here is half a one, that was round a cap I bought of a peddler yesterday." I told him the letter would be ready the next evening. He bade me goodbye, adding, "Keep up your spirits, Linda, brighter days will come by and by." My Uncle Phillip kept watch over the gate until our brief interview was over. Early the next morning, I seated myself near the little aperture to examine the newspaper. It was a piece of the *New York Herald*, and, for once, the paper that systematically abuses the colored people, was made to render them a service. Having obtained what information I wanted concerning streets and numbers, I wrote two letters, one to my grandmother, the other to Dr. Flint.

I reminded him how he, a gray-headed man, had treated a helpless child, who had been placed in his power, and what years of misery he had brought upon her. To my grandmother, I expressed a wish to have my children sent to me at the North, where I could teach them to respect themselves, and set them a virtuous example, which a slave mother was not allowed to do at the South. I asked her to direct her answer to a certain street in Boston, as I did not live in New York, though I went there sometimes. I dated these letters ahead, to allow for the time it would take to carry them, and sent a memorandum of the date to the messenger. When my friend came for the letters, I said, "God bless and reward you, Peter, for this disinterested kindness. Pray be careful. If you are detected, both you and I will have to suffer dreadfully. I have not a relative who would dare to do it for me." He replied, "You may trust to me, Linda. I don't forget that your father was my best friend, and I will be a friend to his children so long as God lets me live." It was necessary to tell my grandmother what I had done, in order that she might be ready for the letter, and prepared to hear what Dr. Flint might say about my being at the North. She was sadly troubled. She felt sure mischief would come of it. I also told my plan to Aunt Nancy, in order that she might report to us what was said at Dr. Flint's house. I whispered it to her through a crack, and she whispered back, "I hope it will succeed. I shan't mind being a slave all *my* life, if I can only see you and the children free." I had directed that my letters should be put into the New York Post Office on the 20th of the month. On the evening of the 24th my aunt came to say that Dr. Flint and his wife had been talking in a low voice about a letter he had received, and that when he went to his office he promised to bring it when he came to tea. So I concluded I should hear my letter read the next morning. I told my grandmother Dr. Flint would be sure to come, and asked her to have him sit near a certain door, and leave it open, that I might hear what he said. The next morning I took my station within sound of that door, and remained motionless as a statue. It was not long before I heard the gate slam, and the well-known footsteps enter the house. He seated himself in the chair that was placed for him, and said, "Well, Martha, I've brought you a letter from Linda. She has sent me a letter, also. I know exactly where to find her, but I don't choose to go to Boston for her. I had rather she would come back of her own accord, in a respectable manner. Her Uncle Phillip is the best person to go for her. With *him*, she would feel perfectly free to act. I am willing to pay his expenses going and returning. She shall be sold to her friends. Her children are free, at least I suppose they are, and when you obtain her freedom, you'll make a happy family. I suppose, Martha, you have no objection to my reading to you the letter Linda has written to you."

He broke the seal, and I heard him read it. The old villain! He had suppressed the letter I wrote to grandmother, and prepared a substitute of his own, the purport of which was as follows—*Dear Grandmother, I have long wanted to write to you, but the disgraceful manner in which I left you and my children made me ashamed to do it. If you knew how much I have suffered since I ran away, you would pity and forgive me. I have purchased freedom at a dear rate. If any arrangement could be made for me to return to the South without being a slave, I would gladly come. If not, I beg of you to send my children to the North. I cannot live any longer without them. Let me know in time, and I will meet them in New York or Philadelphia, whichever place best suits my uncle's convenience, Write as soon as possible to your unhappy daughter, Linda.* "It is very much as I expected it would be," said the old hypocrite, rising to go. "You see the foolish girl has repented of her rashness, and wants to return. We must help her to do it, Martha. Talk with Phillip about it. If he will go for her, she will trust to him, and come back. I should like an answer tomorrow. Good morning, Martha." As he stepped out on the piazza, he stumbled over my little girl. "Ah, Ellen, is that you?" he said, in his most gracious manner. "I didn't see you. How do you do?" "Pretty well, sir," she replied. "I heard you tell grandmother that my mother is coming home. I want to see her." "Yes, Ellen, I am going to bring her home very soon," rejoined he, "and you shall see her as much as you like, you little curly-headed nigger." This was as good as a comedy to me, who had heard it all, but grandmother was frightened and distressed, because the doctor wanted my uncle to go for me. The next evening Dr. Flint called to talk the matter over. My uncle told him that from what he had heard of Massachusetts, he judged he should be mobbed if he went there after a runaway slave. "All stuff and nonsense, Phillip!" replied the doctor. "Do you suppose I want you to kick up a row in Boston? The business can all be done quietly. Linda writes that she wants to come back. You are her relative, and she would trust *you*. The case would be different if I went. She might object to coming with *me*, and the damned abolitionists, if they knew I was her master, would not believe me, if I told them she had begged to go back. They would get up a row, and I should not like to see Linda dragged through the streets like a common Negro. She has been very ungrateful to me for all my kindness, but I forgive her, and want to act the part of a friend towards her. I have no wish to hold her as my slave. Her friends can buy her as soon as she arrives here." Finding that his arguments failed to convince my uncle, the doctor "let the cat out of the bag," by saying that he had written to the mayor of Boston, to ascertain whether there was a person of my description at the street and number from which my letter was dated. He had omitted this date in the letter he had made up to read to my grandmother. If I had dated from New York, the old man would probably have made another journey to that city. But even in that dark region where knowledge is so carefully excluded from the slave, I had heard enough about Massachusetts to come to the conclusion that slaveholders did not consider it a comfortable place to go to in search of a runaway. That was before the Fugitive Slave Law was passed, before Massachusetts had consented to become a "nigger hunter" for the South. My grandmother, who had become skittish by seeing her family always in danger, came to me with a very distressed countenance, and said, "What will you do if the mayor of Boston sends him word that you haven't been there? Then he will suspect the letter was a trick, and maybe he'll find out something about it, and we shall all get into trouble. O Linda, I wish you had never sent the letters." "Don't worry yourself, grandmother," said I. "The mayor of Boston won't trouble himself to hunt niggers for Dr. Flint. The letters will do good in the end. I shall get out of this dark hole sometime or other." "I hope you will, child," replied the good, patient old friend. "You have been here a long time, almost five years, but whenever you do go, it will break your old grandmother's heart. I should be expecting every day to hear that you were brought back in irons and put in jail. God help you, poor child! Let us be thankful that sometime or other we shall go where the wicked cease from troubling, and the weary are at rest." My heart responded, Amen. The fact that Dr. Flint had written to the mayor of Boston convinced me that he believed my letter to be genuine, and of course that he had no suspicion of my being anywhere in the vicinity. It was a great object to keep up this delusion, for it made me and my friends feel less anxious, and it would be very convenient whenever there was a chance to escape. I resolved, therefore, to continue to write letters from the North from time to time. Two or three weeks passed, and as no news came from the mayor of Boston, grandmother began to listen to my entreaty to be allowed to leave my cell, sometimes, and exercise my limbs to prevent my becoming a cripple. I was allowed to slip down into the small storeroom, early in the morning, and remain there a little while. The room was all filled up with barrels, except a small open space under my trapdoor.

This faced the door, the upper part of which was of glass, and purposely left uncurtained, that the curious might look in. The air of this place was close, but it was so much better than the atmosphere of my cell, that I dreaded to return. I came down as soon as it was light, and remained till eight o'clock, when people began to be about, and there was danger that someone might come on the piazza. I had tried various applications to bring warmth and feeling into my limbs, but without avail. They were so numb and stiff that it was a painful effort to move, and had my enemies come upon me during the first mornings I tried to exercise them in the small unoccupied space of the storeroom, it would have been impossible for me to have escaped.

☐☐☐☐☐☐☐☐☐☐

I missed the company and kind attentions of my brother William, who had gone to Washington with his master, Mr. Sands. We received several letters from him, written without any allusion to me, but expressed in such a manner that I knew he did not forget me. I disguised my hand, and wrote to him in the same manner. It was a long session, and when it closed, William wrote to inform us that Mr. Sands was going to the North, to be gone some time, and that he was to accompany him. I knew that his master had promised to give him his freedom, but no time had been specified. Would William trust to a slave's chances?

I remembered how we used to talk together, in our young days, about obtaining our freedom, and I thought it very doubtful whether he would come back to us. Grandmother received a letter from Mr. Sands, saying that William had proved a most faithful servant, and he would also say a valued friend, that no mother had ever trained a better boy. He said he had traveled through the Northern States and Canada, and though the abolitionists had tried to decoy him away, they had never succeeded. He ended by saying they should be at home shortly.

We expected letters from William, describing the novelties of his journey, but none came. In time, it was reported that Mr. Sands would return late in the autumn, accompanied by a bride. Still no letters from William. I felt almost sure I should never see him again on Southern soil, but had he no word of comfort to send to his friends at home? To the poor captive in her dungeon? My thoughts wandered through the dark past, and over the uncertain future. Alone in my cell, where no eye but God's could see me, I wept bitter tears. How earnestly I prayed to him to restore me to my children, and enable me to be a useful woman and a good mother! At last the day arrived for the return of the travelers. Grandmother had made loving preparations to welcome her absent boy back to the old hearthstone. When the dinner table was laid, William's plate occupied its old place. The stagecoach went by empty. My grandmother waited dinner. She thought perhaps he was necessarily detained by his master. In my prison I listened anxiously, expecting every moment to hear my dear brother's voice and step. In the course of the afternoon a lad was sent by Mr. Sands to tell grandmother that William did not return with him, that the abolitionists had decoyed him away. But he begged her not to feel troubled about it, for he felt confident she would see William in a few days. As soon as he had time to reflect he would come back, for he could never expect to be so well off at the North as he had been with him. If you had seen the tears, and heard the sobs, you would have thought the messenger had brought tidings of death instead of freedom.

    Poor old grandmother felt that she should never see her darling boy again. And I was selfish. I thought more of what I had lost, than of what my brother had gained. A new anxiety began to trouble me. Mr. Sands had expended a good deal of money, and would naturally feel irritated by the loss he had incurred.

    I greatly feared this might injure the prospects of my children, who were now becoming valuable property. I longed to have their emancipation made certain. The more so, because their master and father was now married. I was too familiar with slavery not to know that promises made to slaves, though with kind intentions, and sincere at the time, depend upon many contingencies for their fulfillment. Much as I wished William to be free, the step he had taken made me sad and anxious.

The following Sabbath was calm and clear, so beautiful that it seemed like a Sabbath in the eternal world. My grandmother brought the children out on the piazza, that I might hear their voices. She thought it would comfort me in my despondency, and it did. They chatted merrily, as only children can. Benny said, "Grandmother, do you think Uncle Will has gone for good? Won't he ever come back again? Maybe he'll find mother. If he does, *won't* she be glad to see him! Why don't you and Uncle Phillip, and all of us, go and live where mother is? I should like it, wouldn't you, Ellen?" "Yes, I should like it," replied Ellen, "but how could we find her? Do you know the place, grandmother? I don't remember how mother looked—do you, Benny?" Benny was just beginning to describe me when they were interrupted by an old slave woman, a near neighbor, named Aggie. This poor creature had witnessed the sale of her children, and seen them carried off to parts unknown, without any hopes of ever hearing from them again. She saw that my grandmother had been weeping, and she said, in a sympathizing tone, "What's the matter, Aunt Marthy?" "O Aggie," she replied, "it seems as if I shouldn't have any of my children or grandchildren left to hand me a drink when I'm dying, and lay my old body in the ground. My boy didn't come back with Mr. Sands. He stayed at the North."

Poor old Aggie clapped her hands for joy. "Is *dat* what you's crying fur?" she exclaimed. "Git down on your knees and bress de Lord! I don't know whar my poor chillern is, and I nebber 'spect to know. You don't know whar poor Linda's gone to, but you *do* know whar her brudder is. He's in free parts, and dat's de right place. Don't murmur at de Lord's doings, but git down on your knees and tank him for his goodness." My selfishness was rebuked by what poor Aggie said. She rejoiced over the escape of one who was merely her fellow bondman, while his own sister was only thinking what his good fortune might cost her children. I knelt and prayed God to forgive me, and I thanked him from my heart, that one of my family was saved from the grasp of slavery. It was not long before we received a letter from William. He wrote that Mr. Sands had always treated him kindly, and that he had tried to do his duty to him faithfully. But ever since he was a boy, he had longed to be free, and he had already gone through enough to convince him he had better not lose the chance that offered. He concluded by saying, "Don't worry about me, dear grandmother. I shall think of you always, and it will spur me on to work hard and try to do right. When I have earned money enough to give you a home, perhaps you will come to the North, and we can all live happy together." Mr. Sands told my Uncle Phillip the particulars about William's leaving him. He said, "I trusted him as if he were my own brother, and treated him as kindly. The abolitionists talked to him in several places, but I had no idea they could tempt him. However, I don't blame William. He's young and inconsiderate, and those Northern rascals decoyed him. I must confess the scamp was very bold about it. I met him coming down the steps of the Astor House with his trunk on his shoulder, and I asked him where he was going. He said he was going to change his old trunk. I told him it was rather shabby, and asked if he didn't need some money. He said, no, thanked me, and went off. He did not return so soon as I expected, but I waited patiently. At last I went to see if our trunks were packed, ready for our journey. I found them locked, and a sealed note on the table informed me where I could find the keys. The fellow even tried to be religious. He wrote that he hoped God would always bless me, and reward me for my kindness, that he was not unwilling to serve me, but he wanted to be a free man, and that if I thought he did wrong, he hoped I would forgive him. I intended to give him his freedom in five years. He might have trusted me. He has shown himself ungrateful, but I shall not go for him, or send for him. I feel confident that he will soon return to me." I afterwards heard an account of the affair from William himself. He had not been urged away by abolitionists. He needed no information they could give him about slavery to stimulate his desire for freedom.

  He looked at his hands, and remembered that they were once in irons. What security had he that they would not be so again? Mr. Sands was kind to him, but he might indefinitely postpone the promise he had made to give him his freedom. He might come under pecuniary embarrassments, and his property be seized by creditors, or he might die, without making any arrangements in his favor. He had too often known such accidents to happen to slaves who had kind masters, and he wisely resolved to make sure of the present opportunity to own himself. He was scrupulous about taking any money from his master on false pretences, so he sold his best clothes to pay for his passage to Boston. The slaveholders pronounced him a base, ungrateful wretch, for thus requiting his master's indulgence. What would *they* have done under similar circumstances? When Dr. Flint's family heard that William had deserted Mr. Sands, they chuckled greatly over the news. Mrs. Flint made her usual manifestations of Christian feeling, by saying, "I'm glad of it. I hope he'll never get him again. I like to see people paid back in their own coin. I reckon Linda's children will have to pay for it. I should be glad to see them in the speculator's hands again, I'm tired of seeing those little niggers march about the streets."

☐☐☐☐☐☐☐☐☐☐

    Mrs. Flint proclaimed her intention of informing Mrs. Sands who was the father of my children. She likewise proposed to tell her what an artful devil I was, that I had made a great deal of trouble in her family, that when Mr. Sands was at the North, she didn't doubt I had followed him in disguise, and persuaded William to run away. She had some reason to entertain such an idea, for I had written from the North, from time to time, and I dated my letters from various places. Many of them fell into Dr. Flint's hands, as I expected they would, and he must have come to the conclusion that I traveled about a good deal.

    He kept a close watch over my children, thinking they would eventually lead to my detection. A new and unexpected trial was in store for me. One day, when Mr. Sands and his wife were walking in the street, they met Benny. The lady took a fancy to him, and exclaimed, "What a pretty little Negro! Whom does he belong to?" Benny did not hear the answer, but he came home very indignant with the stranger lady, because she had called him a Negro. A few days afterwards, Mr. Sands called on my grandmother, and told her he wanted her to take the children to his house. He said he had informed his wife of his relation to them, and told her they were motherless, and she wanted to see them. When he had gone, my grandmother came and asked what I would do. The question seemed a mockery. What *could* I do? They were Mr. Sands's slaves, and their mother was a slave, whom he had represented to be dead. Perhaps he thought I was. I was too much pained and puzzled to come to any decision, and the children were carried without my knowledge. Mrs. Sands had a sister from Illinois staying with her. This lady, who had no children of her own, was so much pleased with Ellen, that she offered to adopt her, and bring her up as she would a daughter. Mrs. Sands wanted to take Benjamin. When grandmother reported this to me, I was tried almost beyond endurance. Was this all I was to gain by what I had suffered for the sake of having my children free? True, the prospect *seemed* fair, but I knew too well how lightly slaveholders held such "parental relations."

If pecuniary troubles should come, or if the new wife required more money than could conveniently be spared, my children might be thought of as a convenient means of raising funds. I had no trust in thee, O slavery! Never should I know peace till my children were emancipated with all due formalities of law. I was too proud to ask Mr. Sands to do anything for my own benefit, but I could bring myself to become a supplicant for my children. I resolved to remind him of the promise he had made me, and to throw myself upon his honor for the performance of it. I persuaded my grandmother to go to him, and tell him I was not dead, and that earnestly entreated him to keep the promise he had made me, that I had heard of the recent proposals concerning my children, and did not feel easy to accept them, that he had promised to emancipate them, and it was time for him to redeem his pledge. I knew there was some risk in thus betraying that I was in the vicinity, but what will not a mother do for her children? He received the message with surprise, and said, "The children are free. I have never intended to claim them as slaves. Linda may decide their fate. In my opinion, they had better be sent to the North. I don't think they are quite safe here. Dr. Flint boasts that they are still in his power. He says they were his daughter's property, and as she was not of age when they were sold, the contract is not legally binding." So, then, after all I had endured for their sakes, my poor children were between two fires, between my old master and their new master! And I was powerless. There was no protecting arm of the law for me to invoke. Mr. Sands proposed that Ellen should go, for the present, to some of his relatives, who had removed to Brooklyn, Long Island. It was promised that she should be well-taken care of, and sent to school. I consented to it, as the best arrangement I could make for her. My grandmother, of course, negotiated it all, and Mrs. Sands knew of no other person in the transaction.

She proposed that they should take Ellen with them to Washington, and keep her till they had a good chance of sending her, with friends, to Brooklyn. She had an infant daughter. I had, had a glimpse of it, as the nurse passed with it in her arms. It was not a pleasant thought to me, that the bondwoman's child should tend her free-born sister, but there was no alternative. Ellen was made ready for the journey. O, how it tried my heart to send her away, so young, alone, among strangers! Without a mother's love to shelter her from the storms of life, almost without memory of a mother! I doubted whether she and Benny would have for me the natural affection that children feel for a parent. I thought to myself that I might perhaps never see my daughter again, and I had a great desire that she should look upon me, before she went, that she might take my image with her in her memory.

It seemed to me cruel to have her brought to my dungeon. It was sorrow enough for her young heart to know that her mother was a victim of slavery, without seeing the wretched hiding place to which it had driven her. I begged permission to pass the last night in one of the open chambers, with my little girl. They thought I was crazy to think of trusting such a young child with my perilous secret. I told them I had watched her character, and I felt sure she would not betray me, that I was determined to have an interview, and if they would not facilitate it, I would take my own way to obtain it. They remonstrated against the rashness of such a proceeding, but finding they could not change my purpose, they yielded. I slipped through the trapdoor into the storeroom, and my uncle kept watch at the gate while I passed into the piazza and went upstairs, to the room I used to occupy. It was more than five years since I had seen it, and how the memories crowded on me! There I had taken shelter when my mistress drove me from her house, there came my old tyrant, to mock, insult, and curse me, there my children were first laid in my arms, there I had watched over them, each day with a deeper and sadder love, there I had knelt to God, in anguish of heart, to forgive the wrong I had done. How vividly it all came back! And after this long, gloomy interval, I stood there such a wreck! In the midst of these meditations, I heard footsteps on the stairs. The door opened, and my Uncle Phillip came in, leading Ellen by the hard. I put my arms round her, and said, "Ellen, my dear child, I am your mother." She drew back a little, and looked at me, then, with sweet confidence, she laid her cheek against mine, and I foded her to the heart that had been so long desolated. She was the first to speak. Raising her head, she said, inquiringly, "You really *are* my mother?" I told her I really was, that during all the long time she had not seen me, I had loved her most tenderly, and that now she was going away, I wanted to see her and talk with her, that she might remember me. With a sob in her voice, she said, "I'm glad you've come to see me, but why didn't you ever come before? Benny and I have wanted so much to see you! He remembers you, and sometimes he tells me about you. Why didn't you come home when Dr. Flint went to bring you?" I answered, "I couldn't come before, dear. But now that I am with you, tell me whether you like to go away."

"I don't know," said she, crying. "Grandmother says I ought not to cry, that I am going to a good place, where I can learn to read and write, and that by and by I can write her a letter. But I shan't have Benny, or grandmother, or Uncle Phillip, or anybody to love me. Can't you go with me? O, *do* go, dear mother!" I told her I couldn't go now, but sometime I would come to her, and then she and Benny and I would live together, and have happy times. She wanted to run and bring Benny to see me now. I told her he was going to the North, before long, with Uncle Phillip, and then I would come to see him before he went away. I asked if she would like to have me stay all night and sleep with her. "O, yes," she replied. Then, turning to her uncle, she said, pleadingly, "*May* I stay? Please, uncle! She is my own mother." He laid his hand on her head, and said, solemnly, "Ellen, this is the secret you have promised grandmother never to tell. If you ever speak of it to anybody, they will never let you see your grandmother again, and your mother can never come to Brooklyn." "Uncle," she replied, "I will never tell." He told her she might stay with me, and when he had gone, I took her in my arms and told her I was a slave, and that was the reason she must never say she had seen me. I exhorted her to be a good child, to try to please the people where she was going, and that God would raise her up friends. I told her to say her prayers, and remember always to pray for her poor mother, and that God would permit us to meet again. She wept, and I did not check her tears.

Perhaps she would never again have a chance to pour her tears into a mother's bosom. All night she nestled in my arms, and I had no inclination to slumber. The moments were too precious to lose any of them. Once, when I thought she was asleep, I kissed her forehead softly, and she said, "I am not asleep, dear mother." Before dawn they came to take me back to my den. I drew aside the window curtain, to take a last look of my child. The moonlight shone on her face, and I bent over her, as I had done years before, that wretched night when I ran away.

I hugged her close to my throbbing heart, and tears, too sad for such young eyes to shed, flowed down her cheeks, as she gave her last kiss, and whispered in my ear, "Mother, I will never tell." And she never did. When I got back to my den, I threw myself on the bed and wept there alone in the darkness. It seemed as if my heart would burst. When the time for Ellen's departure drew nigh, I could hear neighbors and friends saying to her, "Goodbye, Ellen. I hope your poor mother will find you out. *Won't* you be glad to see her!" She replied, "Yes, ma'am," and they little dreamed of the weighty secret that weighed down her young heart. She was an affectionate child, but naturally very reserved, except with those she loved, and I felt secure that my secret would be safe with her. I heard the gate close after her, with such feelings as only a slave mother can experience. During the day my meditations were very sad. Sometimes I feared I had been very selfish not to give up all claim to her, and let her go to Illinois, to be adopted by Mrs. Sands's sister. It was my experience of slavery that decided me against it. I feared that circumstances might arise that would cause her to be sent back. I felt confident that I should go to New York myself, and then I should be able to watch over her, and in some degree protect her. Dr. Flint's family knew nothing of the proposed arrangement till after Ellen was gone, and the news displeased them greatly. Mrs. Flint called on Mrs. Sands's sister to inquire into the matter. She expressed her opinion very freely as to the respect Mr. Sands showed for his wife, and for his own character, in acknowledging those "young niggers." And as for sending Ellen away, she pronounced it to be just as much stealing as it would be for him to come and take a piece of furniture out of her parlor. She said her daughter was not of age to sign the bill of sale, and the children were her property, and when she became of age, or was married, she could take them, wherever she could lay hands on them. Miss Emily Flint, the little girl to whom I had been bequeathed, was now in her sixteenth year. Her mother considered it all right and honorable for her, or her future husband, to steal my children, but she did not understand how anybody could hold up their heads in respectable society, after they had purchased their own children, as Mr. Sands had done. Dr. Flint said very little. Perhaps he thought that Benny would be less likely to be sent away if he kept quiet. One of my letters, that fell into his hands, was dated from Canada, and he seldom spoke of me now. This state of things enabled me to slip down into the storeroom more frequently, where I could stand upright, and move my limbs more freely.

Days, weeks, and months passed, and there came no news of Ellen. I sent a letter to Brooklyn, written in my grandmother's name, to inquire whether she had arrived there. Answer was returned that she had not. I wrote to her in Washington, but no notice was taken of it. There was one person there, who ought to have had some sympathy with the anxiety of the child's friends at home, but the links of such relations as he had formed with me, are easily broken and cast away as rubbish. Yet how protectingly and persuasively he once talked to the poor, helpless slave girl! And how entirely I trusted him! But now suspicions darkened my mind. Was my child dead, or had they deceived me, and sold her? If the secret memoirs of many members of Congress should be published, curious details would be unfolded. I once saw a letter from a member of Congress to a slave, who was the mother of six of his children. He wrote to request that she would send her children away from the great house before his return, as he expected to be accompanied by friends. The woman could not read, and was obliged to employ another to read the letter. The existence of the colored children did not trouble this gentleman, it was only the fear that friends might recognize in their features a resemblance to him.

At the end of six months, a letter came to my grandmother, from Brooklyn. It was written by a young lady in the family, and announced that Ellen had just arrived. It contained the following message from her, "I do try to do just as you told me to, and I pray for you every night and morning."

I understood that these words were meant for me, and they were a balsam to my heart. The writer closed her letter by saying, "Ellen is a nice little girl, and we shall like to have her with us. My cousin, Mr. Sands, has given her to me, to be my little waiting maid. I shall send her to school, and I hope someday she will write to you herself." This letter perplexed and troubled me. Had my child's father merely placed her there till she was old enough to support herself? Or had he given her to his cousin, as a piece of property? If the last idea was correct, his cousin might return to the South at any time, and hold Ellen as a slave.

I tried to put away from me the painful thought that such a foul wrong could have been done to us. I said to myself, "Surely there must be *some* justice in man," then I remembered, with a sigh, how slavery perverted all the natural feelings of the human heart. It gave me a pang to look on my light-hearted boy.

He believed himself free, and to have him brought under the yoke of slavery, would be more than I could bear. How I longed to have him safely out of the reach of its power.

☐☐☐☐☐☐☐☐☐☐

I have mentioned my great-aunt, who was a slave in Dr. Flint's family, and who had been my refuge during the shameful persecutions I suffered from him. This aunt had been married at twenty years of age, that is, as far as slaves *can* marry. She had the consent of her master and mistress, and a clergyman performed the ceremony. But it was a mere form, without any legal value. Her master or mistress could annul it any day they pleased. She had always slept on the floor in the entry, near Mrs. Flint's chamber door, that she might be within call. When she was married, she was told she might have the use of a small room in an outhouse. Her mother and her husband furnished it. He was a seafaring man, and was allowed to sleep there when he was at home. But on the wedding evening, the bride was ordered to her old post on the entry floor. Mrs. Flint, at that time, had no children, but she was expecting to be a mother, and if she should want a drink of water in the night, what could she do without her slave to bring it? So my aunt was compelled to lie at her door, until one midnight she was forced to leave, to give premature birth to a child. In a fortnight she was required to resume her place on the entry floor, because Mrs. Flint's babe needed her attentions. She kept her station there through summer and winter, until she had given premature birth to six children, and all the while she was employed as night nurse to Mrs. Flint's children. Finally, toiling all day, and being deprived of rest at night, completely broke down her constitution, and Dr. Flint declared it was impossible she could ever become the mother of a living child. The fear of losing so valuable a servant by death, now induced them to allow her to sleep in her little room in the outhouse, except when there was sickness in the family.

  She afterwards had two feeble babes, one of whom died in a few days, and the other in four weeks. I well remember her patient sorrow as she held the last dead baby in her arms. "I wish it could have lived," she said, "it is not the will of God that any of my children should live. But I will try to be fit to meet their little spirits in heaven." Aunt Nancy was housekeeper and waiting maid in Dr. Flint's family. Indeed, she was the *factotum* of the household. Nothing went on well without her. She was my mother's twin sister, and, as far as was in her power, she supplied a mother's place to us orphans, I slept with her all the time I lived in my old master's house, and the bond between us was very strong. When my friends tried to discourage me from running away, she always encouraged me. When they thought I had better return and ask my master's pardon, because there was no possibility of escape, she sent me word never to yield. She said if I persevered I might, perhaps, gain the freedom of my children, and even if I perished in doing it, that was better than to leave them to groan under the same persecutions that had blighted my own life. After I was shut up in my dark cell, she stole away, whenever she could, to bring me the news and say something cheering. How often did I kneel down to listen to her words of consolation, whispered through a crack! "I am old, and have not long to live," she used to say, "and I could die happy if I could only see you and the children free. You must pray to God, Linda, as I do for you, that he will lead you out of this darkness." I would beg her not to worry herself on my account, that there was an end of all suffering sooner or later, and that whether I lived in chains or in freedom, I should always remember her as the good friend who had been the comfort of my life. A word from her always strengthened me, and not me only. The whole family relied upon her judgment, and were guided by her advice. I had been in my cell six years when my grandmother was summoned to the bedside of this, her last remaining daughter. She was very ill, and they said she would die. Grandmother had not entered Dr. Flint's house for several years. They had treated her cruelly, but she thought nothing of that now. She was grateful for permission to watch by the deathbed of her child. They had always been devoted to each other, and now they sat looking into each other's eyes, longing to speak of the secret that had weighed so much on the hearts of both. My aunt had been stricken with paralysis.

She lived but two days, and the last day she was speechless. Before she lost the power of utterance, she told her mother not to grieve if she could not speak to her, that she would try to hold up her hand, to let her know that all was well with her. Even the hard-hearted doctor was a little softened when he saw the dying woman try to smile on the aged mother, who was kneeling by her side. His eyes moistened for a moment, as he said she had always been a faithful servant, and they should never be able to supply her place. Mrs. Flint took to her bed, quite overcome by the shock. While my grandmother sat alone with the dead, the doctor came in, leading his youngest son, who had always been a great pet with Aunt Nancy, and was much attached to her. "Martha," said he, "Aunt Nancy loved this child, and when he comes where you are, I hope you will be kind to him, for her sake." She replied, "Your wife was my foster child, Dr. Flint, the foster sister of my poor Nancy, and you little know me if you think I can feel anything but goodwill for her children." "I wish the past could be forgotten, and that we might never think of it," said he, "and that Linda would come to supply her aunt's place. She would be worth more to us than all the money that could be paid for her. I wish it for your sake also, Martha. Now that Nancy is taken away from you, she would be a great comfort to your old age." He knew he was touching a tender chord. Almost choking with grief, my grandmother replied, "It was not I that drove Linda away. My grandchildren are gone, and of my nine children only one is left. God help me!" To me, the death of this kind relative was an inexpressible sorrow. I knew that she had been slowly murdered, and felt that my troubles had helped to finish the work. After I heard of her illness, I listened constantly to hear what news was brought from the great house, and the thought that I could not go to her made me utterly miserable.

At last, as Uncle Phillip came into the house, I heard someone inquire, "How is she?" and he answered, "She is dead." My little cell seemed whirling round, and I knew nothing more till I opened my eyes and found Uncle Phillip bending over me. I had no need to ask any questions. He whispered, "Linda, she died happy." I could not weep. My fixed gaze troubled him. "Don't look *so*," he said. "Don't add to my poor mother's trouble. Remember how much she has to bear, and that we ought to do all we can to comfort her." Ah, yes, that blessed old grandmother, who for seventy-three years had borne the pelting storms of a slave mother's life. She did indeed need consolation! Mrs. Flint had rendered her poor foster sister childless, apparently without any compunction, and with cruel selfishness had ruined her health by years of incessant, unrequited toil, and broken rest. But now she became very sentimental. I suppose she thought it would be a beautiful illustration of the attachment existing between slaveholder and slave, if the body of her old worn out servant was buried at her feet. She sent for the clergyman and asked if he had any objection to burying Aunt Nancy in the doctor's family burial place. No colored person had ever been allowed interment in the white people's burying ground, and the minister knew that all the deceased of our family reposed together in the old graveyard of the slaves. He therefore replied, "I have no objection to complying with your wish, but perhaps Aunt Nancy's *mother* may have some choice as to where her remains shall be deposited." It had never occurred to Mrs. Flint that slaves could have any feelings. When my grandmother was consulted, she at once said she wanted Nancy to lie with all the rest of her family, and where her own old body would be buried.

Mrs. Flint graciously complied with her wish, though she said it was painful to her to have Nancy buried away from *her*. She might have added with touching pathos, "I was so long *used* to sleep with her lying near me, on the entry floor." My Uncle Phillip asked permission to bury his sister at his own expense, and slaveholders are always ready to grant *such* favors to slaves and their relatives. The arrangements were very plain, but perfectly respectable. She was buried on the Sabbath, and Mrs. Flint's minister read the funeral service. There was a large concourse of colored people, bond and free, and a few white persons who had always been friendly to our family. Dr. Flint's carriage was in the procession, and when the body was deposited in its humble resting place, the mistress dropped a tear, and returned to her carriage, probably thinking she had performed her duty nobly.

It was talked of by the slaves as a mighty grand funeral. Northern travelers, passing through the place, might have described this tribute of respect to the humble dead as a beautiful feature in the "patriarchal institution," a touching proof of the attachment between slaveholders and their servants, and tenderhearted Mrs. Flint would have confirmed this impression, with handkerchief at her eyes. *We* could have told them a different story. We could have given them a chapter of wrongs and sufferings, that would have touched their hearts, if they *had* any hearts to feel for the colored people. We could have told them how the poor old slave mother had toiled, year after year, to earn eight hundred dollars to buy her son Phillip's right to his own earnings, and how that same Phillip paid the expenses of the funeral, which they regarded as doing so much credit to the master. We could also have told them of a poor, blighted young creature, shut up in a living grave for years, to avoid the tortures that would be inflicted on her, if she ventured to come out and look on the face of her departed friend. All this, and much more, I thought of, as I sat at my loophole, waiting for the family to return from the grave, sometimes weeping, sometimes falling asleep, dreaming strange dreams of the dead and the living.

It was sad to witness the grief of my bereaved grandmother. She had always been strong to bear, and now, as ever, religious faith supported her. But her dark life had become still darker, and age and trouble were leaving deep traces on her withered face. She had four places to knock for me to come to the trapdoor, and each place had a different meaning.

She now came oftener than she had done, and talked to me of her dead daughter, while tears trickled slowly down her furrowed cheeks. I said all I could to comfort her, but it was a sad reflection, that instead of being able to help her, I was a constant source of anxiety and trouble. The poor old back was fitted to its burden. It bent under it, but did not break.

□□□□□□□□□□

I hardly expect that the reader will credit me, when I affirm that I lived in that little dismal hole, almost deprived of light and air, and with no space to move my limbs, for nearly seven years. But it is a fact, and to me a sad one, even now, for my body still suffers from the effects of that long imprisonment, to say nothing of my soul. Members of my family, now living in New York and Boston, can testify to the truth of what I say. Countless were the nights that I sat late at the little loophole scarcely large enough to give me a glimpse of one twinkling star. There, I heard the patrols and slave hunters conferring together about the capture of runaways, well-knowing how rejoiced they would be to catch me. Season after season, year after year, I peeped at my children's faces, and heard their sweet voices, with a heart yearning all the while to say, "Your mother is here." Sometimes it appeared to me as if ages had rolled away since I entered upon that gloomy, monotonous existence. At times, I was stupefied and listless, at other times I became very impatient to know when these dark years would end, and I should again be allowed to feel the sunshine, and breathe the pure air.

After Ellen left us, this feeling increased. Mr. Sands had agreed that Benny might go to the North whenever his Uncle Phillip could go with him, and I was anxious to be there also, to watch over my children, and protect them so far as I was able. Moreover, I was likely to be drowned out of my den, if I remained much longer, for the slight roof was getting badly out of repair, and Uncle Phillip was afraid to remove the shingles, lest someone should get a glimpse of me. When storms occurred in the night, they spread mats and bits of carpet, which in the morning appeared to have been laid out to dry, but to cover the roof in the daytime might have attracted attention. Consequently, my clothes and bedding were often drenched, a process by which the pains and aches in my cramped and stiffened limbs were greatly increased. I revolved various plans of escape in my mind, which I sometimes imparted to my grandmother, when she came to whisper with me at the trapdoor. The kind-hearted old woman had an intense sympathy for runaways. She had known too much of the cruelties inflicted on those who were captured.

Her memory always flew back at once to the sufferings of her bright and handsome son, Benjamin, the youngest and dearest of her flock. So, whenever I alluded to the subject, she would groan out, "O, don't think of it, child. You'll break my heart." I had no good old Aunt Nancy now to encourage me, but my brother William and my children were continually beckoning me to the North. And now I must go back a few months in my story. I have stated that the first of January was the time for selling slaves, or leasing them out to new masters. If time were counted by heartthrobs, the poor slaves might reckon years of suffering during that festival so joyous to the free. On the New Year's Day preceding my aunt's death, one of my friends, named Fanny, was to be sold at auction, to pay her master's debts. My thoughts were with her during all the day, and at night I anxiously inquired what had been her fate. I was told that she had been sold to one master, and her four little girls to another master, far distant, that she had escaped from her purchaser, and was not to be found. Her mother was the old Aggie I have spoken of.

She lived in a small tenement belonging to my grandmother, and built on the same lot with her own house. Her dwelling was searched and watched, and that brought the patrols so near me that I was obliged to keep very close in my den. The hunters were somehow eluded, and not long afterwards Benny accidentally caught sight of Fanny in her mother's hut. He told his grandmother, who charged him never to speak of it, explaining to him the frightful consequences, and he never betrayed the trust. Aggie little dreamed that my grandmother knew where her daughter was concealed, and that the stooping form of her old neighbor was bending under a similar burden of anxiety and fear, but these dangerous secrets deepened the sympathy between the two old persecuted mothers. My friend Fanny and I remained many weeks hidden within call of each other, but she was unconscious of the fact. I longed to have her share my den, which seemed a more secure retreat than her own, but I had brought so much trouble on my grandmother, that it seemed wrong to ask her to incur greater risks. My restlessness increased. I had lived too long in bodily pain and anguish of spirit. Always I was in dread that by some accident, or some contrivance, slavery would succeed in snatching my children from me. This thought drove me nearly frantic, and I determined to steer for the North Star at all hazards. At this crisis, Providence opened an unexpected way for me to escape. My friend Peter came one evening, and asked to speak with me. "Your day has come, Linda," said he. "I have found a chance for you to go to the Free States. You have a fortnight to decide." The news seemed too good to be true, but Peter explained his arrangements, and told me all that was necessary was for me to say I would go. I was going to answer him with a joyful yes, when the thought of Benny came to my mind. I told him the temptation was exceedingly strong, but I was terribly afraid of Dr. Flint's alleged power over my child, and that I could not go and leave him behind. Peter remonstrated earnestly. He said such a good chance might never occur again, that Benny was free, and could be sent to me, and that for the sake of my children's welfare I ought not to hesitate a moment. I told him I would consult with Uncle Phillip. My uncle rejoiced in the plan, and bade me go by all means. He promised, if his life was spared, that he would either bring or send my son to me as soon as I reached a place of safety. I resolved to go, but thought nothing had better be said to my grandmother till very near the time of departure. But my uncle thought she would feel it more keenly if I left her so suddenly. "I will reason with her," said he, "and convince her how necessary it is, not only for your sake, but for hers also. You cannot be blind to the fact that she is sinking under her burdens." I was not blind to it. I knew that my concealment was an ever-present source of anxiety, and that the older she grew the more nervously fearful she was of discovery.

My uncle talked with her, and finally succeeded in persuading her that it was absolutely necessary for me to seize the chance so unexpectedly offered. The anticipation of being a free woman proved almost too much for my weak frame. The excitement stimulated me, and at the same time bewildered me. I made busy preparations for my journey, and for my son to follow me. I resolved to have an interview with him before I went, that I might give him cautions and advice, and tell him how anxiously I should be waiting for him at the North. Grandmother stole up to me as often as possible to whisper words of counsel. She insisted upon my writing to Dr. Flint, as soon as I arrived in the Free States, and asking him to sell me to her. She said she would sacrifice her house, and all she had in the world, for the sake of having me safe with my children in any part of the world. If she could only live to know *that* she could die in peace. I promised the dear old faithful friend that I would write to her as soon as I arrived, and put the letter in a safe way to reach her, but in my own mind I resolved that not another cent of her hard earnings should be spent to pay rapacious slaveholders for what they called their property. And even if I had not been unwilling to buy what I had already a right to possess, common humanity would have prevented me from accepting the generous offer, at the expense of turning my aged relative out of house and home, when she was trembling on the brink of the grave. I was to escape in a vessel, but I forbear to mention any further particulars.

I was in readiness, but the vessel was unexpectedly detained several days. Meantime, news came to town of a most horrible murder committed on a fugitive slave, named James. Charity, the mother of this unfortunate young man, had been an old acquaintance of ours. I have told the shocking particulars of his death, in my description of some of the neighboring slaveholders. My grandmother, always nervously sensitive about runaways, was terribly frightened. She felt sure that a similar fate awaited me, if I did not desist from my enterprise. She sobbed, and groaned, and entreated me not to go. Her excessive fear was somewhat contagious, and my heart was not proof against her extreme agony. I was grievously disappointed, but I promised to relinquish my project. When my friend Peter was apprised of this, he was both disappointed and vexed. He said, that judging from our past experience, it would be a long time before I had such another chance to throw away. I told him it need not be thrown away, that I had a friend concealed nearby, who would be glad enough to take the place that had been provided for me.

    I told him about poor Fanny, and the kind-hearted, noble fellow, who never turned his back upon anybody in distress, white or black, expressed his readiness to help her. Aggie was much surprised when she found that we knew her secret. She was rejoiced to hear of such a chance for Fanny, and arrangements were made for her to go on board the vessel the next night. They both supposed that I had long been at the North, therefore my name was not mentioned in the transaction. Fanny was carried on board at the appointed time, and stowed away in a very small cabin. This accommodation had been purchased at a price that would pay for a voyage to England. But when one proposes to go to fine old England, they stop to calculate whether they can afford the cost of the pleasure, while in making a bargain to escape from slavery, the trembling victim is ready to say, "Take all I have, only don't betray me!" The next morning I peeped through my loophole, and saw that it was dark and cloudy. At night I received news that the wind was ahead, and the vessel had not sailed. I was exceedingly anxious about Fanny, and Peter too, who was running a tremendous risk at my instigation. Next day the wind and weather remained the same. Poor Fanny had been half-dead with fright when they carried her on board, and I could readily imagine how she must be suffering now. Grandmother came often to my den, to say how thankful she was I did not go. On the third morning she rapped for me to come down to the storeroom. The poor old sufferer was breaking down under her weight of trouble. She was easily flurried now. I found her in a nervous, excited state, but I was not aware that she had forgotten to lock the door behind her, as usual. She was exceedingly worried about the detention of the vessel. She was afraid all would be discovered, and then Fanny, and Peter, and I, would all be tortured to death, and Phillip would be utterly ruined, and her house would be torn down. Poor Peter! If he should die such a horrible death as the poor slave James had lately done, and all for his kindness in trying to help me, how dreadful it would be for us all! Alas, the thought was familiar to me, and had sent many a sharp pang through my heart. I tried to suppress my own anxiety, and speak soothingly to her. She brought in some allusion to Aunt Nancy, the dear daughter she had recently buried, and then she lost all control of herself. As she stood there, trembling and sobbing, a voice from the piazza called out, "Whar is you, Aunt Marthy?" Grandmother was startled, and in her agitation opened the door, without thinking of me. In stepped Jenny, the mischievous housemaid, who had tried to enter my room, when I was concealed in the house of my white benefactress. "I's bin huntin ebery whar for you, Aunt Marthy," said she. "My missis wants you to send her some crackers." I had slunk down behind a barrel, which entirely screened me, but I imagined that Jenny was looking directly at the spot, and my heart beat violently. My grandmother immediately thought what she had done, and went out quickly with Jenny to count the crackers locking the door after her. She returned to me, in a few minutes, the perfect picture of despair. "Poor child!" she exclaimed, "my carelessness has ruined you. The boat ain't gone yet. Get ready immediately, and go with Fanny. I ain't got another word to say against it now, for there's no telling what may happen this day." Uncle Phillip was sent for, and he agreed with his mother in thinking that Jenny would inform Dr. Flint in less than twenty-four hours. He advised getting me on board the boat, if possible, if not, I had better keep very still in my den, where they could not find me without tearing the house down. He said it would not do for him to move in the matter, because suspicion would be immediately excited, but he promised to communicate with Peter.

I felt reluctant to apply to him again, having implicated him too much already, but there seemed to be no alternative. Vexed as Peter had been by my indecision, he was true to his generous nature, and said at once that he would do his best to help me, trusting I should show myself a stronger woman this time. He immediately proceeded to the wharf, and found that the wind had shifted, and the vessel was slowly beating down stream. On some pretext of urgent necessity, he offered two boatmen a dollar apiece to catch up with her. He was of lighter complexion than the boatmen he hired, and when the captain saw them coming so rapidly, he thought officers were pursuing his vessel in search of the runaway slave he had on board. They hoisted sails, but the boat gained upon them, and the indefatigable Peter sprang on board. The captain at once recognized him.

Peter asked him to go below, to speak about a bad bill he had given him. When he told his errand, the captain replied, "Why, the woman's here already, and I've put her where you or the devil would have a tough job to find her?" "But it is another woman I want to bring," said Peter. "*She* is in great distress, too, and you shall be paid anything within reason, if you'll stop and take her." "What's her name?" inquired the captain. "Linda," he replied. "That's the name of the woman already here," rejoined the captain. "By George! I believe you mean to betray me." "O!" exclaimed Peter, "God knows I wouldn't harm a hair of your head. I am too grateful to you. But there really *is* another woman in great danger. Do have the humanity to stop and take her!"

After a while they came to an understanding. Fanny, not dreaming I was anywhere about in that region, had assumed my name, though she called herself Johnson. "Linda is a common name," said Peter, "and the woman I want to bring is Linda Brent." The captain agreed to wait at a certain place till evening, being handsomely paid for his detention. Of course, the day was an anxious one for us all. But we concluded that if Jenny had seen me, she would be too wise to let her mistress know of it, and that she probably would not get a chance to see Dr. Flint's family till evening, for I knew very well what were the rules in that household. I afterwards believed that she did not see me, for nothing ever came of it, and she was one of those base characters that would have jumped to betray a suffering fellow being for the sake of thirty pieces of silver. I made all my arrangements to go on board as soon as it was dusk. The intervening time I resolved to spend with my son. I had not spoken to him for seven years, though I had been under the same roof, and seen him every day, when I was well enough to sit at the loophole. I did not dare to venture beyond the storeroom, so they brought him there, and locked us up together, in a place concealed from the piazza door. It was an agitating interview for both of us. After we had talked and wept together for a little while, he said, "Mother, I'm glad you're going away. I wish I could go with you. I knew you was here, and I have been *so* afraid they would come and catch you!" I was greatly surprised, and asked him how he had found it out. He replied, "I was standing under the eaves, one day, before Ellen went away, and I heard somebody cough up over the woodshed. I don't know what made me think it was you, but I did think so. I missed Ellen, the night before she went away, and grandmother brought her back into the room in the night, and I thought maybe she'd been to see *you*, before she went, for I heard grandmother whisper to her, 'Now go to sleep, and remember never to tell.' "

I asked him if he ever mentioned his suspicions to his sister. He said he never did, but after he heard the cough, if he saw her playing with other children on that side of the house, he always tried to coax her round to the other side, for fear they would hear me cough, too. He said he had kept a close lookout for Dr. Flint, and if he saw him speak to a constable, or a patrol, he always told grandmother. I now recollected that I had seen him manifest uneasiness, when people were on that side of the house, and I had at the time been puzzled to conjecture a motive for his actions. Such prudence may seem extraordinary in a boy of twelve years, but slaves, being surrounded by mysteries, deceptions, and dangers, early learn to be suspicious and watchful, and prematurely cautious and cunning. He had never asked a question of grandmother, or Uncle Phillip, and I had often heard him chime in with other children, when they spoke of my being at the North. I told him I was now really going to the Free States, and if he was a good, honest boy, and a loving child to his dear old grandmother, the Lord would bless him, and bring him to me, and we and Ellen would live together. He began to tell me that grandmother had not eaten anything all day. While he was speaking, the door was unlocked, and she came in with a small bag of money, which she wanted me to take. I begged her to keep a part of it, at least, to pay for Benny's being sent to the North, but she insisted, while her tears were falling fast, that I should take the whole. "You may be sick among strangers," she said, "and they would send you to the poorhouse to die."

Ah, that good grandmother! For the last time I went up to my nook. Its desolate appearance no longer chilled me, for the light of hope had risen in my soul. Yet, even with the blessed prospect of freedom before me, I felt very sad at leaving forever that old homestead, where I had been sheltered so long by the dear old grandmother, where I had dreamed my first young dream of love, and where, after that had faded away, my children came to twine themselves so closely round my desolate heart.

As the hour approached for me to leave, I again descended to the storeroom. My grandmother and Benny were there. She took me by the hand, and said, "Linda, let us pray." We knelt down together, with my child pressed to my heart, and my other arm round the faithful, loving old friend I was about to leave forever. On no other occasion has it ever been my lot to listen to so fervent a supplication for mercy and protection. It thrilled through my heart, and inspired me with trust in God.

Peter was waiting for me in the street. I was soon by his side, faint in body, but strong of purpose. I did not look back upon the old place, though I felt that I should never see it again.

☐☐☐☐☐☐☐☐☐☐

I never could tell how we reached the wharf. My brain was all of a whirl, and my limbs tottered under me. At an appointed place we met my Uncle Phillip, who had started before us on a different route, that he might reach the wharf first, and give us timely warning if there was any danger. A rowboat was in readiness. As I was about to step in, I felt something pull me gently, and turning round I saw Benny, looking pale and anxious. He whispered in my ear, "I've been peeping into the doctor's window, and he's at home. Goodbye, mother. Don't cry, I'll come." He hastened away. I clasped the hand of my good uncle, to whom I owed so much, and of Peter, the brave, generous friend who had volunteered to run such terrible risks to secure my safety. To this day I remember how his bright face beamed with joy, when he told me he had discovered a safe method for me to escape. Yet that intelligent, enterprising, noble-hearted man was a chattel! Liable, by the laws of a country that calls itself civilized, to be sold with horses and pigs! We parted in silence. Our hearts were all too full for words! Swiftly the boat glided over the water. After a while, one of the sailors said, "Don't be downhearted, madam. We will take you safely to your husband." At first I could not imagine what he meant, but I had presence of mind to think that it probably referred to something the captain had told him, so I thanked him, and said I hoped we should have pleasant weather. When I entered the vessel the captain came forward to meet me. He was an elderly man, with a pleasant countenance. He showed me to little box of a cabin, where sat my friend Fanny. She started as if she had seen a specter. She gazed on me in utter astonishment, and exclaimed, "Linda, can this be *you*? Or is it your ghost?" When we were locked in each other's arms, my overwrought feelings could no longer be restrained. My sobs reached the ears of the captain, who came and very kindly reminded us, that for his safety, as well as our own, it would be prudent for us not to attract any attention. He said that when there was a sail in sight he wished us to keep below, but at other times, he had no objection to our being on deck. He assured us that he would keep a good lookout, and if we acted prudently, he thought we should be in no danger. He had represented us as women going to meet our husbands. We thanked him, and promised to observe carefully all the directions he gave us.

Fanny and I now talked by ourselves, low and quietly, in our little cabin. She told me of the sufferings she had gone through in making her escape, and of her terrors while she was concealed in her mother's house. Above all, she dwelt on the agony of separation from all her children on that dreadful auction day. She could scarcely credit me, when I told her of the place where I had passed nearly seven years. "We have the same sorrows," said I. "No," replied she, "you are going to see your children soon, and there is no hope that I shall ever even hear from mine." The vessel was soon underway, but we made slow progress. The wind was against us. I should not have cared for this, if we had been out of sight of the town, but until there were miles of water between us and our enemies, we were filled with constant apprehensions that the constables would come on board. Neither could I feel quite at ease with the captain and his men. I was an entire stranger to that class of people, and I had heard that sailors were rough, and sometimes cruel. We were so completely in their power, that if they were bad men, our situation would be dreadful. Now that the captain was paid for our passage, might he not be tempted to make more money by giving us up to those who claimed us as property? I was naturally of a confiding disposition, but slavery had made me suspicious of everybody. Fanny did not share my distrust of the captain or his men. She said she was afraid at first, but she had been on board three days while the vessel lay in the dock, and nobody had betrayed her, or treated her otherwise than kindly. The captain soon came to advise us to go on deck for fresh air. His friendly and respectful manner, combined with Fanny's testimony, reassured me, and we went with him. He placed us in a comfortable seat, and occasionally entered into conversation. He told us he was a Southerner by birth, and had spent the greater part of his life in the Slave States, and that he had recently lost a brother who traded in slaves. "But," said he, "it is a pitiable and degrading business, and I always felt ashamed to acknowledge my brother in connection with it." As we passed Snaky Swamp, he pointed to it, and said, "There is a slave territory that defies all the laws." I thought of the terrible days I had spent there, and though it was not called Dismal Swamp, it made me feel very dismal as I looked at it. I shall never forget that night. The balmy air of spring was so refreshing! And how shall I describe my sensations when we were fairly sailing on Chesapeake Bay? O, the beautiful sunshine! The exhilarating breeze! and I could enjoy them without fear or restraint. I had never realized what grand things air and sunlight are till I had been deprived of them.

Ten days after we left land we were approaching Philadelphia. The captain said we should arrive there in the night, but he thought we had better wait till morning, and go on shore in broad daylight, as the best way to avoid suspicion. I replied, "You know best. But will you stay on board and protect us?" He saw that I was suspicious, and he said he was sorry, now that he had brought us to the end of our voyage, to find I had so little confidence in him. Ah, if he had ever been a slave he would have known how difficult it was to trust a white man. He assured us that we might sleep through the night without fear, that he would take care we were not left unprotected. Be it said to the honor of this captain, Southerner as he was, that if Fanny and I had been white ladies, and our passage lawfully engaged, he could not have treated us more respectfully. My intelligent friend, Peter, had rightly estimated the character of the man to whose honor he had intrusted us. The next morning I was on deck as soon as the day dawned. I called Fanny to see the sunrise, for the first time in our lives, on free soil, for such I *then* believed it to be. We watched the reddening sky, and saw the great orb come up slowly out of the water, as it seemed. Soon the waves began to sparkle, and everything caught the beautiful glow. Before us lay the city of strangers. We looked at each other, and the eyes of both were moistened with tears. We had escaped from slavery and we supposed ourselves to be safe from the hunters.

But we were alone in the world, and we had left dear ties behind us, ties cruelly sundered by the demon slavery.

I had heard that the poor slave had many friends at the North. I trusted we should find some of them. Meantime, we would take it for granted that all were friends, till they proved to the contrary. I sought out the kind captain, thanked him for his attentions, and told him I should never cease to be grateful for the service he had rendered us. I gave him a message to the friends I had left at home, and he promised to deliver it.

We were placed in a rowboat, and in about fifteen minutes were landed on a wood wharf in Philadelphia. As I stood looking round, the friendly captain touched me on the shoulder, and said, "There is a respectable-looking colored man behind you. I will speak to him about the New York trains, and tell him you wish to go directly on." I thanked him, and asked him to direct me to some shops where I could buy gloves and veils. He did so, and said he would talk with the colored man till I returned. I made what haste I could. Constant exercise on board the vessel, and frequent rubbing with salt water, had nearly restored the use of my limbs. The noise of the great city confused me, but I found the shops, and bought some double veils and gloves for Fanny and myself. The shop man told me they were so many levies.

I had never heard the word before, but I did not tell him so. I thought if he knew I was a stranger he might ask me where I came from. I gave him a gold piece, and when he returned the change, I counted it, and found out how much a levy was. I made my way back to the wharf, where the captain introduced me to the colored man, as the Reverend Jeremiah Durham, minister of Bethel Church. He took me by the hand, as if I had been an old friend. He told us we were too late for the morning cars to New York, and must wait until the evening, or the next morning. He invited me to go home with him, assuring me that his wife would give me a cordial welcome, and for my friend he would provide a home with one of his neighbors. I thanked him for so much kindness to strangers, and told him if I must be detained, I should like to hunt up some people who formerly went from our part of the country. Mr. Durham insisted that I should dine with him, and then he would assist me in finding my friends. The sailors came to bid us goodbye. I shook their hardy hands, with tears in my eyes. They had all been kind to us, and they had rendered us a greater service than they could possibly conceive of. I had never seen so large a city, or been in contact with so many people in the streets. It seemed as if those who passed looked at us with an expression of curiosity. My face was so blistered and peeled, by sitting on deck, in wind and sunshine, that I thought they could not easily decide to what nation I belonged. Mrs. Durham met me with a kindly welcome, without asking any questions. I was tired, and her friendly manner was a sweet refreshment. God bless her! I was sure that she had comforted other weary hearts, before I received her sympathy. She was surrounded by her husband and children, in a home, made sacred by protecting laws. I thought of my own children, and sighed. After dinner Mr. Durham went with me in quest of the friends I had spoken of. They went from my native town, and I anticipated much pleasure in looking on familiar faces. They were not at home, and we retraced our steps through streets delightfully clean. On the way, Mr. Durham observed that I had spoken to him of a daughter I expected to meet, that he was surprised, for I looked so young he had taken me for a single woman. He was approaching a subject on which I was extremely sensitive. He would ask about my husband next, I thought, and if I answered him truly, what would he think of me? I told him I had two children, one in New York the other at the South. He asked some further questions, and I frankly told him some of the most important events of my life. It was painful for me to do it, but I would not deceive him. If he was desirous of being my friend, I thought he ought to know how far I was worthy of it. "Excuse me, if I have tried your feelings," said he. "I did not question you from idle curiosity. I wanted to understand your situation, in order to know whether I could be of any service to you, or your little girl. Your straight-forward answers do you credit, but don't answer everybody so openly. It might give some heartless people a pretext for treating you with contempt." That word *contempt* burned me like coals of fire. I replied, "God alone knows how I have suffered, and He, I trust, will forgive me. If I am permitted to have my children, I intend to be a good mother, and to live in such a manner that people cannot treat me with contempt." "I respect your sentiments," said he. "Place your trust in God, and be governed by good principles, and you will not fail to find friends." When we reached home, I went to my room, glad to shut out the world for a while. The words he had spoken made an indelible impression upon me. They brought up great shadows from the mournful past. In the midst of my meditations I was startled by a knock at the door. Mrs. Durham entered, her face all beaming with kindness, to say that there was an anti-slavery friend downstairs, who would like to see me. I overcame my dread of encountering strangers, and went with her.

Many questions were asked concerning my experiences and my escape from slavery, but I observed how careful they all were not to say anything that might wound my feelings. How gratifying this was, can be fully understood only by those who have been accustomed to be treated as if they were not included within the pale of human beings. The anti-slavery friend had come to inquire into my plans, and to offer assistance, if needed. Fanny was comfortably established, for the present, with a friend of Mr. Durham. The Anti-Slavery Society agreed to pay her expenses to New York. The same was offered to me, but I declined to accept it, telling them that my grandmother had given me sufficient to pay my expenses to the end of my journey. We were urged to remain in Philadelphia a few days, until some suitable escort could be found for us. I gladly accepted the proposition, for I had a dread of meeting slaveholders, and some dread also of railroads. I had never entered a railroad car in my life, and it seemed to me quite an important event.

That night I sought my pillow with feelings I had never carried to it before. I verily believed myself to be a free woman. I was wakeful for a long time, and I had no sooner fallen asleep, than I was roused by fire bells. I jumped up, and hurried on my clothes. Where I came from, everybody hastened to dress themselves on such occasions. The white people thought a great fire might be used as a good opportunity for insurrection, and that it was best to be in readiness, and the colored people were ordered out to labor in extinguishing the flames. There was but one engine in our town, and colored women and children were often required to drag it to the river's edge and fill it.

Mrs. Durham's daughter slept in the same room with me, and seeing that she slept through all the din, I thought it was my duty to wake her. "What's the matter?" said she, rubbing her eyes. "They're screaming fire in the streets, and the bells are ringing," I replied. "What of that?" said she, drowsily. "We are used to it. We never get up, without the fire is very near. What good would it do?" I was quite surprised that it was not necessary for us to go and help fill the engine. I was an ignorant child, just beginning to learn how things went on in great cities.

At daylight, I heard women crying fresh fish, berries, radishes, and various other things. All this was new to me. I dressed myself at an early hour, and sat at the window to watch that unknown tide of life. Philadelphia seemed to me a wonderfully great place. At the breakfast table, my idea of going out to drag the engine was laughed over, and I joined in the mirth. I went to see Fanny, and found her so well-contented among her new friends that she was in no haste to leave. I was also very happy with my kind hostess. She had, had advantages for education, and was vastly my superior. Every day, almost every hour, I was adding to my little stock of knowledge. She took me out to see the city as much as she deemed prudent. One day she took me to an artist's room, and showed me the portraits of some of her children. I had never seen any paintings of colored people before, and they seemed to me beautiful. At the end of five days, one of Mrs. Durham's friends offered to accompany us to New York the following morning. As I held the hand of my good hostess in a parting clasp, I longed to know whether her husband had repeated to her what I had told him. I supposed he had, but she never made any allusion to it. I presume it was the delicate silence of womanly sympathy. When Mr. Durham handed us our tickets, he said, "I am afraid you will have a disagreeable ride, but I could not procure tickets for the first class cars." Supposing I had not given him enough money, I offered more. "O, no," said he, "they could not be had for any money. They don't allow colored people in the first class cars." This was the first chill to my enthusiasm about the Free States. Colored people were allowed to ride in a filthy box behind white people at the South, but there they were not required to pay. It made me sad to find how the North aped the customs of slavery. We were stowed away in a large, rough car, with windows on each side, too high for us to look out without standing up. It was crowded with people, apparently of all nations. There were plenty of beds and cradles, containing screaming and kicking babies. Every other man had a cigar or pipe in his mouth, and jugs of whiskey were handed round freely. The fumes of the whiskey and the dense tobacco smoke were sickening to my senses, and my mind was equally nauseated by the coarse jokes and ribald songs around me. It was a very disagreeable ride. Since that time there has been some improvement in these matters.

When we arrived in New York, I was half crazed by the crowd of coachmen calling out, "Carriage, ma'am?" We bargained with one to take us to Sullivan Street for twelve shillings. A burly Irishman stepped up and said, "I'll tak' ye for sax shillings." The reduction of half the price was an object to us, and we asked if he could take us right away. "Troth an I will, ladies," he replied. I noticed that the hackmen smiled at each other, and I inquired whether his conveyance was decent. "Yes, it's dacent it is, marm. Devil a bit would I be after takin' ladies in a cab that was not dacent." We gave him our checks. He went for the baggage and soon reappeared, saying, "This way, if you plase, ladies." We followed, and found our trunks on a truck, and we were invited to take our seats on them. We told him that was not what we bargained for, and he must take the trunks off. He swore they should not be touched till we had paid him six shillings. In our situation it was not prudent to attract attention, and I was about to pay him what he required, when a man nearby shook his head for me not to do it. After a great ado we got rid of the Irishman and had our trunks fastened on a hack. We had been recommended to a boardinghouse in Sullivan Street, and thither we drove. There Fanny and I separated. The Anti-Slavery Society provided a home for her, and I afterwards heard of her in prosperous circumstances. I sent for an old friend from my part of the country, who had for some time been doing business in New York. He came immediately. I told him I wanted to go to my daughter, and asked him to aid me in procuring an interview.

 I cautioned him not to let it be known to the family that I had just arrived from the South, because they supposed I had been at the North seven years. He told me there was a colored woman in Brooklyn who came from the same town I did, and I had better go to her house, and have my daughter meet me there. I accepted the proposition thankfully, and he agreed to escort me to Brooklyn. We crossed Fulton Ferry, went up Myrtle Avenue, and stopped at the house he designated. I was just about to enter, when two girls passed. My friend called my attention to them. I turned, and recognized in the eldest, Sarah, the daughter of a woman who used to live with my grandmother, but who had left the South years ago. Surprised and rejoiced at this unexpected meeting, I threw my arms round her, and inquired concerning her mother. "You take no notice of the other girl," said my friend. I turned, and there stood my Ellen! I pressed her to my heart, then held her away from me to take a look at her.

 She had changed a good deal in the two years since I parted from her. Signs of neglect could be discerned by eyes less observing than a mother's. My friend invited us all to go into the house, but Ellen said she had been sent of an errand, which she would do as quickly as possible, and go home and ask Mrs. Hobbs to let her come and see me. It was agreed that I should send for her the next day. Her companion, Sarah, hastened to tell her mother of my arrival. When I entered the house, I found the mistress of it absent, and I waited for her return. Before I saw her, I heard her saying, "Where is Linda Brent? I used to know her father and mother." Soon Sarah came with her mother. So there was quite a company of us, all from my grandmother's neighborhood. These friends gathered round me and questioned me eagerly. They laughed, they cried, and they shouted.

They thanked God that I had got away from my persecutors and was safe on Long Island. It was a day of great excitement. How different from the silent days I had passed in my dreary den! The next morning was Sunday.

My first waking thoughts were occupied with the note I was to send to Mrs. Hobbs, the lady with whom Ellen lived. That I had recently come into that vicinity was evident, otherwise I should have sooner inquired for my daughter. It would not do to let them know I had just arrived from the South, for that would involve the suspicion of my having been harbored there, and might bring trouble, if not ruin, on several people. I like a straightforward course, and am always reluctant to resort to subterfuges. So far as my ways have been crooked, I charge them all upon slavery. It was that system of violence and wrong which now left me no alternative but to enact a falsehood. I began my note by stating that I had recently arrived from Canada, and was very desirous to have my daughter come to see me. She came and brought a message from Mrs. Hobbs, inviting me to her house, and assuring me that I need not have any fears.

The conversation I had with my child did not leave my mind at ease. When I asked if she was well-treated, she answered yes, but there was no heartiness in the tone, and it seemed to me that she said it from an unwillingness to have me troubled on her account. Before she left me, she asked very earnestly, "Mother, when will you take me to live with you?" It made me sad to think that I could not give her a home till I went to work and earned the means, and that might take me a long time. When she was placed with Mrs. Hobbs, the agreement was that she should be sent to school. She had been there two years, and was now nine years old, and she scarcely knew her letters. There was no excuse for this, for there were good public schools in Brooklyn, to which she could have been sent without expense. She stayed with me till dark, and I went home with her. I was received in a friendly manner by the family, and all agreed in saying that Ellen was a useful, good girl. Mrs. Hobbs looked me coolly in the face, and said, "I suppose you know that my cousin, Mr. Sands, has *given* her to my eldest daughter. She will make a nice waiting maid for her when she grows up." I did not answer a word.

How *could* she, who knew by experience the strength of a mother's love, and who was perfectly aware of the relation Mr. Sands bore to my children—how *could* she look me in the face, while she thrust such a dagger into my heart? I was no longer surprised that they had kept her in such a state of ignorance. Mr. Hobbs had formerly been wealthy, but he had failed, and afterwards obtained a subordinate situation in the Custom House. Perhaps they expected to return to the South someday, and Ellen's knowledge was quite sufficient for a slave's condition. I was impatient to go to work and earn money, that I might change the uncertain position of my children. Mr. Sands had not kept his promise to emancipate them. I had also been deceived about Ellen. What security had I with regard to Benjamin?

I felt that I had none. I returned to my friend's house in an uneasy state of mind. In order to protect my children, it was necessary that I should own myself. I called myself free, and sometimes felt so, but I knew I was insecure. I sat down that night and wrote a civil letter to Dr. Flint, asking him to state the lowest terms on which he would sell me, and as I belonged by law to his daughter, I wrote to her also, making a similar request.

Since my arrival at the North I had not been unmindful of my dear brother William. I had made diligent inquiries for him, and having heard of him in Boston, I went thither. When I arrived there, I found he had gone to New Bedford. I wrote to that place and was informed he had gone on a whaling voyage, and would not return for some months. I went back to New York to get employment near Ellen. I received an answer from Dr. Flint, which gave me no encouragement. He advised me to return and submit myself to my rightful owners, and then any request I might make would be granted. I lent this letter to a friend, who lost it, otherwise I would present a copy to my readers.

My greatest anxiety now was to obtain employment. My health was greatly improved, though my limbs continued to trouble me with swelling whenever I walked much. The greatest difficulty in my way was, that those who employed strangers required a recommendation, and in my peculiar position, I could, of course, obtain no certificates from the families I had so faithfully served. One day an acquaintance told me of a lady who wanted a nurse for her babe, and I immediately applied for the situation. The lady told me she preferred to have one who had been a mother, and accustomed to the care of infants. I told her I had nursed two babes of my own. She asked me many questions, but, to my great relief, did not require a recommendation from my former employers. She told me she was an English woman, and that was a pleasant circumstance to me, because I had heard they had less prejudice against color than Americans entertained. It was agreed that we should try each other for a week.

The trial proved satisfactory to both parties, and I was engaged for a month. The heavenly Father had been most merciful to me in leading me to this place. Mrs. Bruce was a kind and gentle lady, and proved a true and sympathizing friend. Before the stipulated month expired, the necessity of passing up and downstairs frequently, caused my limbs to swell so painfully, that I became unable to perform my duties. Many ladies would have thoughtlessly discharged me, but Mrs. Bruce made arrangements to save me steps, and employed a physician to attend upon me. I had not yet told her that I was a fugitive slave. She noticed that I was often sad, and kindly inquired the cause. I spoke of being separated from my children, and from relatives who were dear to me, but I did not mention the constant feeling of insecurity which oppressed my spirits. I longed for someone to confide in, but I had been so deceived by white people, that I had lost all confidence in them. If they spoke kind words to me, I thought it was for some selfish purpose. I had entered this family with the distrustful feelings I had brought with me out of slavery but ere six months had passed, I found that the gentle deportment of Mrs. Bruce and the smiles of her lovely babe were thawing my chilled heart. My narrow mind also began to expand under the influences of her intelligent conversation, and the opportunities for reading, which were gladly allowed me whenever I had leisure from my duties. I gradually became more energetic and more cheerful. The old feeling of insecurity, especially with regard to my children, often threw its dark shadow across my sunshine. Mrs. Bruce offered me a home for Ellen, but pleasant as it would have been, I did not dare to accept it, for fear of offending the Hobbs family. Their knowledge of my precarious situation placed me in their power, and I felt that it was important for me to keep on the right side of them, till, by dint of labor and economy, I could make a home for my children. I was far from feeling satisfied with Ellen's situation. She was not well-cared for. She sometimes came to New York to visit me, but she generally brought a request from Mrs. Hobbs that I would buy her a pair of shoes, or some article of clothing. This was accompanied by a promise of payment when Mr. Hobbs's salary at the Custom House became due, but somehow or other the payday never came. Thus many dollars of my earnings were expended to keep my child comfortably clothed. That, however, was a slight trouble, compared with the fear that their pecuniary embarrassments might induce them to sell my precious young daughter. I knew they were in constant communication with Southerners, and had frequent opportunities to do it. I have stated that when Dr. Flint put Ellen in jail, at two years old, she had an inflammation of the eyes, occasioned by measles. This disease still troubled her, and kind Mrs. Bruce proposed that she should come to New York for a while, to be under the care of Dr. Elliott, a well-known oculist. It did not occur to me that there was anything improper in a mother's making such a request, but Mrs. Hobbs was very angry, and refused to let her go. Situated as I was, it was not politic to insist upon it. I made no complaint, but I longed to be entirely free to act a mother's part towards my children. The next time I went over to Brooklyn, Mrs. Hobbs, as if to apologize for her anger, told me she had employed her own physician to attend to Ellen's eyes, and that she had refused my request because she did not consider it safe to trust her in New York. I accepted the explanation in silence, but she had told me that my child *belonged* to her daughter, and I suspected that her real motive was a fear of my conveying her property away from her. Perhaps I did her injustice, but my knowledge of Southerners made it difficult for me to feel otherwise. Sweet and bitter were mixed in the cup of my life, and I was thankful that it had ceased to be entirely bitter. I loved Mrs. Bruce's babe. When it laughed and crowed in my face, and twined its little tender arms confidingly about my neck, it made me think of the time when Benny and Ellen were babies, and my wounded heart was soothed. One bright morning, as I stood at the window, tossing baby in my arms, my attention was attracted by a young man in sailor's dress, who was closely observing every house as he passed. I looked at him earnestly. Could it be my brother William? It *must* be he—and yet, how changed! I placed the baby safely, flew downstairs, opened the front door, beckoned to the sailor, and in less than a minute I was clasped in my brother's arms. How much we had to tell each other! How we laughed, and how we cried, over each other's adventures! I took him to Brooklyn, and again saw him with Ellen, the dear child whom he had loved and tended so carefully, while I was shut up in my miserable den.

He stayed in New York a week. His feelings of affection for me and Ellen were as lively as ever. There are no bonds so strong as those which are formed by suffering together.

❑❑❑❑❑❑❑❑❑❑

My young mistress, Miss Emily Flint, did not return any answer to my letter requesting her to consent to my being sold. But after a while, I received a reply, which purported to be written by her younger brother. In order rightly to enjoy the contents of this letter, the reader must bear in mind that the Flint family supposed I had been at the North many years. They had no idea that I knew of the doctor's three excursions to New York in search of me, that I had heard his voice, when he came to borrow five hundred dollars for that purpose, and that I had seen him pass on his way to the steamboat. Neither were they aware that all the particulars of Aunt Nancy's death and burial were conveyed to me at the time they occurred. I have kept the letter, of which I herewith subjoin a copy—*Your letter to sister was received a few days ago. I gather from it that you are desirous of returning to your native place, among your friends and relatives. We were all gratified with the contents of your letter, and let me assure you that if any members of the family have had any feeling of resentment towards you, they feel it no longer. We all sympathize with you in your unfortunate condition, and are ready to do all in our power to make you contented and happy. It is difficult for you to return home as a free person. If you were purchased by your grandmother, it is doubtful whether you would be permitted to remain, although it would be lawful for you to do so. If a servant should be allowed to purchase herself, after absenting herself so long from her owners, and return free, it would have an injurious effect. From your letter, I think your situation must be hard and uncomfortable. Come home. You have it in your power to be reinstated in our affections. We would receive you with open arms and tears of joy. You need not apprehend any unkind treatment, as we have not put ourselves to any trouble or expense to get you. Had we done so, perhaps we should feel otherwise. You know my sister was always attached to you, and that you were never treated as a slave. You were never put to hard work, nor exposed to field labor. On the contrary, you were taken into the house, and treated as one of us, and almost as free, and we, at least, felt that you were above disgracing yourself by running away. Believing you may be induced to come home voluntarily has induced me to write for my sister. The family will be rejoiced to see you, and your poor old grandmother expressed a great desire to have you come, when she heard your letter read. In her old age she needs the consolation of having her children round her. Doubtless you have heard of the death of your aunt. She was a faithful servant, and a faithful member of the Episcopal Church. In her Christian life she taught us how to live—and, O, too high the price of knowledge, she taught us how to die! Could you have seen us round her deathbed, with her mother, all mingling our tears in one common stream, you would have thought the same heartfelt tie existed between a master and his servant, as between a mother and her child. But this subject is too painful to dwell upon. I must bring my letter to a close. If you are contented to stay away from your old grandmother, your child, and the friends who love you, stay where you are. We shall never trouble ourselves to apprehend you. But should you prefer to come home, we will do all that we can to make you happy. If you do not wish to remain in the family, I know that father, by our persuasion, will be induced to let you be purchased by any person you may choose in our community. You will please answer this as soon as possible, and let us know your decision. Sister sends much love to you. In the meantime believe me your sincere friend and well-wisher.* This letter was signed by Emily's brother, who was as yet a mere lad. I knew, by the style, that it was not written by a person of his age, and though the writing was disguised, I had been made too unhappy by it, in former years, not to recognize at once the hand of Dr. Flint.

O, the hypocrisy of slaveholders! Did the old fox suppose I was goose enough to go into such a trap? Verily, he relied too much on "the stupidity of the African race." I did not return the family of Flints any thanks for their cordial invitation—a remissness for which I was, no doubt, charged with base ingratitude. Not long afterwards I received a letter from one of my friends at the South, informing me that Dr. Flint was about to visit the North. The letter had been delayed, and I supposed he might be already on the way. Mrs. Bruce did not know I was a fugitive. I told her that important business called me to Boston where my brother then was, and asked permission to bring a friend to supply my place as nurse, for a fortnight.

I started on my journey immediately, and as soon as I arrived, I wrote to my grandmother that if Benny came, he must be sent to Boston. I knew she was only waiting for a good chance to send him North, and, fortunately, she had the legal power to do so, without asking leave of anybody. She was a free woman and when my children were purchased, Mr. Sands preferred to have the bill of sale drawn up in her name. It was conjectured that he advanced the money, but it was not known. At the South, a gentleman may have a shoal of colored children without any disgrace, but if he is known to purchase them, with the view of setting them free, the example is thought to be dangerous to their "peculiar institution" and he becomes unpopular.

There was a good opportunity to send Benny in a vessel coming directly to New York. He was put on board with a letter to a friend, who was requested to see him off to Boston. Early one morning, there was a loud rap at my door, and in rushed Benjamin, all out of breath. "O mother!" he exclaimed, "Here I am! I run all the way, and I come all alone. How d'you do?" O reader, can you imagine my joy? No, you cannot, unless you have been a slave mother. Benjamin rattled away as fast as his tongue could go. "Mother, why don't you bring Ellen here? I went over to Brooklyn to see her, and she felt very bad when I bid her goodbye. She said, 'O Ben, I wish I was going too.' I thought she'd know ever so much, but she don't know so much as I do, for I can read, and she can't. And, mother, I lost all my clothes coming. What can I do to get some more? I 'spose free boys can get along here at the North as well as white boys." I did not like to tell the sanguine, happy little fellow how much he was mistaken. I took him to a tailor, and procured a change of clothes.

The rest of the day was spent in mutual asking and answering of questions, with the wish constantly repeated that the good old grandmother was with us, and frequent injunctions from Benny to write to her immediately, and be sure to tell her everything about his voyage, and his journey to Boston.

Dr. Flint made his visit to New York and made every exertion to call upon me, and invite me to return with him, but not being able to ascertain where I was, his hospitable intentions were frustrated, and the affectionate family, who were waiting for me with "open arms," were doomed to disappointment. As soon as I knew he was safely at home, I placed Benjamin in the care of my brother William, and returned to Mrs. Bruce. There I remained through the winter and spring, endeavoring to perform my duties faithfully, and finding a good degree of happiness in the attractions of baby Mary, the considerate kindness of her excellent mother, and occasional interviews with my darling daughter. But when summer came, the old feeling of insecurity haunted me. It was necessary for me to take little Mary out daily, for exercise and fresh air, and the city was swarming with Southerners, some of whom might recognize me.

Hot weather brings out snakes and slaveholders, and I like one class of the venomous creatures as little as I do the other.

What a comfort it is, to be free to *say* so.

It was a relief to my mind to see preparations for leaving the city. We went to Albany in the steamboat *Knickerbocker*. When the gong sounded for tea, Mrs. Bruce said, "Linda, it is late, and you and baby had better come to the table with me." I replied, "I know it is time baby had her supper, but I had rather not go with you, if you please. I am afraid of being insulted." "O no, not if you are with *me*," she said. I saw several white nurses go with their ladies, and I ventured to do the same. We were at the extreme end of the table. I was no sooner seated, than a gruff voice said, "Get up! You know you are not allowed to sit here." I looked up, and, to my astonishment and indignation, saw that the speaker was a colored man. If his office required him to enforce the by-laws of the boat, he might, at least, have done it politely. I replied, "I shall not get up, unless the captain comes and takes me up." No cup of tea was offered me, but Mrs. Bruce handed me hers and called for another. I looked to see whether the other nurses were treated in a similar manner. They were all properly waited on. Next morning, when we stopped at Troy for breakfast, everybody was making a rush for the table. Mrs. Bruce said, "Take my arm, Linda, and we'll go in together." The landlord heard her, and said, "Madam, will you allow your nurse and baby to take breakfast with my family?" I knew this was to be attributed to my complexion, but he spoke courteously, and therefore I did not mind it. At Saratoga we found the United States Hotel crowded, and Mr. Bruce took one of the cottages belonging to the hotel. I had thought, with gladness, of going to the quiet of the country, where I should meet few people, but here I found myself in the midst of a swarm of Southerners. I looked round me with fear and trembling, dreading to see someone who would recognize me. I was rejoiced to find that we were to stay but a short time. We soon returned to New York, to make arrangements for spending the remainder of the summer at Rockaway. While the laundress was putting the clothes in order, I took an opportunity to go over to Brooklyn to see Ellen. I met her going to a grocery store, and the first words she said, were, "O, mother, don't go to Mrs. Hobbs's. Her brother, Mr. Thorne, has come from the South, and maybe he'll tell where you are." I accepted the warning. I told her I was going away with Mrs. Bruce the next day, and would try to see her when I came back. Being in servitude to the Anglo-Saxon race, I was not put into a "Jim Crow car" on our way to Rockaway, neither was I invited to ride through the streets on the top of trunks in a truck, but every where I found the same manifestations of that cruel prejudice, which so discourages the feelings, and represses the energies of the colored people. We reached Rockaway before dark, and put up at the Pavilion—a large hotel, beautifully situated by the seaside—a great resort of the fashionable world. Thirty or forty nurses were there, of a great variety of nations. Some of the ladies had colored waiting maids and coachmen, but I was the only nurse tinged with the blood of Africa. When the tea bell rang, I took little Mary and followed the other nurses. Supper was served in a long hall (room). A young man, who had the ordering of things, took the circuit of the table two or three times, and finally pointed me to a seat at the lower end of it. As there was but one chair, I sat down and took the child in my lap. Whereupon the young man came to me and said, in the blandest manner possible, "Will you please to seat the little girl in the chair, and stand behind it and feed her? After they have done, you will be shown to the kitchen, where you will have a good supper." This was the climax! I found it hard to preserve my self-control, when I looked round, and saw women who were nurses, as I was, and only one shade lighter in complexion, eyeing me with a defiant look, as if my presence were a contamination. However, I said nothing. I quietly took the child in my arms, went to our room, and refused to go to the table again. Mr. Bruce ordered meals to be sent to the room for little Mary and I. This answered for a few days, but the waiters of the establishment were white, and they soon began to complain, saying they were not hired to wait on Negroes. The landlord requested Mr. Bruce to send me down to my meals, because his servants rebelled against bringing them up, and the colored servants of other boarders were dissatisfied because all were not treated alike. My answer was that the colored servants ought to be dissatisfied with *themselves*, for not having too much self-respect to submit to such treatment, that there was no difference in the price of board for colored and white servants, and there was no justification for difference of treatment. I stayed a month, and finding I was resolved to stand up for my rights, they concluded to treat me well.

Let every colored man and woman do this, and eventually we shall cease to be trampled by our oppressors.

□□□□□□□□□□

After we returned to New York, I took the earliest opportunity to go and see Ellen. I asked to have her called downstairs, for I supposed Mrs. Hobbs's Southern brother might still be there, and I was desirous to avoid seeing him, if possible. But Mrs. Hobbs came to the kitchen, and insisted on my going upstairs. "My brother wants to see you," said she, "and he is sorry you seem to shun him. He knows you are living in New York. He told me to say to you that he owes thanks to good old Aunt Martha for too many little acts of kindness for him to be base enough to betray her grandchild." This Mr. Thorne had become poor and reckless long before he left the South, and such persons had much rather go to one of the faithful old slaves to borrow a dollar, or get a good dinner, than to go to one whom they consider an equal. It was such acts of kindness as these for which he professed to feel grateful to my grandmother. I wished he had kept at a distance, but as he was here, and knew where I was, I concluded there was nothing to be gained by trying to avoid him, on the contrary, it might be the means of exciting his ill will. I followed his sister upstairs. He met me in a very friendly manner, congratulated me on my escape from slavery, and hoped I had a good place, where I felt happy. I continued to visit Ellen as often as I could. She, good thoughtful child, never forgot my hazardous situation, but always kept a vigilant lookout for my safety.

She never made any complaint about her own inconveniences and troubles, but a mother's observing eye easily perceived that she was not happy. On the occasion of one of my visits I found her unusually serious. When I asked her what was the matter, she said nothing was the matter. But I insisted upon knowing what made her look so very grave. Finally, I ascertained that she felt troubled about the dissipation that was continually going on in the house. She was sent to the store very often for rum and brandy, and she felt ashamed to ask for it so often, and Mr. Hobbs and Mr. Thorne drank a great deal, and their hands trembled so that they had to call her to pour out the liquor for them. "But for all that," said she, "Mr. Hobbs is good to me, and I can't help liking him. I feel sorry for him." I tried to comfort her, by telling her that I had laid up a hundred dollars, and that before long I hoped to be able to give her and Benjamin a home, and send them to school. She was always desirous not to add to my troubles more than she could help, and I did not discover till years afterwards that Mr. Thorne's intemperance was not the only annoyance she suffered from him. Though he professed too much gratitude to my grandmother to injure any of her descendants, he had poured vile language into the ears of her innocent great-grandchild. I usually went to Brooklyn to spend Sunday afternoon. One Sunday, I found Ellen anxiously waiting for me near the house. "O, mother," said she, "I've been waiting for you this long time. I'm afraid Mr. Thorne has written to tell Dr. Flint where you are. Make haste and come in. Mrs. Hobbs will tell you all about it!" The story was soon told. While the children were playing in the grapevine arbor, the day before, Mr. Thorne came out with a letter in his hand, which he tore up and scattered about. Ellen was sweeping the yard at the time, and having her mind full of suspicions of him, she picked up the pieces and carried them to the children, saying, "I wonder who Mr. Thorne has been writing to." "I'm sure I don't know, and don't care," replied the oldest of the children, "and I don't see how it concerns you." "But it does concern me," replied Ellen, "for I'm afraid he's been writing to the South about my mother." They laughed at her, and called her a silly thing, but good-naturedly put the fragments of writing together, in order to read them to her.

They were no sooner arranged, than the little girl exclaimed, "I declare, Ellen, I believe you are right." The contents of Mr. Thorne's letter, as nearly as I can remember, were as follows, "*I have seen your slave, Linda, and conversed with her. She can be taken very easily, if you manage prudently. There are enough of us here to swear to her identity as your property. I am a patriot, a lover of my country, and I do this as an act of justice to the laws.*" He concluded by informing the doctor of the street and number where I lived. The children carried the pieces to Mrs. Hobbs, who immediately went to her brother's room for an explanation. He was not to be found. The servants said they saw him go out with a letter in his hand, and they supposed he had gone to the post office. The natural inference was, that he had sent to Dr. Flint a copy of those fragments. When he returned, his sister accused him of it, and he did not deny the charge.

He went immediately to his room, and the next morning he was missing. He had gone over to New York, before any of the family were astir. It was evident that I had no time to lose, and I hastened back to the city with a heavy heart. Again I was to be torn from a comfortable home, and all my plans for the welfare of my children were to be frustrated by that demon slavery! I now regretted that I never told Mrs. Bruce my story. I had not concealed it merely on account of being a fugitive, that would have made her anxious, but it would have excited sympathy in her kind heart. I valued her good opinion, and I was afraid of losing it, if I told her all the particulars of my sad story. But now I felt that it was necessary for her to know how I was situated. I had once left her abruptly, without explaining the reason, and it would not be proper to do it again. I went home resolved to tell her in the morning. But the sadness of my face attracted her attention, and, in answer to her kind inquiries, I poured out my full heart to her, before bedtime. She listened with true womanly sympathy, and told me she would do all she could to protect me. How my heart blessed her! Early the next morning, Judge Vanderpool and Lawyer Hopper were consulted. They said I had better leave the city at once, as the risk would be great if the case came to trial. Mrs. Bruce took me in a carriage to the house of one of her friends, where she assured me I should be safe until my brother could arrive, which would be in a few days. In the interval my thoughts were much occupied with Ellen. She was mine by birth, and she was also mine by Southern law, since my grandmother held the bill of sale that made her so. I did not feel that she was safe unless I had her with me. Mrs. Hobbs, who felt badly about her brother's treachery, yielded to my entreaties, on condition that she should return in ten days. I avoided making any promise. She came to me clad in very thin garments, all outgrown, and with a school satchel on her arm, containing a few articles. It was late in October, and I knew the child must suffer, and not daring to go out in the streets to purchase anything, I took off my own flannel skirt and converted it into one for her. Kind Mrs. Bruce came to bid me goodbye, and when she saw that I had taken off my clothing for my child, the tears came to her eyes. She said, "Wait for me, Linda," and went out. She soon returned with a nice warm shawl and hood for Ellen. Truly, of such souls as hers are the kingdom of heaven. My brother reached New York on Wednesday. Lawyer Hopper advised us to go to Boston by the Stonington route, as there was less Southern travel in that direction. Mrs. Bruce directed her servants to tell all inquirers that I formerly lived there, but had gone from the city. We reached the steamboat *Rhode Island* in safety. That boat employed colored hands, but I knew that colored passengers were not admitted to the cabin. I was very desirous for the seclusion of the cabin, not only on account of exposure to the night air, but also to avoid observation. Lawyer Hopper was waiting on board for us. He spoke to the stewardess, and asked, as a particular favor, that she would treat us well. He said to me, "Go and speak to the captain yourself by and by. Take your little girl with you, and I am sure that he will not let her sleep on deck." With these kind words and a shake of the hand he departed.

The boat was soon on her way, bearing me rapidly from the friendly home where I had hoped to find security and rest. My brother had left me to purchase the tickets, thinking that I might have better success than he would. When the stewardess came to me, I paid what she asked, and she gave me three tickets with clipped corners. In the most unsophisticated manner I said, "You have made a mistake, I asked you for cabin tickets. I cannot possibly consent to sleep on deck with my little daughter."

She assured me there was no mistake. She said on some of the routes colored people were allowed to sleep in the cabin, but not on this route, which was much traveled by the wealthy. I asked her to show me to the captain's office, and she said she would after tea. When the time came, I took Ellen by the hand and went to the captain, politely requesting him to change our tickets, as we should be very uncomfortable on deck. He said it was contrary to their custom, but he would see that we had berths below, he would also try to obtain comfortable seats for us in the cars, of that he was not certain, but he would speak to the conductor about it, when the boat arrived. I thanked him, and returned to the ladies cabin. He came afterwards and told me that the conductor of the cars was on board, that he had spoken to him, and he had promised to take care of us. I was very much surprised at receiving so much kindness. I don't know whether the pleasing face of my little girl had won his heart, or whether the stewardess inferred from Lawyer Hopper's manner that I was a fugitive, and had pleaded with him in my behalf. When the boat arrived at Stonington, the conductor kept his promise, and showed us to seats in the first car, nearest the engine. He asked us to take seats next the door, but as he passed through, we ventured to move on toward the other end of the car.

No incivility was offered us, and we reached Boston in safety. The day after my arrival was one of the happiest of my life. I felt as if I was beyond the reach of the bloodhounds, and, for the first time during many years, I had both my children together with me. They greatly enjoyed their reunion, and laughed and chatted merrily. I watched them with a swelling heart.

Their every motion delighted me. I could not feel safe in New York, and I accepted the offer of a friend, that we should share expenses and keep house together. I represented to Mrs. Hobbs that Ellen must have some schooling, and must remain with me for that purpose. She felt ashamed of being unable to read or spell at her age, so instead of sending her to school with Benny, I instructed her myself till she was fitted to enter an intermediate school. The winter passed pleasantly, while I was busy with my needle, and my children with their books.

☐☐☐☐☐☐☐☐☐☐

In the spring, sad news came to me. Mrs. Bruce was dead. Never again, in this world, should I see her gentle face, or hear her sympathizing voice. I had lost an excellent friend, and little Mary had lost a tender mother. Mr. Bruce wished the child to visit some of her mother's relatives in England, and he was desirous that I should take charge of her. The little motherless one was accustomed to me, and attached to me, and I thought she would be happier in my care than in that of a stranger. I could also earn more in this way than I could by my needle. So I put Benny to a trade, and left Ellen to remain in the house with my friend and go to school. We sailed from New York, and arrived in Liverpool after a pleasant voyage of twelve days. We proceeded directly to London, and took lodgings at the Adelaide Hotel. The supper seemed to me less luxurious than those I had seen in American hotels, but my situation was indescribably more pleasant. For the first time in my life I was in a place where I was treated according to my deportment, without reference to my complexion. I felt as if a great millstone had been lifted from my breast. Ensconced in a pleasant room, with my dear little charge, I laid my head on my pillow, for the first time, with the delightful consciousness of pure, unadulterated freedom. As I had constant care of the child, I had little opportunity to see the wonders of that great city, but I watched the tide of life that flowed through the streets, and found it a strange contrast to the stagnation in our Southern towns. Mr. Bruce took his little daughter to spend some days with friends in Oxford Crescent, and of course it was necessary for me to accompany her. I had heard much of the systematic method of English education, and I was very desirous that my dear Mary should steer straight in the midst of so much propriety. I closely observed her little playmates and their nurses, being ready to take any lessons in the science of good management.

The children were more rosy than American children, but I did not see that they differed materially in other respects. They were like all children—sometimes docile and sometimes wayward. We next went to Steventon, in Berkshire. It was a small town, said to be the poorest in the county. I saw men working in the fields for six shillings, and seven shillings, a week, and women for sixpence, and sevenpence, a day, out of which they boarded themselves. Of course they lived in the most primitive manner, it could not be otherwise, where a woman's wages for an entire day were not sufficient to buy a pound of meat. They paid very low rents, and their clothes were made of the cheapest fabrics, though much better than could have been procured in the United States for the same money. I had heard much about the oppression of the poor in Europe. The people I saw around me were, many of them, among the poorest poor. But when I visited them in their little thatched cottages, I felt that the condition of even the meanest and most ignorant among them was vastly superior to the condition of the most favored slaves in America. They labored hard, but they were not ordered out to toil while the stars were in the sky, and driven and slashed by an overseer, through heat and cold, till the stars shone out again. Their homes were very humble, but they were protected by law. No insolent patrols could come, in the dead of night, and flog them at their pleasure. The father, when he closed his cottage door, felt safe with his family around him. No master or overseer could come and take from him his wife, or his daughter. They must separate to earn their living, but the parents knew where their children were going, and could communicate with them by letters.

The relations of husband and wife, parent and child, were too sacred for the richest noble in the land to violate with impunity. Much was being done to enlighten these poor people. Schools were established among them, and benevolent societies were active in efforts to ameliorate their condition. There was no law forbidding them to learn to read and write, and if they helped each other in spelling out the Bible, they were in no danger of thirty-nine lashes, as was the case with myself and poor, pious, old Uncle Fred. I repeat that the most ignorant and the most destitute of these peasants was a thousand-fold better off than the most pampered American slave. I do not deny that the poor are oppressed in Europe. I am not disposed to paint their condition so rose-colored as the "honorable" Miss Murray paints the condition of the slaves in the United States. A small portion of *my* experience would enable her to read her own pages with anointed eyes. If she were to lay aside her title, and, instead of visiting among the fashionable, become domesticated, as a poor governess, on some plantation in Louisiana or Alabama, she would see and hear things that would make her tell quite a different story. My visit to England is a memorable event in my life, from the fact of my having there received strong religious impressions. The contemptuous manner in which the communion had been administered to colored people, in my native place, the church membership of Dr. Flint, and others like him, and the buying and selling of slaves, by professed ministers of the gospel, had given me a prejudice against the Episcopal Church. The whole service seemed to me a mockery and a sham. But my home in Steventon was in the family of a clergyman, who was a true disciple of Jesus. The beauty of his daily life inspired me with faith in the genuineness of Christian professions. Grace entered my heart, and I knelt at the communion table, I trust, in true humility of soul. I remained abroad ten months, which was much—longer than I had anticipated. During all that time, I never saw the slightest symptom of prejudice against color. Indeed, I entirely forgot it, till the time came for us to return to America.

☐☐☐☐☐☐☐☐☐☐

We had a tedious winter passage, and from the distance, specters seemed to rise up on the shores of the United States. It is a sad feeling to be afraid of one's native country. We arrived in New York safely, and I hastened to Boston to look after my children. I found Ellen well, and improving at her school, but Benny was not there to welcome me. He had been left at a good place to learn a trade, and for several months everything worked well. He was liked by the master, and was a favorite with his fellow-apprentices, but one day they accidentally discovered a fact they had never before suspected—that he was colored! This at once transformed him into a different being. Some of the apprentices were Americans, others American-born Irish, and it was offensive to their dignity to have a "nigger" among them, after they had been told that he *was* a "nigger." They began by treating him with silent scorn, and finding that he returned the same, they resorted to insults and abuse. He was too spirited a boy to stand that, and he went off. Being desirous to do something to support himself, and having no one to advise him, he shipped for a whaling voyage. When I received these tidings I shed many tears, and bitterly reproached myself for having left him so long. But I had done it for the best, and now all I could do was to pray to the heavenly Father to guide and protect him.

Not long after my return, I received the following letter from Miss Emily Flint, now Mrs. Dodge—*In this you will recognize the hand of your friend and mistress. Having heard that you had gone with a family to Europe, I have waited to hear of your return to write to you. I should have answered the letter you wrote to me long since, but as I could not then act independently of my father, I knew there could be nothing done satisfactory to you. There were persons here who were willing to buy you and run the risk of getting you. To this I would not consent. I have always been attached to you, and would not like to see you the slave of another, or have unkind treatment. I am married now, and can protect you. My husband expects to move to Virginia this spring, where we think of settling. I am very anxious that you should come and live with me. If you are not willing to come, you may purchase yourself, but I should prefer having you live with me. If you come, you may, if you like, spend a month with your grandmother and friends, then come to me in Norfolk, Virginia. Think this over, and write as soon as possible, and let me know the conclusion. Hoping that your children are well, I remain you friend and mistress.* Of course I did not write to return thanks for this cordial invitation. I felt insulted to be thought stupid enough to be caught by such professions.

Come up into my parlor, said the spider to the fly, tis the prettiest little parlor that ever you did spy. It was plain that Dr. Flint's family were apprised of my movements, since they knew of my voyage to Europe. I expected to have further trouble from them, but having eluded them thus far, I hoped to be as successful in the future. The money I had earned, I was desirous to devote to the education of my children, and to secure a home for them. It seemed not only hard, but unjust, to pay for myself. I could not possibly regard myself as a piece of property. Moreover, I had worked many years without wages, and during that time had been obliged to depend on my grandmother for many comforts in food and clothing. My children certainly belonged to me, but though Dr. Flint had incurred no expense for their support, he had received a large sum of money for them. I knew the law would decide that I was his property, and would probably still give his daughter a claim to my children, but I regarded such laws as the regulations of robbers, who had no rights that I was bound to respect. The Fugitive Slave Law had not then passed. The judges of Massachusetts had not then stooped under chains to enter her courts of justice, so called. I knew my old master was rather skittish of Massachusetts. I relied on her love of freedom, and felt safe on her soil. I am now aware that I honored the old Commonwealth beyond her deserts.

○○○○○○○○○○

For two years my daughter and I supported ourselves comfortably in Boston. At the end of that time, my brother William offered to send Ellen to a boarding school. It required a great effort for me to consent to part with her, for I had few near ties, and it was her presence that made my two little rooms seem home-like. But my judgment prevailed over my selfish feelings. I made preparations for her departure. During the two years we had lived together I had often resolved to tell her something about her father, but I had never been able to muster sufficient courage. I had a shrinking dread of diminishing my child's love.

I knew she must have curiosity on the subject, but she had never asked a question. She was always very careful not to say anything to remind me of my troubles. Now that she was going from me, I thought if I should die before she returned, she might hear my story from someone who did not understand the palliating circumstances, and that if she were entirely ignorant on the subject, her sensitive nature might receive a rude shock.

When we retired for the night, she said, "Mother, it is very hard to leave you alone. I am almost sorry I am going, though I do want to improve myself. But you will write to me often, won't you, mother?" I did not throw my arms round her. I did not answer her. But in a calm, solemn way for it cost me great effort I said, "Listen to me, Ellen, I have something to tell you!"

I recounted my early sufferings in slavery, and told her how nearly they had crushed me. I began to tell her how they had driven me into a great sin, when she clasped me in her arms, and exclaimed "O, don't, mother! Please don't tell me anymore." I said, "But, my child, I want you to know about your father."

"I know all about it, mother," she replied, "I am nothing to my father, and he is nothing to me. All my love is for you. I was with him five months in Washington, and he never cared for me. He never spoke to me as he did to his little Fanny. I knew all the time he was my father, for Fanny's nurse told me so, but she said I must never tell anybody, and I never did. I used to wish he would take me in his arms and kiss me, as he did Fanny, or that he would sometimes smile at me, as he did at her. I thought if he was my own father, he ought to love me. I was a little girl then, and didn't know any better. But now I never think anything about my father. All my love is for you." She hugged me closer as she spoke, and I thanked God that the knowledge I had so much dreaded to impart had not diminished the affection of my child. I had not the slightest idea she knew that portion of my history.

If I had, I should have spoken to her long before, for my pent-up feelings had often longed to pour themselves out to someone I could trust. But I loved the dear girl better for the delicacy she had manifested towards her unfortunate mother. The next morning, she and her uncle started on their journey to the village in New York, where she was to be placed at school. It seemed as if all the sunshine had gone away. My little room was dreadfully lonely. I was thankful when a message came from a lady, accustomed to employ me, requesting me to come and sew in her family for several weeks. On my return, I found a letter from brother William. He thought of opening an anti-slavery reading room in Rochester, and combining with it the sale of some books and stationery, and he wanted me to unite with him. We tried it, but it was not successful. We found warm anti-slavery friends there, but the feeling was not general enough to support such an establishment. I passed nearly a year in the family of Isaac and Amy Post, practical believers in the Christian doctrine of human brotherhood. They measured a man's worth by his character, not by his complexion. The memory of those beloved and honored friends will remain with me to my latest hour.

☐☐☐☐☐☐☐☐☐☐

My brother, being disappointed in his project, concluded to go to California, and it was agreed that Benjamin should go with him. Ellen liked her school, and was a great favorite there. They did not know her history, and she did not tell it, because she had no desire to make capital out of their sympathy. But when it was accidentally discovered that her mother was a fugitive slave, every method was used to increase her advantages and diminish her expenses. I was alone again. It was necessary for me to be earning money, and I preferred that it should be among those who knew me. On my return from Rochester, I called at the house of Mr. Bruce, to see Mary, the darling little babe that had thawed my heart, when it was freezing into a cheerless distrust of all my fellow beings. She was growing a tall girl now, but I loved her always. Mr. Bruce had married again, and it was proposed that I should become nurse to a new infant. I had but one hesitation, and that was my feeling of insecurity in New York, now greatly increased by the passage of the Fugitive Slave Law. However, I resolved to try the experiment. I was again fortunate in my employer. The new Mrs. Bruce was an American, brought up under aristocratic influences, and still living in the midst of them, but if she had any prejudice against color, I was never made aware of it, and as for the system of slavery, she had a most hearty dislike of it. No sophistry of Southerners could blind her to its enormity. She was a person of excellent principles and a noble heart. To me, from that hour to the present, she has been a true and sympathizing friend. Blessings be with her and hers.

 About the time that I reentered the Bruce family, an event occurred of disastrous import to the colored people. The slave Hamlin, the first fugitive that came under the new law, was given up by the bloodhounds of the North to the bloodhounds of the South. It was the beginning of a reign of terror to the colored population. The great city rushed on in its whirl of excitement taking no note of the "short and simple annals of the poor."

 But while fashionables were listening to the thrilling voice of Jenny Lind in Metropolitan Hall, the thrilling voices of poor hunted colored people went up, in an agony of supplication, to the Lord, from Zion's church. Many families, who had lived in the city for twenty years, fled from it now. Many a poor washerwoman, who, by hard labor, had made herself a comfortable home, was obliged to sacrifice her furniture, bid a hurried farewell to friends, and seek her fortune among strangers in Canada. Many a wife discovered a secret she had never known before—that her husband was a fugitive, and must leave her to insure his own safety. Worse still, many a husband discovered that his wife had fled from slavery years ago, and as "the child follows the condition of its mother," the children of his love were liable to be seized and carried into slavery. Everywhere, in those humble homes, there was consternation and anguish. But what cared the legislators of the "dominant race" for the blood they were crushing out of trampled hearts? When my brother William spent his last evening with me, before he went to California, we talked nearly all the time of the distress brought on our oppressed people by the passage of this iniquitous law, and never had I seen him manifest such bitterness of spirit, such stern hostility to our oppressors. He was himself free from the operation of the law, for he did not run from any slaveholding State, being brought into the Free States by his master. But I was subject to it, and so were hundreds of intelligent and industrious people all around us. I seldom ventured into the streets, and when it was necessary to do an errand for Mrs. Bruce, or any of the family, I went as much as possible through back streets and by-ways. What a disgrace to a city calling itself free, that inhabitants, guiltless of offense, and seeking to perform their duties conscientiously, should be condemned to live in such incessant fear, and have nowhere to turn for protection.

This state of things, of course, gave rise to many impromptu vigilance committees. Every colored person, and every friend of their persecuted race, kept their eyes wide open. Every evening I examined the newspapers carefully, to see what Southerners had put up at the hotels. I did this for my own sake, thinking my young mistress and her husband might be among the list, I wished also to give information to others, if necessary, for if many were "running to and fro," I resolved that "knowledge should be increased." This brings up one of my Southern reminiscences, which I will here briefly relate. I was somewhat acquainted with a slave named Luke, who belonged to a wealthy man in our vicinity. His master died, leaving a son and daughter heirs to his large fortune. In the division of the slaves, Luke was included in the son's portion. This young man became a prey to the vices growing out of the "patriarchal institution," and when he went to the North, to complete his education, he carried his vices with him. He was brought home, deprived of the use of his limbs, by excessive dissipation. Luke was appointed to wait upon his bedridden master, whose despotic habits were greatly increased by exasperation at his own helplessness. He kept a cowhide beside him, and, for the most trivial occurrence, he would order his attendant to bare his back, and kneel beside the couch, while he whipped him till his strength was exhausted.

Some days he was not allowed to wear anything but his shirt, in order to be in readiness to be flogged. A day seldom passed without his receiving more or less blows. If the slightest resistance was offered, the town constable was sent for to execute the punishment, and Luke learned from experience how much more the constable's strong arm was to be dreaded than the comparatively feeble one of his master. The arm of his tyrant grew weaker, and was finally palsied, and then the constable's services were in constant requisition. The fact that he was entirely dependent on Luke's care, and was obliged to be tended like an infant, instead of inspiring any gratitude or compassion towards his poor slave, seemed only to increase his irritability and cruelty. As he lay there on his bed, a mere degraded wreck of manhood, he took into his head the strangest freaks of despotism, and if Luke hesitated to submit to his orders, the constable was immediately sent for. Some of these freaks were of a nature too filthy to be repeated. When I fled from the house of bondage, I left poor Luke still chained to the bedside of this cruel and disgusting wretch. One day, when I had been requested to do an errand for Mrs. Bruce, I was hurrying through back streets, as usual, when I saw a young man approaching, whose face was familiar to me, As he came nearer, I recognized Luke. I always rejoiced to see or hear of anyone who had escaped from the black pit, but, remembering this poor fellow's extreme hardships, I was peculiarly glad to see him on Northern soil, though I no longer called it *free* soil. I well-remembered what a desolate feeling it was to be alone among strangers, and I went up to him and greeted him cordially. At first, he did not know me, but when I mentioned my name, he remembered all about me. I told him of the Fugitive Slave Law, and asked him if he did not know that New York was a city of kidnappers. He replied, "De risk ain't so bad for me, as 'tis fur you. 'Cause I runned away from de speculator, and you runned away from de Massa. Dem speculators vont spen dar money to come here fur a runaway, if dey ain't sartin sure to put dar hans right on him. An I tell you I's tuk good car 'bout dat. I had too hard times down dar, to let 'em ketch dis nigger." He then told me of the advice he had received, and the plans he had laid. I asked if he had money enough to take him to Canada. " 'Pend upon it, I hab," he replied. "I tuk car fur dat. I'd bin workin all my days fur dem cussed whites, an got no pay but kicks and cuffs. So I tought dis nigger had a right to money nuff to bring him to de Free States. Massa Henry he lib till ebery body vish him dead, an ven he did die, I knowed de debbil would hab him, an vouldn't vant him to bring his money 'long too. So I tuk some of his bills, and put 'em in de pocket of his ole trousers. An ven he was buried, dis nigger ask fur dem ole trousers, an dey gub 'em to me." With a low, chuckling laugh, he added, "You see I didn't *steal* it, dey *gub* it to me. I tell you, I had mighty hard time to keep de speculator from findin it, but he didn't git it." This is a fair specimen of how the moral sense is educated by slavery. When a man has his wages stolen from him, year after year, and the laws sanction and enforce the theft, how can he be expected to have more regard to honesty than has the man who robs him? I have become somewhat enlightened, but I confess that I agree with poor, ignorant, much-abused, Luke, in thinking he had a *right* to that money, as a portion of his unpaid wages. He went to Canada forthwith, and I have not since heard from him. All that winter I lived in a state of anxiety.

When I took the children out to breathe the air, I closely observed the countenances of all I met. I dreaded the approach of summer, when snakes and slaveholders make their appearance. I was, in fact, as slave in New York, as subject to slave laws as I had been in a Slave State. Strange incongruity in a State called free! Spring returned, and I received warning from the South that Dr. Flint knew of my return to my old place, and was making preparations to have me caught. I learned afterwards that my dress, and that of Mrs. Bruce's children, had been described to him by some of the Northern tools, which slaveholders employ for their base purposes, and then indulge in sneers at their cupidity and mean servility. I immediately informed Mrs. Bruce of my danger, and she took prompt measures for my safety. My place as nurse could not be supplied immediately, and this generous, sympathizing lady proposed that I should carry her baby away. It was a comfort to me to have the child with me, for the heart is reluctant to be torn away from every object it loves. But how few mothers would have consented to have one of their own babes become a fugitive, for the sake of a poor, hunted nurse, on whom the legislators of the country had let loose the bloodhounds. When I spoke of the sacrifice she was making, in depriving herself of her dear baby, she replied, "It is better for you to have baby with you, Linda, for if they get on your track, they will be obliged to bring the child to me, and then, if there is a possibility of saving you, you shall be saved." This lady had a very wealthy relative, a benevolent gentleman in many respects, but aristocratic and pro-slavery. He remonstrated with her for harboring a fugitive slave, told her she was violating the laws of her country, and asked her if she was aware of the penalty. She replied, "I am very well aware of it. It is imprisonment and one thousand dollars fine. Shame on my country that it *is* so! I am ready to incur the penalty. I will go to the state's prison, rather than have any poor victim torn from *my* house, to be carried back to slavery." The noble heart! The brave heart! The tears are in my eyes while I write of her. May the God of the helpless reward her for her sympathy with my persecuted people! I was sent into New England, where I was sheltered by the wife of a senator, whom I shall always hold in grateful remembrance. This honorable gentleman would not have voted for the Fugitive Slave Law, as did the senator in *Uncle Tom's Cabin*, on the contrary, he was strongly opposed to it, but he was enough under its influence to be afraid of having me remain in his house many hours. So I was sent into the country, where I remained a month with the baby. When it was supposed that Dr. Flint's emissaries had lost track of me, and given up the pursuit, I returned to New York.

☐☐☐☐☐☐☐☐☐☐

Mrs. Bruce, and every member of her family, were exceedingly kind to me. I was thankful for the blessings of my lot, yet I could not always wear a cheerful countenance. I was doing harm to no one, on the contrary, I was doing all the good I could in my small way, yet I could never go out to breathe God's free air without trepidation at my heart. This seemed hard, and I could not think it was a right state of things in any civilized country.

From time to time I received news from my good old grandmother. She could not write, but she employed others to write for her. The following is an extract from one of her last letters—*Dear Daughter, I cannot hope to see you again on earth, but I pray to God to unite us above, where pain will no more rack this feeble body of mine, where sorrow and parting from my children will be no more. God has promised these things if we are faithful unto the end. My age and feeble health deprive me of going to church now, but God is with me here at home. Thank your brother for his kindness. Give much love to him, and tell him to remember the Creator in the days of his youth, and strive to meet me in the Father's kingdom. Love to Ellen and Benjamin. Don't neglect him. Tell him for me, to be a good boy. Strive, my child, to train them for God's children. May he protect and provide for you, is the prayer of your loving old mother.* These letters both cheered and saddened me. I was always glad to have tidings from the kind, faithful old friend of my unhappy youth, but her messages of love made my heart yearn to see her before she died, and I mourned over the fact that it was impossible. Some months after I returned from my flight to New England, I received a letter from her, in which she wrote, "*Dr. Flint is dead. He has left a distressed family. Poor old man! I hope he made his peace with God.*"

I remembered how he had defrauded my grandmother of the hard earnings she had loaned, how he had tried to cheat her out of the freedom her mistress had promised her, and how he had persecuted her children, and I thought to myself that she was a better Christian than I was, if she could entirely forgive him. I cannot say, with truth, that the news of my old master's death softened my feelings towards him. There are wrongs which even the grave does not bury. The man was odious to me while he lived, and his memory is odious now. His departure from this world did not diminish my danger. He had threatened my grandmother that his heirs should hold me in slavery after he was gone, that I never should be free so long as a child of his survived. As for Mrs. Flint, I had seen her in deeper afflictions than I supposed the loss of her husband would be, for she had buried several children, yet I never saw any signs of softening in her heart. The doctor had died in embarrassed circumstances, and had little to will to his heirs, except such property as he was unable to grasp. I was well-aware what I had to expect from the family of Flints, and my fears were confirmed by a letter from the South, warning me to be on my guard, because Mrs. Flint openly declared that her daughter could not afford to lose so valuable a slave as I was. I kept close watch of the newspapers for arrivals, but one Saturday night, being much occupied, I forgot to examine the *Evening Express* as usual. I went down into the parlor for it, early in the morning, and found the boy about to kindle a fire with it. I took it from him and examined the list of arrivals.

Reader, if you have never been a slave, you cannot imagine the acute sensation of suffering at my heart, when I read the names of Mr. and Mrs. Dodge, at a hotel in Courtland Street. It was a third-rate hotel, and that circumstance convinced me of the truth of what I had heard, that they were short of funds and had need of my value, as *they* valued me, and that was by dollars and cents. I hastened with the paper to Mrs. Bruce. Her heart and hand were always open to everyone in distress, and she always warmly sympathized with mine. It was impossible to tell how near the enemy was. He might have passed and repassed the house while we were sleeping. He might at that moment be waiting to pounce upon me if I ventured out of doors. I had never seen the husband of my young mistress, and therefore I could not distinguish him from any other stranger. A carriage was hastily ordered, and, closely veiled, I followed Mrs. Bruce, taking the baby again with me into exile. After various turnings and crossings, and returnings, the carriage stopped at the house of one of Mrs. Bruce's friends, where I was kindly received.

Mrs. Bruce returned immediately, to instruct the domestics what to say if anyone came to inquire for me. It was lucky for me that the evening paper was not burned up before I had a chance to examine the list of arrivals. It was not long after Mrs. Bruce's return to her house, before several people came to inquire for me. One inquired for me, another asked for my daughter Ellen, and another said he had a letter from my grandmother, which he was requested to deiver in person. They were told, "She *has* lived here, but she has left." "How long ago?" "I don't know, sir." "Do you know where she went?" "I do not, sir." And the door was closed. This Mr. Dodge, who claimed me as his property, was originally a Yankee peddler in the South, then he became a merchant, and finally a slaveholder. He managed to get introduced into what was called the first society, and married Miss Emily Flint. A quarrel arose between him and her brother, and the brother cowhided him. This led to a family feud, and he proposed to remove to Virginia. Dr. Flint left him no property, and his own means had become circumscribed, while a wife and children depended upon him for support. Under these circumstances, it was very natural that he should make an effort to put me into his pocket. I had a colored friend, a man from my native place, in whom I had the most implicit confidence.

I sent for him, and told him that Mr. and Mrs. Dodge had arrived in New York. I proposed that he should call upon them to make inquiries about his friends at the South, with whom Dr. Flint's family were well-acquainted. He thought there was no impropriety in his doing so, and he consented. He went to the hotel, and knocked at the door of Mr. Dodge's room, which was opened by the gentleman himself, who gruffly inquired, "What brought you here? How came you to know I was in the city?" "Your arrival was published in the evening papers, sir, and I called to ask Mrs. Dodge about my friends at home. I didn't suppose it would give any offense." "Where's that Negro girl, that belongs to my wife?" "What girl, sir?" "You know well enough. I mean Linda, that ran away from Dr. Flint's plantation, some years ago. I dare say you've seen her, and know where she is." "Yes, sir, I've seen her, and know where she is. She is out of your reach, sir." "Tell me where she is, or bring her to me, and I will give her a chance to buy her freedom." "I don't think it would be of any use, sir. I have heard her say she would go to the ends of the earth, rather than pay any man or woman for her freedom, because she thinks she has a right to it. Besides, she couldn't do it, if she would, for she has spent her earnings to educate her children."

    This made Mr. Dodge very angry, and some high words passed between them. My friend was afraid to come where I was but in the course of the day I received a note from him.

    I supposed they had not come from the South, in the winter, for a pleasure excursion, and now the nature of their business was very plain. Mrs. Bruce came to me and entreated me to leave the city the next morning. She said her house was watched, and it was possible that some clue to me might be obtained. I refused to take her advice. She pleaded with an earnest tenderness, that ought to have moved me, but I was in a bitter, disheartened mood. I was weary of flying from pillar to post. I had been chased during half my life, and it seemed as if the chase was never to end. There I sat, in that great city, guiltless of crime, yet not daring to worship God in any of the churches.

    I heard the bells ringing for afternoon service, and, with contemptuous sarcasm, I said, "Will the preachers take for their text, 'Proclaim liberty to the captive, and the opening of prison doors to them that are bound?' Or will they preach from the text 'Do unto others as ye would they should do unto you?'"

Oppressed Poles and Hungarians could find a safe refuge in that city, John Mitchell was free to proclaim in the City Hall his desire for "a plantation well-stocked with slaves," but there I sat, an oppressed American, not daring to show my face. God forgive the black and bitter thoughts I indulged on that Sabbath day.

The Scripture says, "Oppression makes even a wise man mad," and I was not wise. I had been told that Mr. Dodge said his wife had never signed away her right to my children, and if he could not get me, he would take them. This it was, more than anything else, that roused such a tempest in my soul. Benjamin was with his Uncle William in California, but my innocent young daughter had come to spend a vacation with me. I thought of what I had suffered in slavery at her age, and my heart was like a tiger when a hunter tries to seize her young. Dear Mrs. Bruce! I seem to see the expression of her face, as she turned away discouraged by my obstinate mood. Finding her expostulations unavailing, she sent Ellen to entreat me. When ten o'clock in the evening arrived and Ellen had not returned, this watchful and unwearied friend became anxious. She came to us in a carriage, bringing a well-filled trunk for my journey—trusting that by this time I would listen to reason. I yielded to her, as I ought to have done before. The next day, baby and I set out in a heavy snowstorm, bound for New England again. I received letters from the City of Iniquity, addressed to me under an assumed name.

In a few days one came from Mrs. Bruce, informing me that my new master was still searching for me, and that she intended to put an end to this persecution by buying my freedom. I felt grateful for the kindness that prompted this offer, but the idea was not so pleasant to me as might have been expected. The more my mind had become enlightened, the more difficult it was for me to consider myself an article of property, and to pay money to those who had so grievously oppressed me seemed like taking from my sufferings the glory of triumph. I wrote to Mrs. Bruce, thanking her, but saying that being sold from one owner to another seemed too much like slavery, that such a great obligation could not be easily cancelled, and that I preferred to go to my brother in California. Without my knowledge, Mrs. Bruce employed a gentleman in New York to enter into negotiations with Mr. Dodge. He proposed to pay three hundred dollars down, if Mr. Dodge would sell me, and enter into obligations to relinquish all claim to me or my children forever after. He who called himself my master said he scorned so small an offer for such a valuable servant. The gentleman replied, "You can do as you choose, sir. If you reject this offer you will never get anything, for the woman has friends who will convey her and her children out of the country." Mr. Dodge concluded that "half a loaf was better than no bread," and he agreed to the proffered terms.

By the next mail I received this brief letter from Mrs. Bruce, "I am rejoiced to tell you that the money for your freedom has been paid to Mr. Dodge. Come home tomorrow. I long to see you and my sweet babe." My brain reeled as I read these lines. A gentleman near me said, "It's true, I have seen the bill of sale." "The bill of sale!" Those words struck me like a blow. So I was *sold* at last! A human being *sold* in the free city of New York! The bill of sale is on record, and future generations will learn from it that women were articles of traffic in New York, late in the nineteenth century of the Christian religion. It may hereafter prove a useful document to antiquaries, who are seeking to measure the progress of civilization in the United States. I well know the value of that bit of paper, but much as I love freedom, I do not like to look upon it. I am deeply grateful to the generous friend who procured it, but I despise the miscreant who demanded payment for what never rightfully belonged to him or his. I had objected to having my freedom bought, yet I must confess that when it was done I felt as if a heavy load had been lifted from my weary shoulders. When I rode home in the cars I was no longer afraid to unveil my face and look at people as they passed. I should have been glad to have met Daniel Dodge himself, to have had him seen me and known me, that he might have mourned over the untoward circumstances which compelled him to sell me for three hundred dollars. When I reached home, the arms of my benefactress were thrown round me, and our tears mingled. As soon as she could speak, she said, "O Linda, I'm *so* glad it's all over! You wrote to me as if you thought you were going to be transferred from one owner to another. But I did not buy you for your services. I should have done just the same, if you had been going to sail for California tomorrow. I should, at least, have the satisfaction of knowing that you left me a free woman."

My heart was exceedingly full. I remembered how my poor father had tried to buy me, when I was a small child, and how he had been disappointed. I hoped his spirit was rejoicing over me now. I remembered how my good old grandmother had laid up her earnings to purchase me in later years, and how often her plans had been frustrated. How that faithful, loving old heart would leap for joy, if she could look on me and my children now that we were free! My relatives had been foiled in all their efforts, but God had raised me up a friend among strangers, who had bestowed on me the precious, long-desired boon. Friend! It is a common word, often lightly used. Like other good and beautiful things, it may be tarnished by careless handling, but when I speak of Mrs. Bruce as my friend, the word is sacred. My grandmother lived to rejoice in my freedom, but not long after, a letter came with a black seal. She had gone "where the wicked cease from troubling, and the weary are at rest." Time passed on, and a paper came to me from the South, containing an obituary notice of my Uncle Phillip. It was the only case I ever knew of such an honor conferred upon a colored person. It was written by one of his friends, and contained these words, "Now that death has laid him low, they call him a good man and a useful citizen, but what are eulogies to the black man, when the world has faded from his vision? It does not require man's praise to obtain rest in God's kingdom." So they called a colored man a *citizen!* Strange words to be uttered in that region! Reader, my story ends with freedom, not in the usual way, with marriage. I and my children are now free! We are as free from the power of slaveholders as are the white people of the North, and though that, according to my ideas, is not saying a great deal, it is a vast improvement in *my* condition. The dream of my life is not yet realized. I do not sit with my children in a home of my own. I still long for a hearthstone of my own, however humble. I wish it for my children's sake far more than for my own. But God so orders circumstances as to keep me with my friend Mrs. Bruce. Love, duty, gratitude, also bind me to her side. It is a privilege to serve her who pities my oppressed people, and who has bestowed freedom on me and my children. It has been painful to me, in many ways, to recall the dreary years I passed in bondage. I would gladly forget them if I could. Yet the retrospection is not altogether without solace, for with those gloomy recollections come tender memories of my good old grandmother, like light fleecy clouds floating over a dark and troubled sea.

Afterword

With the publication of his autobiography Moses Roper was able to achieve brief fame as his writings exposed the horrible reality about American slavery. It was assumed at first by many who read his memoir that he had "imagined" a large portion of what he described until other escaped slaves came forward and began telling similar stories about life in the southern United States. Up to that point, American slavery had been an ugly reality that was kept hidden from the rest of the country to some extent for over a century. People either didn't know or chose to ignore the stories they had heard from others. But it can be assumed that despite the ignorance displayed by many "good" citizens in the North—most people knew what was going on but simply turned a blind eye to it—and that it wasn't until abolitionists became involved that the ugly images about slave life amid the palatial plantations in the South was accurately described and exposed in their infamous glory. From that moment onward it should be noted that so-called Christian plantation owners (both sadistic and mild) had bounties placed on their heads as more and more memoirs written by escaped slaves made their way into people's hands, and the "happy" view of slavery began to change rapidly. Books written by slaves were rare before the Civil War and for the most part most who read the accounts about what was happening didn't act upon the knowledge. But as more and more accounts began turning up in bookstores the scab was ripped off and calls to end slavery became shouts. Abolitionists began their crusade and whether slave owners liked it or not their world was put under extreme scrutiny—especially their so-called Christian "beliefs." The events of Moses Roper's later life after his memoir was published seemed destined for greatness. Unfortunately things didn't go as planned. In December 1839 Roper married a British citizen named Ann Price and had four daughters. The Roper family traveled between Canada and Great Britain during the next decade on the lecture circuit, first moving to Nova Scotia and living there until 1857. His wife and daughters moved back to Great Britain sometime in the late 1850s, living in Wales at the home of her father in 1861 according to records. As for Moses Roper, he ended up living in a boardinghouse miles away in Cambridge, England during this time but there seems to be no record if he and his wife were separated. It appears, though not proven, that Roper had a midlife crisis or possibly a nervous breakdown which led to the spiraling of his life even further. He apparently returned to the United States, living in the New England area but from records it appears he had no further contact with his family. Roper died in April 1891 in Boston at the Boston City Hospital after being found at a train station in poor health. He was buried in an unmarked grave at Mount Hope Cemetery. Moses Roper's life held so much promise yet the traumatic events of his early years probably had an effect on his mindset and it eventually led to mental problems Roper couldn't overcome. At the end of the Civil War, Roper's autobiography found a new audience and was reprinted endlessly throughout the remaining part of the nineteenth century and into the twentieth. Today his autobiography is considered one of the best firsthand accounts about the life of a slave and escape from slavery. Roper's relatives and descendants can be found in the United States as well as England and Australia. Some of his Australian relatives bear his name according to records found.

Harriet Jacobs began her life as a slave during the early years of the nineteenth century—but through perseverance and determination she survived her ordeal to become one of the most important historical figures in American history. Her story made it possible for future generations to remember the past and this personal memoir written by Jacobs after her daring escape from slavery is one of the most riveting accounts ever published before the Civil War about life as a slave. Her vivid descriptions detailing her life and the forgotten lives of so many others still seem impossible to believe—even today. Her story is unforgettable.

Harriet Jacobs began writing her memoir of her incredible life while working for writer Nathaniel Parker Willis and his family. Selections of her writings were first published in the *New York Tribune*—but the newspaper ceased publishing her entire story because it was deemed too shocking for the time. Jacobs then tried to find a publisher for her book but encountered obstacles, including having noted novelist Harriet Beecher Stowe turn down her request to write a preface to the now-famous memoir due to hurt feelings Stowe harbored because Jacobs didn't want to meld her story into a novel Stowe was writing at the time. Jacobs then met noted abolitionist and writer, Lydia Maria Child, who agreed to edit her writings, becoming a lifelong friend following the publication of her memoir, first published in 1861 under the title *Incidents in the Life of a Slave Girl*.

Though the book was received well, it wasn't an immediate bestseller as many who read it could not believe such things had actually occurred. Jacobs changed the names of everyone mentioned in her book, including herself, using the pen name "Linda Brent." Though names were changed, everyone who read it knew exactly whom Jacobs was writing about. The Norcom family was probably the most upset with the publication of the book since their personal lives became public knowledge and subjected them to harsh scrutiny. Not that it mattered much at that point as the Norcom family had fallen on hard times since Dr. James Norcom's death in 1850. The worst off was probably Mary Norcom Messmore whose husband was not above resorting to sleazy tactics to obtain money as described in the book. Though not known for sure, one shouldn't doubt that in later years he probably pimped out his wife to whoever would pay for her "services" in order to make ends meet. He was a lowlife individual but nevertheless Norcom's daughter deserved her lot in life after how she behaved toward Jacobs. The whole Norcom family pretty much ended up being nothing more than white trash after the Civil War—of which was a just-deserving end resulting from their horrible behavior toward their fellow human beings—a high fall from the society they originally belonged to. What is not clearly seen however by most historians is of Norcom's apparent feelings for Jacobs. It appears he may have actually been in love with her but either he refused to admit it to himself or foolishly thought he could get her to love him with his misguided attempts to control her through veiled threats. The fact he supposedly never severely punished her and prevented others from doing so as well—when he clearly could of—gives credence to this theory. Nevertheless, whether he loved her or not, how he treated Jacobs certainly didn't endear him further to her—and probably led to her justifiably disliking him even further as the years slipped by and his behavior turned sadistic.

    Molly Horniblow and her son, Mark Ramsey died in 1853 and 1858. Samuel Tredwell Sawyer died in 1865 without ever publicly acknowledging his children with Jacobs. Nathaniel Parker Willis died in 1867 and was buried at the Mount Auburn Cemetery in Cambridge, near Boston, Massachusetts. Harriet's brother, John S. Jacobs died in 1875 and was buried at Mount Auburn Cemetery also. Lydia Maria Child died in 1880 and Amy Post died in 1889. Joseph Jacobs (Sawyer) wandered throughout his entire adult life trying desperately to find himself. He spent time in California and later Australia—but never seemed to find the happiness he so desperately sought. Exactly what happened to him after he returned to the United States from Australia remains somewhat unclear. Meanwhile, Louisa Jacobs (Sawyer) focused her life in helping others—and strived for women's rights. She remained close to her mother—maintaining a boardinghouse with her in Cambridge, Massachusetts, lobbying for civil rights on behalf of former slaves, and later working for writer Charles Nordhoff during her mother's final years in the 1890s.

Harriet remained close to the Willis family in the decades that followed the Civil War, especially Bailey Willis, the son of Nathaniel Parker Willis and Cornelia Grinnell Willis. Willis would later become known for his efforts to have Mount Rainier declared a national park in 1899 as well as being one of the leading earthquake experts at the time. Harriet Jacobs died in March 1897 and was buried next to her younger brother at Mount Auburn Cemetery. Cornelia Grinnell Willis died in March 1904 and her stepdaughter Imogen Willis Eddy passed away several months later in September 1904. Louisa Jacobs (Sawyer) passed away in April 1917. She was laid to rest next to her mother at the Mount Auburn Cemetery just outside of Boston. Bailey Willis died in 1949 in Palo Alto, California. What became of Joseph Jacobs (Sawyer) and where is he buried officially remains unknown.

It should be noted that Jacobs is buried in the same cemetery as Nathaniel Parker Willis and Mary Stace Willis and their daughter Imogen Willis Eddy. However, for some reason the first name and birthdate on the headstone for Jacobs at Mount Auburn is misspelled and mislabeled—as well as one of the dates on her daughter's headstone. Why this error was never addressed or corrected by the cemetery is unclear. Cornelia Grinnell Willis was buried next to her parents at the Oak Grove Cemetery in nearby New Bedford, Massachusetts upon her death at 79.

Though her mesmerizing memoir wasn't a huge bestseller during her lifetime, in the succeeding decades following her death *Incidents in the Life of a Slave Girl* has became a classic of American literature. As with Anne Frank's now world-famous diary, the credibility of Jacobs's writings fell under scrutiny by unbelieving historians or closeted racists. Nevertheless shameless attempts to discredit her memoir have come up short as evidence supporting the events described in her book have surfaced. Still, there will always be historians who refuse to believe that the unbelievable events portrayed in *Incidents in the Life of a Slave*

Girl really happened, and they will continually spew forth their comments in books and Internet sites stating that the life of a slave wasn't as bad as it was portrayed to be. Of course it wasn't them who experienced it and therefore they have no idea what they're talking about when they open their mouths to repeat lies and make inaccurate statements. Sometimes even the most intelligent people, or those who think they're intelligent, can be absolutely ignorant. This memoir is one of those rare books that seem like it only could have happened in a movie, but this was a true story written by a former slave. Seeming very much like the diary written by Anne Frank almost a century later, the narrative contained in these pages defy reality. Could human beings have treated each other with such cruelty? The answer is yes. Jacobs details her harrowing experiences as a slave and her eventual escape to freedom with such clarity that time hasn't diminished its power. Though the real names of those described were changed before publication to protect their privacy, the people described were real. Very few books written by former slaves are this eloquent, this real, and this sad at revealing the truth.

    This memoir by Harriet Jacobs spares no one, including the author—it is a no-holds-barred brutal account of life as a slave—describing exactly how life was for her and so many others in the South before Abraham Lincoln dared to change the course of United States history forever. Today it seems absolutely impossible that the incredible events described in this book actually happened. But for Jacobs and countless others—*this* was their life, their reality—the only existence they knew from birth until death. Words alone cannot describe what took place in the years before 1863, but it certainly helps. It should be noted that though Jacobs had an editor to help finish her autobiography, she wrote it herself and therefore the tragic accounts of her life mentioned are her own firsthand views, and not the editor's.

Additional Notes

Transcription from a clipping mentioning Moses Roper's death in April 1891 as described in a local Boston newspaper.

Though the detailed account below seemed sourced from truthful information pertaining to public records or possibly from notes found on his body—several statements about Roper's life is incorrect. It is unknown if stated material was provided from acquaintances who knew Moses Roper prior to his death.

MOTHER WAS A SLAVE

Death of Moses Roper at the City Hospital—was suffering from skin disease and kidney complaint.

Moses Roper, the man who was found in the Eastern Depot in a very weak condition, apparently suffering from dropsy, last Saturday evening, died at the City Hospital early last evening. After Roper was taken to the hospital Saturday evening, it was discovered by Dr. Higgins that the man was suffering from a complication of diseases of the heart and kidneys, and also from eczema, and these diseases combined were the cause of the man's death. Roper was a very eccentric individual, and the officials at the hospital say that his is one of the most peculiar cases received there for a long time. When Roper was received he was well-protected from the cold, having on four shirts, two overcoats and three pairs of pantaloons. He was born in North Carolina about 65 years ago, his mother being a mulatto and a slave, while his father was a white laborer. As soon as he was old enough he ran away, going to England, where, by his own efforts, he gained a fair education. A number of years ago he began a lecture tour, delivering lectures upon "Africa and the African People" "Causes of the Colors of the Races" and also upon the "Holy Land." His success as a lecturer was limited, and a few months ago he hired out as a farm laborer with a man named Skillings in Strong, Maine, where he worked until his strength gave out. Roper's sole and faithful companion has been his dog, which has stuck to him through thick and thin, remaining by his bedside until he was taken away after his master's death. Roper had $100 in his pocket, but as he has no friends in this part of the country it is not known how the money will be disposed of.

Though Moses Roper wrote in his memoir he was born in 1815, he was probably born much earlier, possibly as early as 1810 according to his own writings, since he stated that his father's new wife tried to kill him soon after his birth because of his resemblance to her new husband. His father, Henry H. Roper, was a white planter who impregnated one of his slaves, resulting in the birth of Moses Roper. From the papers on the Roper family, Henry Roper's wife was named Rachel Farley, whom he married in October 1810. It can be assumed *she* was the *wife* that tried to kill Moses Roper soon after his birth with a knife. Obviously old records could be mislabeled or confused for whatever reasons (though unlikely) since Roper and Farley's first child together was born in 1814, four years after their marriage and of which records survive. So, the year given for his birth is clearly wrong (by a few years) or the story he was told by his mother's (slave) relatives was somewhat factually inaccurate based on their inability to read. There are other minor discrepancies found throughout

Roper's memoir also—but it remains unknown if it was simply a publishing error or Roper himself misstated something that he thought was correct when in fact it was actually incorrect.

Harriet Jacobs was born on February 11, 1813 in North Carolina. Though born a slave, she was able to learn to read and write, due to a kindly woman named Margaret Horniblow. After Horniblow's death in 1825, Jacobs ended up in the household of Dr. James Norcom, a sadistic, cruel tyrant who sexually harassed her for nearly a decade. Jacobs eventually escaped after spending years in hiding and later found refuge in the household of writer Nathaniel Parker Willis. While living with the Willis family, Jacobs began composing a memoir in her free time. Edited by Lydia Maria Child, it was originally turned down by several publishers but eventually became one of the most widely read books of its time. Harriet Jacobs died on March 7, 1897 in Massachusetts.

Lydia Maria Child was born in February 1802 in Medford, Massachusetts. She was an abolitionist, human rights activist, novelist, and journalist. Her entire life was focused in helping others, especially women and American Indians. Child was also known for her classic 1844 poem *Over the River and through the Wood* which was later rendered into a song that became a Christmas tradition for over a century. Child was married to social activist David Lee Child, a well-known journalist known for his outspoken views. He died in September 1874. Lydia Maria Child died in October 1880 in Wayland, Massachusetts. She was 78.

About the Series Editor

Gary Brin was born in 1965 and has lived in the United States Virgin Islands, Hawaii and California. He has edited numerous original literary works over the years—both new and revised. In 2019 he established Standish Press to bring forth interesting fictional and historical material usually ignored by mainstream publishers because of specific views or content. In addition to publishing books, he also created the Nancy Hanks Lincoln Public Library (named after the mother of Abraham Lincoln) in 2014 to make available hard-to-find books to a worldwide audience.

Production Notes

Written by Moses Roper and Harriet Jacobs
Manuscripts edited by Gary Brin
Front cover design and book layout by Gary Brin
Cover layout and additional design by Victoria Valentine
Additional help provided by Carlton J. Young
Series created by Gary Brin

For free public domain books please visit
www.nancyhankslincolnpubliclibrary.org

Marie Laplace
February 13, 1892
August 16, 1981

Robert J. Questel
June 22, 1911
August 4, 1990

Marie Anicia Berry Questel
January 13, 1912
April 9, 1997

Eugene Albery Brin
March 21, 1932
May 26, 1977

Lucille Questel Brin
February 21, 1940
December 10, 2000

They never got to have the dreams they wanted or expected but their lives were important nevertheless.

Moses Roper
and
Harriet Jacobs

Published by
Standish Press

www.ingramcontent.com/pod-product-compliance
Lightning Source LLC
Chambersburg PA
CBHW071959110526
44592CB00012B/1144